WASHE

FROM DARKNESS

A MEMOIR BY

NIKKI DUBOSE

WITH **JAMES JOHANSON**

outskirts
press

Outskirts Press, Inc.
http://www.outskirtspress.com

ISBN: 978-1-4787-7745-8

Library of Congress Control Number: 2016910897

Outskirts Press and the "OP" logo are trademarks belonging to Outskirts Press, Inc.

PRINTED IN THE UNITED STATES OF AMERICA

In memory of my late cousin, Ryan,
and the late American journalist James Foley, two heroes.

Without the love of God, none of this would have been possible.

To my dad, for your continued love, support, and inspiration.

To my brother, I love you for you.

To my mom, your spirit lives on forever.

To my family and friends, the staff at CalSouthern University, Linda,
Dr. Carroll, Dr. Sanon, Olivier & family, thank you for believing in me.

To James, thank you for embarking upon this incredible journey with me.

Everyone at NEDA, Project HEAL, Eating Disorder Hope, C.A.R.I.
and Recovery Warriors, for giving me a second chance.

Contributors

Author: Nikki DuBose
nikkidubose.com

Collaborator: James Johanson
Editor: Mary Duffy

Cover Photography: Seth Karecha
sethkarecha.com

Cover Artist: Marushka Mikulas
marushkamikulas.com

Inside Photography: Federico Peltretti
federicopeltretti.com

Media & Public Relations: Kelsey Butts
bookpublicityservices.com

Mentors: Brian Cuban
briancuban.com

Christopher Kai
christopherkai.com

I have tried to recreate events, locales, and conversations from my memories of them. In some instances, I have changed the names of individuals and places to maintain their anonymity; I may have changed some identifying characteristics and details such as dates and times, physical properties, occupations, and places of residence.

The contents of this book are presented in such a way as to capture the raw emotion and vulnerability of my experiences. I felt it would be unfair to you, the reader, to edit the manuscript in such a way that would lose the authenticity and inflection that characterizes my story. These are my memories, and I wanted to leave them as such.

Contents

If you or someone you know is a victim of child abuse, domestic violence, or rape, please dial 911 immediately—don't wait a single second.

Preface

Washed Away: From Darkness to Light covers a broad range of mental health issues as well as the dark side of the modeling industry. This book even dips into the paranormal; as a child I experienced one mysterious phenomenon after another, and those occurrences followed me into adulthood. In 2015, my psychiatrist diagnosed me with having a set of symptoms known as psychosis, and the primary psychiatric cause is still unknown; however, he also said that I could *probably* see ghosts, so you take your pick. Some websites suggest that there may be a link between trauma and the paranormal (1). It is a belief that poltergeist will haunt an area where individuals are under extreme duress. The types of activity that members of my family and I witnessed growing up - banging on the walls, physical touching, and objects being destroyed by an unseen force - went hand in hand with a classic poltergeist haunting.

As a result of the trauma that I experienced as a child, I developed binge eating disorder at eight years old, which later turned into bulimia nervosa at age ten. During my early teenage years, I binged on drugs and alcohol, which coincided with a dark, downward spiral ridden with hallucinations, delusions, sexual promiscuity, body dysmorphic disorder, self-harm, and constant suicidal thoughts.

In 2010, after roughly fifteen years of engaging in my eating disorder behaviors, I became so ill that my modeling agents urged me to seek professional treatment. I experienced a brief period of abstinence, then relapsed and developed anorexia nervosa in 2012. Having anorexia combined with body dysmorphic disorder as a professional model nearly killed me; I didn't know what I really looked like, and everyone around me in the business told me that I was beautiful, even when, by clinical standards, I was severely underweight and needed to be in a treatment center. My strict, competitive environment combined with my mental health issues consistently triggered my warped self-image, which caused me to think and behave in self-destructive ways. Negative voices controlled many of my thoughts, and I was unable, at times, to discern between fantasy and reality.

Thankfully, after years of spiritual and professional guidance, care, and support, I have been delivered from the darkness, and I live one day at a time in the light of the Holy Spirit. In this book, I will share my personal experiences in the hopes to reduce the shame around mental illness, educate the public, and with the desire that you, too, may come to know your genuine beauty that exists within.

Here are some excellent organizations ready to help you or a loved one:

- **Alcoholics Anonymous (AA):** http://www.aa.org/
- **National Institute on Drug Abuse:** http://www.drugabuse.gov/
- **Suicide Prevention:** 1-800-273-8255 24/7
- http://www.suicidepreventionlifeline.org/
- **Peaceful Hearts Foundation:**
- http://www.peacefulheartsfoundation.org/
- **National Eating Disorders Association (NEDA):** 1.800.931.2237 http://www.nationaleatingdisorders.org/
- **Project HEAL:** http://www.theprojectheal.org/
- **Recovery Warriors:** https://www.recoverywarriors.com/
- **Eating Disorders Coalition:**
- http://www.eatingdisorderscoalition.org/
- **Eating Disorder Hope:** http://www.eatingdisorderhope.com/

- **RAINN:** 1.800.656.HOPE https://www.rainn.org/
- **The Model Alliance:** http://modelalliance.org/
- **Prevent Child Abuse:** http://www.preventchildabuse.org/
- **Mental Health America:** http://www.mentalhealthamerica.net/
- **Art Therapy Association:** http://www.arttherapy.org/
- **The National Domestic Violence Hotline:** 1.800.799.7233
- http://www.thehotline.org/
- **Stop Bullying:** http://www.stopbullying.gov/what-is-bullying/
- **BDD:** http://bddfoundation.org/
- **Schizophrenia:** http://schizophrenia.com

References

1. http://bullyonline.org/old/related/paranorm.htm

Prologue

Darkness descends upon the room, signaling my arrival. Behind the curtain, I can feel my breath, waiting for permission to exhale. My knees quiver with apprehension as whispers drone from the crowd outside. From my spot behind the platform, I notice the flares from cameras and spotlights, like shooting stars in a strange, forsaken sky. I can already feel the eyes of the people as they stare at the empty runway, waiting for their goddesses to strut. My throat clenches and my mind empties—anxiety has taken control. What will *they* think of me?

There is no time to think; a lady dressed in black flies to my side and grabs my arm. Her face in a twisted panic, she begs me to step onto the stage. I agree, but deep within, I sense the devil laughing among the restless souls in the crowd, draped in a dark Armani suit.

I prance down the runway like a queen, my body dripping with jewels. Like a lioness, I sway from side to side, moving to entice all who look my way; I am the beast who no one can touch, and no one can tame. As I glance at the rows of curious faces, however, the darkness begins to take over. Before I know it, my worst nightmare has returned: the demons have revealed themselves, with their black eyes and mouths full of jagged teeth. I cannot escape them; they are my masters, and I am their slave.

Voices command me to keep moving. *"Look forward bitch and keep walking. Don't screw it up! They're all going to laugh at you."* I force my head higher and put my shoulders back as I push through the noise and approach the end of the runway. As my feet carry me to the edge, I hear no sound, experience no sensation. Despite the music and commotion, I am lost in a dreamland. How long have I waited to arrive in this spectacular moment? I never imagined I would feel so numb, so vacant. Dozens of cameras pop and crackle as they capture the magnificent creature before them. I perform, but inside I feel trapped, imprisoned within my mind. I struggle to remember which turn I should take next, and instead act like the beautiful model I am supposed to be.

Stiffening my quivering thighs, I manage to hold my broken body up higher than before. I turn to leave and feel thousands of eyeballs latch onto my back; they're all stabbing me with their eyes like butcher knives. My brain is on fire, but I continue to sashay down the runway like a glamorous mannequin. The masters hold tremendous power over me—they are my gods. Their convictions weigh upon my back until it begins to shatter. Whispers trickle into the air like a dark swarm of ghoulish obscurities, filled with gossip and mockery. As I turn around for my final pose, the whispers mutate into the buzzing of a million angry, swarming bees.

"NIKKI, NIKKI, NIKKI!"

Sweating, I look out into the crowd once more. I see nothing and can feel only the beating of my heart. Thoughts of my meaty thighs consume my mind, and distress blinds me. Flashbacks of my stomach bouncing under the sweltering lights drive me to the breaking point, and all at once I fear I might implode from insanity.

"Nikki! Nikki! You are unbelievable, just incredible, darling!"

A leggy model grabs my arm as I step off the stage. Thick adrenaline rushes through my veins.

"We were all watching you back here on the monitor, cheering you on the *entire time!* What are you doing after the show? A bunch of us girls are going out to dinner and dancing."

The tall, thin redhead joins me in a huddle by the exit. She watches my face, but her smile fades as she realizes that I have no interest in talking.

"Thanks, honestly it was nothing. I—I gotta go."

I change into my clothes and slip out the side door before the designer can discover I've left. I stash the jeweled lingerie in my purse and call a cab. Inside the taxi, I replay the scenes over and over again; the memories are suffocating, far from the life I had always imagined. My moments of fame and brilliance are over. Who am I? I'm certainly not special, but a joke, a clothes hanger for everyone to admire and forget. My only happiness lies in destroying myself.

I slam the door of my apartment and run to the refrigerator to get my hands on anything that will quiet the painful memories; whatever will kill the maniacal voices . . . hell, will kill me too. Tearing open package after package of chips and cookies, I shove them into my mouth and fall onto the kitchen floor. After an hour of binging, my swollen stomach signals me to crawl into the bathroom and purge. I need to get rid of the voices, release the misery. Blood rushes to my head and my veins flood with adrenaline. The filth leaves my body in unforgiving streams of regret and terror. I want to look away as my eyes fill with tears, but the insanity demands my attention. *"Look at it, you stupid whore. Get it out before it's too late!"* My body, throat and brain cry out in agony as I continue to purge and punch my stomach, each time harder than the last; as I do, scenes of the fashion show flash in front of me. I want to expel all of those memories out; I want to get the demons out. I stare at the vomit as it swirls in the toilet—*this* is my value, this I am sure of. Coughing and wheezing through each forceful push, I feel torn between feelings of vulgarity and relief as I watch every bit spew out of my aching mouth. Blinded by my tears, I clean up any clues and spray perfume to erase the memories. The voices are exhausting, but I can't stop succumbing to their callings; at the end of it all, the sickness lets me know I'm alive.

I cleanse my stinging mouth, puffy face, and bloated body in the shower, asking a God I do not know to forgive me for the sins I have just committed. I run my hands over my soaking flesh and gasp for air. Already insanity is creeping back, taunting me to consume more food in isolation. I try to ignore the voices, but the obsession grows as I divert my attention to the mirror and brush my thinning hair. For a fleeting moment I recognize myself, but the demonic voices slither in and steal my sanity.

"You ugly monster, you call yourself a model? You're not even attractive! You're a worthless piece of shit, that's what you are. You made a fool of yourself out there tonight. They were all laughing at you. Everyone is always laughing at you!" I suddenly travel back to my childhood and my stepfather's vitriolic insults. I wonder if I have ever been worthy of anything valuable in my life; if anything has ever been real. Despair slices away at my insides slowly, deeply.

My churning desire for food rises to a level beyond anything that I can handle, and my senses radiate with fire as the voices talk to me again, this time taking on a clever, tempting tone. *"There's all that delicious food in the kitchen, you know you can't wait to get your fat hands on it. What's the big deal? You'll just get rid of it."* My heart races with excitement and fear as I think about the food; I cannot separate myself from my delirium any longer.

Nothing is safe from my frenzy as I choke on more fistfuls of cookies and cake. I am unrecognizable, a savage seeking to destroy herself. I crawl over to the bedroom and flick on the television as I continue to binge, but can hear no sound over the voices. *"Finish your food . . . now! It's such a shame you can't eat this for real, fat ass! If only you could. Hurry up and purge before it reaches your stomach!"* The longer it takes to consume the enormous portions, the more I sweat, the harder my heart beats and the greater my stomach swells until it reaches a size I cannot bear. I can barely breathe, and I wipe my mouth with the back of my hand, spreading crumbs all over my clothes and carpet. I sit in my shame and flip through the channels, stopping on an episode of *The Nanny*.

As I watch Fran's smiling face, I feel sadness come over my body. I yearn to be with Momma, The Momma I knew long ago. I ache for the day when we will be a happy, healthy family, but as the credits begin to roll, I feel the dream slipping away and fall into a deep sleep.

Suddenly, the evil voices interrupt my rest. *"Wake up! Do you know what will happen if you fall asleep? You'll fucking DIE, that's what!"* My stomach feels as if it's ripping apart; I reach down and notice that the button and zipper on my pants have busted. *"That's because you're FAT! FAT, FAT, FAT!"*

I can't handle the voices any longer. I want to bash my head on the wall and make them stop, but I grab a gallon of milk instead and begin chugging it as I approach the bathroom. I glance at myself in the mirror: my stomach is protruding, and my pants are hanging down around my calves. The milk is nauseating but comforting; my throat burns from the vomit, but I swallow more creamy liquid to control the heat. Blended concoctions of body fluids, food, and milk splash up from the toilet and hit me in the face, but I don't care—I gladly accept the abuse. I flush, swallow, purge and repeat until all evidence is gone.

My head pounds like a swarm of heavy-footed soldiers fighting for freedom in my brain, and I collapse on the ground, attempting to cry but unable to make a sound. All I can feel, smell, taste, and know is the putrid universe that traps me. I drag my body back to my bedroom and crash on my silky comforter, faint and unable to move. I open my eyes and for a moment gaze at my surroundings: a lavish apartment with all of the things money can buy. However, on closer inspection, it is evident that my luxurious surroundings are decaying; my velvet curtains remain shut at all times, and I shun anyone from entering, food from Casa Tua is scattered everywhere, and there is the faint smell of vomit in the air. Perhaps I could have a nice life, filled with real friends, love, and laughter. Instead, I'm a prisoner in a glass cage, but I don't want to break it; to do so will mean a death of some kind. I'm not ready to face that.

CHAPTER 1

Childhood

My birth name is Tara Nicole DuBose. My momma called me Tara after the plantation in the movie, *Gone with the Wind*, when she developed an affinity for the main character, Scarlett O'Hara. I never viewed myself as a movie star; for most of my life, I detested my looks. I felt like a monster on the inside, and this reflected on the outside—those deformed feelings trickled into almost every area of my life. For seventeen years I struggled with eating disorders, psychosis, addictions, body dysmorphic disorder, self-harm, and other maladaptive behaviors. My misery began when I was four years old. The genetics I inherited, combined with the events I experienced, left traumatic imprints on my mind, emotions, and spirit, which triggered a battle with many demons from childhood into adulthood. This is the story of how my life became imprisoned by this evil, and how I learned to overcome these demons and discover my true self.

During the first few years of my life, the world did not feel dark and hopeless. From what I remember, life was simple then. As a little girl, I was what others called a pretty child: tall and medium-built with vanilla hair, olive skin, and massive gray-green eyes. I had big feet, even as a baby my feet were rather large for my size. I had a tiny, soft voice and a deep laugh. Some might say it was an odd combination, but I was proud of my unique makeup! And then there were the moles on the right side of my face, two distinct moles that formed a straight line. I was honored to carry those moles, and I often fantasized that I was like Cinderella with my "beauty marks."

Our family was not wealthy, and Daddy labored for long hours, seven days a week, in various positions in the food industry. He worked for companies that produced products like potato chips, bread, and doughnuts. After work, he was never too tired for a laugh, however, and he liked to joke that I resembled the Sunbeam Girl and Coppertone Baby. I knew my daddy was a kind-hearted man, and I loved him. Thoughtful, well-mannered, and humble, Daddy made his love clear to me through his words and actions. He hailed from country-living Charlestonians who were altruistic and not fond of materialism. Everyone knew the DuBoses around Johns Island and the Lowcountry; they had hearts that longed to serve others, and they treated people based on their inner worth.

As with many folks who basked in the presence of the balmy, southern country lifestyle, Daddy had a weakness for two things: food and sports. In high school, he earned a college scholarship to play football. He met Momma while in his senior year of high school, and they dated while attending separate campuses. When the news broke that Momma was pregnant with the likings of me, Daddy dropped the football scholarship to be a full-time father. He never seemed to regret his decision of becoming a father over pursuing his football dreams; he was the kind of man who put family first and was unselfish about his actions. Momma and Daddy married in a small ceremony surrounded by family and close friends; she was nineteen, and he was twenty, and he loved my mother with a fiery passion.

My parents took me to the local Chuck E. Cheese's as a means of entertainment. Momma and Daddy couldn't afford the hot, bubbling pizza, so we would sit and watch the other families having fun, and lose ourselves in their excitement. We created our private cocoon of laughter and escape, and love was our wealth.

It often rained against the glass doors outside, which lulled me into a trance as the lights and noises from the games dazzled and honked like a wonderland; everything seemed to spin and swirl like a merry-go-round. The furry dolls gathered together on the dark stage with their instruments; their bulging eyes and giant movements made them seem otherworldly as they jostled about with their clunky robot dances.

My Momma's name was Sandy. She was the queen of my universe and astounded me with her physical beauty and grace. Sandy made even the most elegant actress jaundiced with her voluminous, raven hair, creamy skin, and mischievous, honey-colored eyes. She possessed a crook in her smile and a move in her hip that compelled every man and woman to take a second look when she passed. Tall and slim, yet athletic, Momma was a mixture of a delicate lady and a tomboy. She always appeared as if she had just waltzed off the pages of a fashion magazine, and she took great pride in that knowledge. And her nails: Momma would have rather died than be seen without her nails painted in her favorite shade of garnet wine, and she *never* wasted an opportunity to boast about how lovely they were. Momma worked hard to make sure the home matched her appearance; it was always pristine. The furniture, décor, and gardens resembled the latest cover of *Southern Living* magazine.

Momma loved nature, and some of her hobbies included painting landscape portraits, fishing, and helping the wildlife control remove alligators from our reservoir in the backyard. She was also unafraid to knock a catfish out with a mallet and taught me a thing or two about hammering fish from a young age.

I look back often and think of the countless days we spent together planted in front of her cherry wood dresser, where she kept a mirror with large, Hollywood-style bulbs. The bright lights couldn't outshine Momma's beauty as she spent hours every morning crafting her hair and painting on her makeup. When I peered into the mirror, I fantasized about my idols: Julia Roberts, Grace Kelly, and Princess Diana all exemplified refinement and poise that I dared to possess. I didn't regard myself as special; instead, I admired Momma and the way her eyes reflected against the mirror, producing a sparkling, intense energy that seemed exotic. Perhaps the intensity that shone in her eyes was something that did not belong in this world, something greater than this life could embrace.

Momma was the best chef you could ever imagine, and just about every meal was homemade. Warm banana nut bread, freshly churned vanilla ice cream, and southern-style sweet tea was always on hand to soothe my belly. And the cookies: somehow she discovered the secret to baking the world's best chocolate-chip cookies. Every night, the small white timer signaled that supper was ready, and she called out in a Gullah accent.

"Alright now, suppuh's ready, come'yuh 'n git it while it's hot, chillun!"

She referred to everyone as "chillun" no matter their age, and she freely swapped between spouting off in Gullah and plain English. Supper consisted of dishes such as crispy fried chicken, salted string beans, and, of course, creamy mashed potatoes with steak gravy. I was expected to devour every item on my plate, and indulging in seconds, thirds, and desserts were frequent occurrences. Life was peaceful at the dinner table; we shared stories and exchanged smiles.

I itched with anticipation for every year to end, as the changes from copper leaves to stark branches signified the coming of Christmas. The energies that emerged with the wintry season permeated my spirit with illusion and wonder. Sparkling lights illuminated pockets of space in every room of the house and accentuated the twilight with their glow. Intoxicating aromas of cinnamon, vanilla, and pumpkin beckoned me to the kitchen as confections were baked around-the-clock. The majestic evergreen emanated strength from its embellished limbs.

On Christmas Eve of 1989, as I poked around in the branches, I caught a glimpse of my reflection in the window. For a fleeting moment, I was intrigued by my appearance and experienced a sense of worthiness and individuality. There was something else in the reflection: a loving family, laughing and sitting close together. I began to wonder about all of the goodies that might welcome me on Christmas Day, and I could barely contain my joy. I raced throughout the house, my feet pattering on the cold ground as the melodies and incense glided through the air like a fragrant, warm-hearted dance. As I stopped to whisper secrets to the nutcrackers, I lost track of time; our private stories filled my mind with enchantment.

In her heavy Georgian accent, Nana called me into the kitchen. Covered in a quilted apron and thick glasses, she labored for hours to produce her signature pecan and pumpkin pies. The nutcrackers lost their charm once the sweet smells came to my attention, and I rushed to her side. Nana has been one of the most influential people in my life: a woman of grace and strength, her character ingrained within me what a female role model should be. Her affectionate nature wrapped around my soul like an electric blanket on the iciest of nights, and to this day her memory, and the manner by which she chose to live her life, dwells in my spirit and provides me with eternal nourishment. She shielded me from harm at times when others wouldn't, and my respect for her flows wide like a river.

Nana was born to a large, loving family from the South and grew up in a farming community in Georgia. Rather than experiencing a comfortable lifestyle, she journeyed along a path filled with hardship and recessions. Married twice, her first husband perished in a plane crash, and her second spouse, Momma's adopted father, Matthew, died from a heart attack one day as he was traveling to work. Although Nana suffered from these traumatic events, she never allowed them to break her spirit. Her world revolved around the grace and promises of God, and she believed that they symbolized goodness and hope. She used the adversities she encountered to draw closer to God instead of pushing away from Him, which strengthened her character and enabled her to grow into someone capable of easing the sadness of others.

Nana enriched my soul with a critical concept that has become a rock during my darkest days: she taught me to trust in God and lean upon His everlasting love *at all times*. She helped me to understand that His love and grace are regularly available and that no matter how far into the depths of despair my heart might fall, or how much the world around me may seem to crumble, God's light has the power to lead me through the darkness.

Momma and Nana shared a powerful bond that began the moment Nana brought Momma home from the hospital in Charleston. Nana and Matthew selected a closed adoption, meaning that the records of the birth parents were sealed, although some information was released. The process was bittersweet; Nana wasn't able to conceive, and Sandy's biological mother passed away after the delivery due to complications from cirrhosis of the liver. A long and hard battle with alcohol ravaged her body, and she was unable to care for Momma. Momma grew up with a faint knowledge of her background, as Nana never wanted to reveal any information.

As a young lady, Momma overflowed with a rainbow of emotions, from profound happiness to buried despair. She internalized many of her feelings about her mysterious biological family and tried to sustain the strict Christian environment that surrounded her. When Matthew died, a metamorphosis took place, and she began to forsake her spiritual side. Momma transformed into a fragmented child, and her reality adopted a darker tone, one vacant of hope and layered in anxiety and fear. Matthew's death flooded Momma with unresolved issues about her biological family and feelings of abandonment. Creating art became her favorite method of therapy during difficult times, sometimes by sketching abstract objects, and other times by painting local landscapes and wildlife.

Momma's artwork revealed to me her raw essence, a soul overflowing with profound passion and appreciation for natural beauty. But of all the works of art crafted by Momma's hands, none stole my heart like her picture of Shem Creek. Dreamy pearl overtones lingered over the azure waters of the harbor, where herds of humble boats unwound for the day. Set apart from the others was a tiny boat etched with the name *Tara Nicole* on its side. To behold my name tattooed in watercolor sealed the union between Momma and me for all time; I felt I was a rare, precious child. The painted seagulls soared along breezy streams as they cried out to anyone who dared to follow them along their voyages. Momma had amassed a soft spot for birds, for to her they illustrated freedom and song. Now whenever I witness seagulls drifting along the waters, or a hummingbird zipping about honeysuckles, I am reminded that freedom is not without difficulty and suffering. As the birds ascend and sing beautiful melodies, I too can choose to rejoice throughout any circumstance.

One of my happier moments

CHAPTER **2**

Stolen Innocence

Perhaps the first few years of my life weren't as magical as I'd like to remember. After all, what child doesn't like to live in a world of make-believe? Especially when the physical world is anything but enchanting. In 1987, at the age of two, the earth shattered, and the stars plunged from the heavens. Momma and Daddy's divorce gave birth to a darkness which threatened to consume me. At the time they parted ways, Daddy was an energetic twenty years old, and Momma was nineteen. According to Momma, Daddy's noggin could boil to an intolerable intensity when he got angry, never mind his immaturity and knack for mishandling money. Daddy declared Momma to be mentally unstable, revealing her affinity for engaging in lengthy conversations with paintings. They couldn't salvage the marriage and Momma found herself braving a mass of uncertainties at a young age, with a baby girl in her arms and a high school education to guide her. Although her future seemed vague, it would not be long before another man would fall under her spell and steal her away. While working as a secretary at a local car dealership, she met Stephen, a man quite her senior, who provided Momma with the promise of a fairy-tale life.

Daddy's love for Momma only grew deeper as time flew forward. He attempted to win back her affection and paid an unannounced visit to Nana's residence one evening in the spring, unaware of the new suitor inside. Upon catching a glimpse of me cradled in another man's arms, Daddy's passions overwhelmed him, and in a rage he crushed the front door, questioning the Romeo who had waltzed into our lives. Violence ensued, and for a brief period, Daddy resided in the slammer.

As unfortunate circumstances had it, the jailhouse was directly across from where Momma and her charmer worked together, and the window from his cell allowed him to see the front entrance. Day after day, through the unforgiving bars, Daddy was powerless as he observed Stephen's gleaming Cadillac pull up with the lovebirds nestled inside. His dreams of working things out with Momma seemed to have washed right on down the Ashley River. In the spring of 1987, while sitting in jail, he learned that Momma and The Wolf had run off and gotten hitched. A part of Daddy died and never recovered; his crumbled heart was now the property of the woman he loved.

Life carried on as I attempted to adapt to my redesigned family. Where had my daddy gone and *who did* this new man reckon himself to be? On the surface, he appeared charismatic and chivalrous, but whenever I cried or did something that wasn't to his liking, he reacted in a harsh manner. This man, this *stepdaddy* was much harder to please than Daddy. If I did anything deemed as incorrect in his judging eyes, it set his emotions on fire like a demon straight out of Hades. Stephen shifted from a charming caretaker to an angry drill sergeant who screamed at me on a moment's notice. His bullying behaviors were written off as displays of paternal love, and at first, I felt guilty for questioning his motives. Over time, however, I began to recognize his cruelty. Even through my child eyes, I knew that my pain was his pleasure. Later in life, I learned that he had suffered all kinds of abuse as a kid. It was common for his father to wake him up in the mornings and command him to stare into the ceiling light. Pain was all he had ever known, and inflicting pain was his way of loving.

Momma was taken by Stephen's ways and did whatever he asked; she even gave me my first taste of a Long Island Iced Tea when I was three. They thought it was the funniest thing and told everyone in the family about it, but I couldn't understand why they were laughing.

My life was changing fast; before I knew it, Stephen had taken over completely. He moved us far away from Daddy and into a house on James Island.

Perched beneath its Spanish moss bonnet, our saffron-colored house harbored somber wooden paneling, sullied gray carpet, and a vast, sinister hallway. The original structure was completed in the 1930s, and an addition was built in the 1970s for function and supposed charm. Momma arranged the rooms to the best of her ability, given the hodge-podge of contrasting furniture sprinkled about. A musty, pea-colored couch, towering grandfather clock, and a rusty pump organ became my friends and distractions from reality. Looming above the head of my bed was a window that displayed a hauntingly beautiful magnolia tree, which projected its gloomy shadow over my walls. The backyard boasted magnolia and oak trees that stained the entire lawn in various shades of chestnut and wine in autumn.

The unsettling aura that surrounded the home seemed to emanate from some otherworldly source. Two weeks after moving in, I peeked into the dark, wicked hallway and was confident Beelzebub and I rubbed eyeballs. Afterward, I pledged never to roam down the hall alone. My existence became contaminated with hallucinations and restless spirits who wandered the yard at night; their chained bodies tortured my soul and disrupted my dreams. And oh, how I despised that icebox Momma referred to as "*de kitch'n.*" The kitchen was so chilly that even during the dog days of summer you had to bundle up in a parka. Momma liked to joke that *de kitch'n* was the spirit's meeting grounds, and that was the reason for its abnormally low temperature.

As the unearthly occurrences increased, I became possessed with paranoia and anxiety. I was traumatized by the relentless antics the ghosts played: the unplugged telephone rang at all hours of the night, the microwave buttons beeped, and the television turned off and on. I tried to seek out someone or something for comfort; ghosts, the concept of divorce and accepting the new father figure in my life were obstacles that seemed insurmountable to my child self.

As a four-year-old, I loved to frolic around the lawn sprinkler in the backyard with my cocker spaniel, Ruby, until one day in the summer of 1989 when my slick-talking cousin Thomas came over to play, too. He pointed out the birthmark on my butt cheek that was popping out of my swimsuit. To me, it was a myriad of itsy-bitsy brown dots that resembled the profile of a man's face. My ego ballooned with pride the instant I realized I had a silhouette on my heinie; could it be Jesus? Surely Jesus loved me, but not enough to carry out a Biblical phenomenon on my bottom. Upon further inspection of my birthmark, Thomas asked with a serpentine grin if it was, indeed, poop. *Poop!* The nerve of that youngin'. He began to whoop and holler as my face contorted in purple rage. Teasing or not, I now felt ashamed of my beauty mark. In a flash, I covered the mark with my clammy hands and from that moment on I vowed to cover up my body and exercise modesty to the best of my ability.

Being picked on for my birthmark was the first time I remember feeling self-consciousness. I trusted that Thomas had innocent intentions when he referred to my mark as "poop," however, anyone who has had to cope with mental health conditions or even stress might attest to the disastrous effects that teasing and bullying can have. A simple joke can strip off layers of self-esteem from a person. My unique birthmark was no less a part of my body than my arms or legs, and I was powerless to change it. Once my body became subject to ridicule, I believed that who I was as a human being was a mistake, and feelings of worthlessness replaced my natural joy. As time rolled on, this sense of inadequacy sealed itself into my psyche, and I relived the intense judgment every day of my life. Countless eyes penetrated through my every weakness, and their words of criticism fired straight to my soul, validating my innermost fears and crushing my courage.

Stephen was wealthier than Daddy, and he knew it too. Momma and I were taken on fancy trips and lavished with expensive gifts. We were *his* girls, and he loved to show us off. I wore frilly clothes and had expensive toys, and Momma . . . Well, Momma looked like a queen. Whenever Stephen came near Momma, she stood to attention and showed off her elegant clothes like a doll. Stephen showered her with compliments but was quick to correct her whenever he thought she could look more beautiful. One day he yelled at us for hours, and the next, he showed up at the door with an armful of presents and a story about where our next adventure was going to be.

Daddy didn't earn much and was struggling to make ends meet. He saw his life spiral downward quickly: from promising football star, to jail, to coming home without a child and wife. He knew about the extravagant gifts Stephen was buying because Momma and I called him from our trips and told him about our adventures. Daddy fell deeper into depression as he realized that he could never give Momma the kind of lifestyle that she desired. To Momma, Daddy became an old friend and a distant memory of love that once was but could never be again. The good life was everything to her, and she grew into it mighty fine. Daddy continued to work hard, over twelve hours a day delivering food to stores across Charleston. In the evenings, he came home and was faced with the reality that the woman he loved was married to a man who had more money and prestige than he ever could.

One day toward the end of summer of '89, Stephen came home from work with a charming grin wrapped around his face. When he leaned down, I could smell his funny breath.

"I have something you might like!"

Over dinner, he revealed that he had bought us all tickets to Disney World. The moment I heard the word "Disney," I jumped out of my seat and hugged him. Disney movies and books were my favorite, and my imagination ran wild at the thought of visiting such a magical place. My dream was about to come true—Stephen was my hero! My emotions fell, however, when I realized that one special person wasn't going to be there.

"What's wrong?"

Stephen seemed puzzled by my sudden change in character.

"Nuthin'. I—I thought that Daddy would come too."

"*Daddy?*"

His smile twisted into a grimace. He turned and positioned me so that I was forced to stare into his enraged eyes.

"*I'm* your dad, your father, do you understand? I'm the one who provides for you, who gives you everything. *He's* not your dad, and I don't ever want to hear you say that again."

One week later, on a record hot August afternoon, Momma, Stephen, Nana, and I packed for our splashy vacation. The seven hours spent traveling to Orlando, Florida, was accompanied by the blast of the air-conditioning, sing-a-long tapes, frequent bathroom breaks, and the sound of soft bickering in the front seat. My head rested on Nana's soft belly, whose snores rose within me like the creek tides half-past six in the evening. We arrived at our swanky hotel on the Disney grounds late in the night, after filling up on steaks, milkshakes, and fries just outside of Daytona Beach. Momma and Stephen kissed me on the cheek and retreated to their room close by. Nana carried me over her shoulder and placed me beside her in the bed where I slept until early the next morning.

Rays of sunlight squinted through the window and hovered over my face. I awoke with nothing other than the knowledge that on this day, I would meet the characters from my favorite movies. I peered over at Nana and shook her cushy shoulder. She turned and wrapped me in her arms, planting endless kisses on the top of my head.

"Good mornin', sugar! Are you ready to go to Disney World today? We better get up and get ready before your momma and Stephen come over to get us."

I looked at the clock: 6:30 am. Nana wasted no time picking out my frilly white sundress and pink jellies that squeaked from my sweat whenever I walked in them too long. She then put on beige pants, a pink blouse and heavy perfume that made me sneeze. I sat on the edge of the bed and kicked my feet back and forth, as I watched Nana color her face with blue and peach powder. She was more beautiful and bright than a bowl of fruit ice cream.

Stephen and Momma came over soon after and we ate breakfast in the hotel. My tummy was rumbling as I devoured my stack of Mickey pancakes and eggs. I finished before everyone and became impatient as Momma and Nana sipped their coffees; I was ready for the day ahead!

The park was a real, live dream world. I roamed along enchanted gardens where apricot tulips held whispering butterflies, I flew through space, and I traveled to faraway lands. As I approached Cinderella's Kingdom, Goofy, Pluto, Mickey Mouse, and Minnie ran over to greet me. They rolled out a velvet carpet just for me, and as my feet touched the end, I jumped into Mickey's arms and embraced him with every ounce of my childhood energy. Minnie Mouse complimented my dress, and Goofy and Pluto sent me into a fit of giggles with their silly jokes. We had a tea party in the center of the kingdom and nibbled on mouse-shaped cake and cookies—I was floating in my heart's desire.

I was lost deep in conversation with Mickey about nothingness when I heard the most familiar sound. *Horses!* Trotting down the cobblestone, in my direction! I dropped a half-eaten cookie on my plate and smiled as Cinderella picked me up and placed me in her royal carriage. She commanded the horses to take us all around the kingdom, and I took in the sights and sounds in style.

After our grand tour, Cinderella said goodbye and delivered me back into Momma's arms. We spent the next hour on the Golden Carrousel; around and around we went on the strawberry-colored pony, as the sky washed away in brilliant colored whirls. Momma smelled of vanilla, and her ponytail swayed and shimmered like the night sky. Then she scooped me up, and we sat down in a magical teacup. Nana and Stephen watched from afar as Momma and I sat on opposite sides of the pastel cup.

"Ready, my sweetheart?"

"Ready, Mommy!"

We began to turn the giant wheel in the middle. Fervently we spiraled, as we stared into each other's eyes, soul to soul, as only mother and daughter can do. Our teacup rolled madly on the slick floor, and everything blended: Momma, the ceiling, the ground, my mind. Pale curls fluttered around my head, and Momma and I laughed and snorted. It was the best day of my little life.

We stayed a week and toured every park. In the midst of all the fun and rides, I often caught myself admiring Momma and her beauty; she was a princess in the flesh. When we visited Snow White and the Seven Dwarfs, I was taken aback by how much she resembled Momma. Porcelain skin, raven hair, and cocoa eyes; they could have been sisters.

Momma liked to stop and take photos of herself kissing different characters throughout the parks. Inside MGM Studios, we stumbled upon a statue of a tall Native American man, and Momma became overwhelmed.

"Oh, I just *have* to take a picture with him! Isn't he cute?"

She leaned over and gave him a juicy smooch on his frozen cheek. Stephen appeared bothered, but he forced a chuckle and planted a kiss on the statue, too. He knew how valuable Momma was; even amidst thousands of people at the park, she shone like a rare diamond. Momma was only wearing tennis shoes, jean shorts, and a cotton shirt with padded shoulders, but it was the way she carried herself that suggested she could have been a queen in disguise—she surely was a queen to me. Not even the sweltering Florida sun could melt her immaculate features, which she enhanced with charcoal eyeliner and ruby red lipstick. *"How can her face be so perfect, when my body sweats and my feet stink in my jelly shoes?"* I thought. I felt sloppy compared to her, but knowing she was mine gave me hope. *"Someday, I'll make my face as pretty as Momma's. As soon as I can, I'll be perfect, too."*

We rode back to Charleston late Sunday afternoon, with a van full of souvenirs and sunburned bodies. I was exhausted from the endless sunshine and sheer magnitude of the sights and sounds and passed out in Nana's arms. I dreamt of floating tea parties with Cinderella and Winnie the Pooh atop a serene, vast ocean.

The noise from the minivan disrupted my dreams as it halted in front of our house. It was black outside, and as Stephen slid the door open, I heard the familiar sounds of frogs and crickets croaking and chirping in the grass. He plucked me up, hauled me into the house, and placed me on my bed with my bags of presents settled beside me.

I closed my eyes, but as soon as he pulled the door to a crack, I crept out of bed and opened my bags. I couldn't wait to give Daddy his special present, a statue from one of the parks that read, "World's Best Dad." I hid the lustrous gold figure under a pile of socks in the chest of drawers for fear that Stephen could steal it.

The next morning, I woke up earlier than usual and wrestled in bed with uncertainty. Should I wake up or should I go back to sleep? My body hurt from the sun, and I wanted to rest, but I couldn't bring my stubborn brain to listen to my heart. I slipped out of bed in my baggy T-shirt and roamed all over the house, looking for any sight of Nana. I felt confused; my thoughts trickled between Nana and breakfast. I was hungry, and I couldn't go back to bed just yet. I needed Nana to cuddle with and lull me back to sleep. I tiptoed toward the guest bedroom and knocked softly on the door. All of a sudden, a raging BOOM rattled my core and made me jump.

I dared to peek over my shoulder, for I *knew* who was behind me: it was Stephen, as angry as a bull. Whatever I had done, I had done wrong, and he was ready to punish me. He snatched my arm like a noodle and shook me about; the pain was profound, but the fear was greater. He threw me over his shoulder, exposed my cotton panties, and spanked my bottom hard and fast with his bare hand; I didn't have a moment to catch my breath. He flipped me around, and his merciless eyes dug into mine.

"What are you doing up? Your mom and I are trying to sleep! You're makin' *too much* noise. Go take a nap, *you hear me?*"

"Yes, sir!"

He stormed into my room, slammed the door, shoved me onto the bed, and began his torments. Digging into my arms, he twisted them until they felt scorching hot. He wrung them harder than the cloth towels Momma used to wash the dishes.

Over and over he struck my body with his hands. As the beatings pummeled up and down my head, back, and tail, he hissed through his teeth and told me that I ought *never* forget to take a nap again! I held my breath hoping that the absence of air could soften the pain, but even through my clenched eyes and mouth, my child soul was on fire—it was dying. My neck, legs, and back were in agony; I begged for him to stop, but he didn't. The more fear I showed, the harder he hit me. I was sorry I hadn't taken my nap.

Suddenly, he stopped and calmly left. I remained face down, in tears. I raised my head and surveyed my body and my surroundings. The happy memories from Disney World were gone; my dreams of a happy family were an illusion. This man was not here to love me, he was here to hurt me.

From that point on, I became Stephen's little doll: a doll that he could abuse whenever he saw fit. I felt powerless and confused; after he threatened and hurt me, he told me how much he loved me. Sometimes I sat in total darkness, listening for any signs of life, for any connection with the world around me. Sounds of thunder and rain soothed me and brought relief to my distressed mind. When I gazed out my bedroom window at the billowing clouds, it felt as if the strands of reality were being pulled apart, too.

〰〰〰

It was common in the spooky house for Momma to stand beside my bed at night, plant her hand over my head, and pray boldly in a language that I just *did not* understand. I couldn't wrap my mind around what I was hearing. All I knew was that Momma enjoyed blabbering in some foreign language, and it scared me.

After Momma's bedside exorcisms and the other chilling occurrences in our home, Stephen decided that we were due for a move. So in the fall of 1990, we found ourselves in a Victorian house tinted in the precise shade of my favorite gum, the original Hubba Bubba. We were the envy of Manor Boulevard, and, oh, was Momma proud! We were living in a life-sized dollhouse, a dream to call our own.

However, even in our new dream house, there were rarely any avenues of relief from the constant stresses. Only a few things brought comfort to me: visits with Nana was one, and junk food was another. With Nana, I enjoyed both comforts freely. She lived across town in a mobile home, the same one where the police had arrested Daddy. During some weekend nights, we had sleepovers and fun "parties with her baby," as she called them. Everything we shared seemed to be the happiest moments of our lives; we had so much fun that sometimes I couldn't tell who the kid was.

Whenever Momma dropped me off, I didn't feel as though I was driving up to a trailer; instead, I believed that I was arriving in a horse-drawn carriage, dressed in a sparkling gown, coming toward a beautiful palace filled with wonder and mystery. I couldn't wait to get away from the evil King Stephen; as soon as I entered through the jewel-covered gates, I knew I was free. Nana's love strengthened me and made me feel like an empress.

We had our special routine once the weekend started. We plopped down on her hard, itchy gray sofa and talked about each other's week. Barbie was typically the highlight of the conversation as I could never tell her what was *really* happening back home. Stephen's temper, the beatings; I was afraid of what he would do to me if he found out.

Mealtime was my favorite time of the weekend. Whenever food was around, we could be found stuck to a movie screen or tied to the television. One day during the winter of '90 - a rather sticky, warm winter's day, mind you - we went to the video store. I dragged my two Cabbage Patch dolls inside her Oldsmobile and buckled them in their seats. Nana smiled at me with her wide, wrinkly smile as we drove off. I adored my Cabbage Patch dolls with their yarn hair and plastic, sturdy bodies, and I carried them with me wherever I went; we were the *three amigos*, as Momma called us. When we walked into the store, I felt free and happy; I could have any movie I wanted.

We headed on over to the "Kids" section and chose a video that had characters on the front with looks similar to my Cabbage Patch Dolls. The title read: *The Garbage Pail Kids Movie*. Nana squinted at the cover.

"What movie is that?"

"Cabbage Patch!"

Nana and I armored ourselves with the movie, a couple of pepperoni pizzas, some extra-long sticks of Tootsie Rolls, a two-liter diet soda, and headed back to the castle. I was floating; all that mattered was that I had the video, and I had Nana. In our world, there was no stress, and I could be myself. Not to mention the chocolate, pizza, and soda; it was a five-and-a-half-year-old's fantasy!

Shortly after we popped in *The Garbage Pail Kids Movie,* however, we realized that it was not like the Cabbage Patch Dolls. We watched the disgusting film in wide-eyed horror and simultaneously stuffed our faces with junk food. I glanced at Nana; she was furious, yet she didn't lose control.

"Honey, this movie is *vulgar*. Not for young girls."

It was. The dolls peed, vomited, and burped; my dolls never did that. I was overwhelmed by their repulsive behavior, and I felt uneasy in my stomach. The cheesy pizza didn't taste so delicious anymore, and I ran to the toilet. Our party ended early, and Nana stayed by my side the rest of the night while I threw up until the early morning, sick from the vile images and filling food. I was afraid that she was going to tell Momma, but she never said a word; I think she knew better than to ruffle Stephen's feathers.

The following February, life began to change again. It was a Wednesday, and I was playing on my bedroom floor with my dolls. Momma called me into the living room. She was sitting on the couch with Stephen; both of them had smiles pinching their cheeks, and their hands were clasped tightly together. They told me to sit down, and that they had something important to say. I couldn't imagine what it could be, and I hoped that I wasn't in trouble. Momma leaned forward with round, shining eyes like diamonds.

"We're having a baby! You're gonna be a sister!"

My mind flurried with excitement as I pondered the word "baby." I didn't exactly understand, but I promised myself that I would love this new arrival.

As the months soared by like bronzed cowbirds on their journey, I grew fond of the giant bump on Momma's stomach. I stayed by her side and rubbed my hands up and down her belly because it felt like rubber. The size of her tummy was incredible; it resembled the beach balls we brought down to the shore during the summer. Momma just laughed when I told her that. She said I was her precious girl for thinking that way.

One sweltering evening in May, while we were alone in the house, Momma called me into her bedroom. She pulled out a thread with a needle attached at the end.

"This is an old trick. With this thread, we will be able to tell if the baby inside of me is a little sister or brother for you."

I was mesmerized; she held the needle and thread over the middle of her full belly until it stopped swinging.

"Now, the needle must be completely still. But when I release my grip, if the thread goes around in a circle, then the baby inside is a girl, like you. If the thread moves back and forth, then it's a boy!"

I watched as she held the needle and thread still again, just above her stomach. Then she let go, and the thread started to move by itself, faster and faster, back and forth across her belly. I held my breath and watched as the thread continued to sway all by itself.

"Momma! You're playin' a trick! Are you movin' it with your hand?"

"No, I promise. One day soon, you will have a baby brother. Mark my words."

She gazed down at my face with loving eyes and planted a gentle kiss on my forehead. Then she leaned over and whispered three words that sent a wave of comfort through my body.

"My little girl . . ."

I breathed in the scent of her natural, warm skin, and soft, silky robe. Content and at peace, I fell asleep. My head rested in the dimple of her arm, dreaming of this love, a love that could last for all time.

"Nikki . . . Nikki!"

Momma interrupted my daydream with her annoyed voice. During the dog days of summer, I often lost myself in my imagination.

"Yes, ma'am?"

Embarrassed, I sat up at the dinner table and straightened my back, barely able to make eye contact.

"Are you gonna eat your supper? Now I spent all day making this pumpernickel bread in that new machine your dad got me, the least you can do is eat a slice!"

She glanced at Stephen. *"I suppose she also expects me to call him Daddy, now,"* I thought. She pranced over to his lap and sat down. They looked at me and smiled. Stephen leaned back in his chair, and they chatted and told jokes for a little while. Momma wrapped her arms around him, and they began to kiss. *"How can she sit in his lap, hugging and kissing him like a monkey? After everything he's done, she still loves him?"* I thought. I picked up my fork and stared at my food; water began to rise in my eyes and throat. *"I hate them,"* I thought. I contemplated a way to break free from their love torture, but it was no use. I stabbed the fork into each portion of my food and chewed it mechanically, with my fist rested on my left cheek.

"How does it taste?"

Stephen smiled. I wanted to respond, but an overwhelming feeling of nausea came over me.

"I *said*, how *does* it taste?"

"I—I . . ."

"You know, you're acting like a spoiled brat!"

Immediately, I shut my eyes and covered my body. I waited for Stephen to hit me but nothing happened. I peeked and saw his red, angry face and cold eyes staring back at me. Momma looked furious, too. Instead of beating or yelling, however, she turned and kissed Stephen, ignoring the tears that began to pour down my cheeks. Who was this woman? Why did Momma care more about him than me? Something inside of me died a bit at that moment. I placed a napkin over my face and continued eating, but a few loud sniffles and hiccups made their way out. Suddenly, Stephen began to scream.

"NIKKI! What the HELL is wrong with you? Next time you feel like that, go to the bathroom! Don't you EVER, EVER blow your nose again at the dinner table! DO YOU UNDERSTAND ME?"

SMACK! He slammed his hand against the table so hard I was sure he broke both. Pee drizzled down my thighs.

"Ye-yes, sir."

I couldn't stop looking at Stephen's face; it was still bloody crimson, smeared with a sick smile.

"You better *mind your daddy* little girl!"

For a moment, Momma woke up, and she wrinkled her brows.

"Please, don't act like that! She didn't mean anything by it, give her a break."

Stephen turned and grabbed her firmly by the arms. She fell backward and began to talk in a tiny voice like mine. I was frozen solid, afraid to move a muscle. The scene was like a scary movie, but I couldn't find the "off" button.

"You don't tell me what to do, *do you understand*?"

He shook her violently, causing her to sob uncontrollably.

"Y-yes, I'm sorry . . ."

Her helplessness drowned me; it choked every ounce of air from my body. Stephen's grin was gone, and his cruelty was exposed. He released Momma and eased back in his chair. With his arms folded, he turned and stared at me. I noticed his left eye twitching.

"What are *you* looking at?"

I prayed to God, but I didn't hear his voice or feel any warmth in my stomach. Then I prayed to Nancy Drew; of all the times I had read about my beloved heroine, I needed her by my side more than ever. More than anything, I wished to *be* Nancy Drew, so that I could whip across the table and rescue Momma and the baby inside. But as I mentally prepared to pounce on the evil Stephen, I felt my courageous spirit sink. He was too big; his strength would overpower me. I was witty, but he was able to knock me to the ground in less than a second, as he had done so many times before. I knew in my heart there was nothing I could do. I desperately wanted to save them, but I was powerless. I glanced at Momma: her eyes were blank. I wanted to run away, far away into my mystery books and see if someone would come searching for me.

Visitations with Daddy were normally every other weekend. The courts allowed us to see each other in limited amounts, but as Momma's feet and stomach started to swell like baking sausages, she asked Daddy to pick me up more.

He lived on an island in the countryside. Situated on a dirt road that spilled onto a pebble path was an old, pea-green, one-story home that his daddy had built long ago. With only two bedrooms and one bath, it raised all six of Daddy's brothers and sisters, their children, and neighborhood children to spare. I was particularly fond of Dad's sister Aunt Sarah and spent quite a lot of time with her whenever Dad worked double shifts. Aunt Sarah didn't have any children of her own, so she spoiled me rotten. She regularly gave me Barbie purses, coloring books, and my favorite: lots of boiled shrimp.

Daddy was the only member of the family who stayed behind in the home, and he cared for Granny and Pappy, up until Pappy's death. "Bug-bug," as he was known, passed away when I was three. He liked to sit me on his lap and slip me suckers that matched the colors of the rainbow. He was magic, and his memory filled the home, long after he was gone.

Daddy and I often walked around the house and talked about how it was falling to pieces. He said that even though it was only a thousand feet and sat on cinder blocks, it was held together by more love than any mansion in the world. Daddy had a way of saying things that made them easy for me to understand.

The house was old, but it had soul. Laughter and smiles saturated the walls from sunrise to sunset and back again. Outside in the yard was a statue of Kermit the Frog atop a stone fountain, and he held an umbrella in his hand to protect himself from the frequent storms. Daddy and I liked to sit on the handmade bench and have tea parties with my *Sesame Street* friend.

I was as excited about the drive to Daddy's house as I was about being at his house. During the long ride through the dusty back roads, Daddy allowed things that Momma and Stephen never did. As soon as he hit the gas pedal, I reclined back on the velvety cushions of his '88 Cutlass Supreme and stacked my bare feet up on the dashboard. He let me turn the radio up loud and listen to anything my heart desired, even if it was rock or country music. Momma and Stephen only listened to boring talk radio. I liked to bang on the outside of the glove compartment and pretend that it was *my* fancy piano. And we *never* passed the Piggly Wiggly without stopping at the boiled peanut stand on the corner.

"You want some peanuts? I know you do! Ain't nobody gonna tell me that my daughter don't want a bag of hot boiled peanuts!"

Daddy would ruffle my hair with his hands, and I nodded my head with vigor; Daddy was always thinking about me. He didn't make a lot of money, Stephen liked to remind me of that, but I knew that my daddy loved me with all of his heart. He put me first and treated me with respect and kindness. With Daddy, I could be myself.

Our time together was an escape from my troubles. Sometimes I dreamed about revealing the truth to Daddy, though. If he knew that Stephen was hurting us, he could make the pain go away. But the fear stopped me and kept me up at night. Even when I couldn't see Stephen's face or hear his voice, the fear was there, painting a frightening picture in my mind. Instead of telling Daddy, I put on a mask with a drawn-on smile and pretended everything was all right.

Momma's stomach swallowed more space as time went on, and I became increasingly protective of her and the mysterious baby inside. Thoughts of the new arrival filled my mind day and night: what was life going to be like with a little person around? Would Momma and Stephen forget about me? I hoped not, but if Stephen did, that wasn't such a bad thing.

My protective instincts were not far off. The accident happened in August, and no one saw it coming, especially Momma. It was early in the afternoon, and I had just come home from school. I sat in the dining room and attempted a crack at my homework. My elbows were sprawled all over the table, and my swinging feet provided a distraction from the humdrum lesson about synonyms, along with our cat, Miss Tess, as she beat her tail against the carpet.

Then I heard it. *The sound.* A deafening, sickening scream upstairs, followed by harsh banging. Before I knew it, Momma was lying in a crooked heap at the foot of the stairs. Her fingers scraped the railing, and her wide eyes stared at an unknown place. I raced over, grabbed her by the shoulders, and she rubbed her belly and muttered something about "911."

Within thirty minutes we were in the emergency room. Stephen, Nana, and I sat in an anxious circle while the doctor and nurses watched over Momma. As each second passed, I waited for the doctor to return with the news that the baby was dead; in my mind, my sibling dreams were dying, too. After an hour, however, the doctor entered the room, smiling. He said that Momma had checked out all right, and so had the baby. I was relieved but felt powerless over how quickly Momma had fallen. The baby who almost never was: it was the newspaper headline of the day. I breathed a heavy sigh and fell into Nana's chest, thankful for our good luck, but unsure of how long it would last.

On September 5, 1991, my brother was born. I held him moments after he arrived, his skin wrinkled and purple. His high-pitched cries were a soothing melody for my soul. This fascinating new creature named Christian Luke, Jr., had my heart, and one look at his tiny face made all of my worries sink to the bottom of the ocean. I was certain that I was going to break him into a million pieces if I touched or held him the wrong way. Later, I sat in the corner of the hospital room and watched as everyone else crowded around him, "oohing" and "ahhing." Jealousy was not my friend, however; I was just grateful that I had someone I could share life with.

‿‿‿

Momma slept more after she gave birth to Christian. She also didn't cook as much, so we ate frozen pizzas and tacos a couple of nights a week. I never imagined that I would miss fresh tomatoes or carrots, but secretly, I began to crave vegetables. After months of consuming junk food, Nana convinced Momma to plant again, and so the next spring, Momma spent all of her free time outside. The baby and the garden, that was Momma's life. Her obsession with vegetables and flowers earned our yard the title of "Garden of the Month," every time the sun shined. It was all Stephen talked about; another achievement to add to our perfect family, another lie to add to our story.

When Christmas of 1992 arrived, Momma must have been exhausted because she didn't decorate the house. And although there were piles of presents underneath the tree, most of them were for Christian. I received a teddy bear with the year sewn on the feet, and watched as Stephen opened Christian's shiny boxes filled with clothes, toys, and books. Just before he unwrapped the last present, Momma disappeared into the kitchen.

"I have one more present for *you*, Nikki!"

I whipped my head around, curious.

"Another present for *me*?"

"One last special surprise, just for you."

I tore open the thin paper, and inside was a smooth, green box. The sides of the box held together with holiday tape, and I dug my stubby nails into them until the strips ripped apart. Stephen didn't approve of my unwrapping method and yelled. Momma shot him a look and stopped him right then and there.

"Stephen *quit.*"

I removed the lid and uncovered a large, antique doll, with western-style clothing, pale skin, and hair as dark as the night. Her glassy, black eyes seemed to follow me as I moved my head from side to side. The more I studied the doll, the more I sensed an odd familiarity. Suddenly, I realized that she starkly resembled Momma, only she was creepy. Her mouth hung open and her face revealed no emotion—it was eerily blank. Every hair on my arm began to stand up. I peeked at Momma: she was beaming from ear to ear.

"How do you like her?"

"I—I love her."

Lying was not easy, but if I didn't accept the present, I was sure to receive a beating.

"I'm so happy you like her! Nana and Aunt Tally found her from the antique shop downtown when I was a little girl, and now I want to pass her on to you! I want you to take good care of her, okay? We're gonna put her high up on your dresser with your other collectibles because she's very delicate. Oh, and *one more thing.* You'll need to dust her often."

I looked at the spooky doll and mumbled.

"Ye-yes, ma'am. Thank you. Thank you so much."

After Christmas, I became restless. My room felt unsafe, especially while I tried to fall sleep. My night terrors multiplied, and I wet the sheets often. Many times I felt an unexplainable presence in my room. In my mind, I knew it was the doll, but to Momma and Stephen, that was a joke.

The doll began to appear in my dreams, even in nightmares that lingered long after I was awake. She tormented my mind; with just one thought of her dreadful face, my heart raced, and my body perspired profusely.

Right before my eighth birthday, the doll got the best of me. It was after two in the morning, and I had just awoken from a deep sleep. I immediately felt numb and couldn't move. I heard someone, no, *something* shuffling in the room. My mind swirled around who or what could be making these sounds because *my door was locked.*

All of a sudden, a finger poked me in the back. *A finger. In my back.* I dared not turn around to face the mystifying presence. Who was it? What was it? I shivered in fear, wanting to close my eyes, but closing my eyes meant that I would risk yielding to the darkness; there was evil in the darkness. Instead, I remained petrified, waiting for another touch, another sound until morning, but nothing ever came.

For months while I slept, my soul traveled to faraway lands, and I fell into my body. Scenes of waterfalls over lush greenery welcomed me, and as I explored, I felt a freedom I had never known before. Fairies and centaurs guided me through dimensions of blazing colors, golden rays, and bodily sensations that felt transcendental. The worlds in my dreams often seemed more real than in my waking life. When I dropped down the waterfalls and returned into my body, I was terrified, but I couldn't wait to fall asleep and ascend into the celestial realm again.

I became so lost in the dreams that I didn't want to return to the real world; I was obsessed with the idea of living in my imagination. Sometimes in the middle of the night, I awoke in my bed, saturated in a heavy perspiration. The memories from reality came flooding in, and I realized I was no longer a traveler in a universe of fantasy. It was then that I returned to the old feelings of being alone, afraid, and tragically empty.

❧❧❧

Stephen did nothing to improve my self-confidence; if anything, he demolished it. Especially after I had to get oversized, turquoise-rimmed glasses to see in school. He was hell-bent on reminding me of how ugly I was and referred to me as his "idiot," "imbecile," and "whore." Over time, I lost my strength to resist his words of torture and became powerless over the emotional pain. He also demanded that I maintain perfect grades at Northside Christian School and stay involved in extracurricular activities and sports. At home I was ordered to inspect my room every day; if I missed a spot or made up the bed the wrong way, I was sure to receive a beating all over my head and body.

I constructed a world of rigorous rituals and behaviors to muffle his voices in my mind. Every evening, I checked my bedroom to make sure that all was in perfect order. With every passing *tick* on the clock, I knew, oh God did I know, that he was one second closer to coming home. One second closer to pulling out his leather belt and skinning my back. My heart raced when I reviewed my mental checklist.

Was the carpet clear of all debris and toys? Check. Did my shoes line up so that each heel touched to form a straight line in my closet? Check. Did my clothes hang with precisely the right amount of space in between so that he could effortlessly run his hand through them? Check. Was my dollhouse meticulously arranged and dusted? Check. Was my comforter smooth like silk? Were my bedsheets tightly folded, military-style, just the way he liked? Check and check.

I depended on my crazed routine, and Stephen terrified me. After all, Stephen had a lot of friends in the community and at work; who was ever going to believe me over him? Everyone thought that Stephen was a golden man, a shining example of a father.

One person in particular, my unofficial Uncle Robbie, adored Stephen and visited often. Robbie and his wife, Cynthia, were neighborhood friends of my parents who became like an aunt and uncle to me. Stephen and Robbie often told loud stories about cars and money over a couple of glasses of wine while I played in my bedroom alone. While Stephen was good at raking in the big bucks, he was all thumbs at fixing things around the house. Uncle Robbie was the one Momma called when the washer started leaking, or the air-conditioner blew hot air instead. Although Uncle Robbie was quick to ruffle my hair or call me a pretty princess, I got a nervous feeling in my stomach when he was around. He always asked me to sit on his lap, and when I refused he smiled, but the smile never reached his eyes. I hated sitting on his lap and feeling his breath on my skin. Sometimes he tickled me and didn't know when to stop; he often didn't stop until Momma laughingly told him to. She said that he was just clumsy because he and Cynthia didn't have any children of their own.

My parents trusted Robbie since he played Mr. Fix-it, but Uncle Robbie played other games—secret games that only he and I knew about. Whenever he fixed something in my house, and no one was around, he asked me to play. At first, I agreed, but soon I discovered that these were not fun games, they were painful. These were games I never won.

When the winter came, Uncle Robbie decided that I was old enough to partake in activities of a different sort, the kind that exposed me to a more mature side of life. He primed me by stripping away of all my self-worth and offered me the promise of love and gifts in exchange. His sly personality and unpredictable violence rattled me to my core. I loathed myself and yet was helpless as I witnessed my agonizing transformation into a monster; he abused my body *and* used it for his pleasure. When Uncle Robbie finished his games, he wrapped me in his arms and professed his love for me, coupled with threats if I ever told a soul.

Then one afternoon in January, just after a quarter past three, I heard the tires on Uncle Robbie's truck come to a halt outside. The fridge was making stale, warm air; Momma ran to the store with Christian to replace the spoiled groceries and make supper. I knew the games would begin soon. The heater blew in a fury; sweat caused my pantyhose and hair to stick to my body. My glasses repeatedly slipped down my wet, piggish face and I prayed that Jesus would take me to Heaven because I knew I was about to be dragged into the pits of Hell.

The front door opened and shut slowly. I wanted to turn on the television as a distraction, but my body wouldn't budge from my bedroom door. Uncle Robbie's heavy footsteps intensified up the stairs until the shadows of his work boots lingered outside my door, then . . . silence. I gasped for air but couldn't nab a breath, and my bladder threatened to spill its urine. One by one the hairs on my arms and legs stiffened. My eyes darted in all directions, finally landing on the brass door handle. *"When is he going to come in, when is he going to come in, when is he going to come in?"* The thought replayed like a broken record. Suddenly, Uncle Robbie pummeled his fists against the door and growled.

"This better not be locked, little girl!"

He rattled the knob ferociously. The door burst open, and we met face-to-face. I stood, rigid as a soldier, while he appeared crazed, ready for action.

"What did I *tell you* about locked doors, huh? You trying to hide from me?"

I backed up toward my bedpost and clawed for the corner of my comforter.

"No, no sir, I didn't I promise, I just shut it becau—"

There was no time to explain. Uncle Robbie had already decided that my right forearm could make a fine substitute for a sponge, and he began to wring and manipulate it in a thousand directions. His light eyes sank deeper and deeper into his scarlet face; with every brutal twist he sucked his teeth and bit his tongue. The pain was unbearable, but I couldn't fight back.

All of a sudden, he violently flung me into the air. I smashed into the bed, and my head snapped back, causing my teeth to reunite in a grisly collision. I tried to breathe and saw his hands removing his tool belt. *One licks, two licks, three licks, four;* the belt sliced through my back. Uncle Robbie didn't stop there, though; he tore off my underwear and beat my bare bottom. I buried my head into the cotton and inhaled, desperate to escape the pain.

Suddenly, he stopped, and I couldn't hear or see him. My body was on *fire;* with my face still down, I pulled up my panties and winced as the raw gashes burned in the open air.

Out of nowhere, my body flipped over, and my head snapped back again. Uncle Robbie was on top of me; his agonizing strength crushed the life right out of me. He spread my arms wide open, then pinched up and down my thighs. He breathed all over my neck and face, and then he stared dead into my eyes. I managed a scream, but he covered my mouth with his other hand, and then I felt a pain so horrible, I left my body for some time.

I woke up, and he was still on top of me.

"Get off me!"

I scratched and bit at his shirt. I pushed him with all of my power until he rolled off of me. He smiled while I sat in blistering pain and fluids, crippled and unable to process what had occurred.

This incident altered my world and turned into a recurrent night-mare. Uncle Robbie repeatedly abused me on a regular basis during critical times of my development. He was well aware of his charm with adults and wasted no opportunity to use it for his gain. Taking advantage of another's trust, he performed his despicable acts on me anytime the mood struck him, and his threats prevented me from speaking up. I felt defenseless in my surroundings and thought I had no one to turn to for guidance and protection.

☽☽☽

Momma's temper quickly turned into rage these days; any little mistake sent her flying into an uncontrollable state. She often screamed at Christian and me in a deep voice until her face became inflamed.

"Nikki! For God's sake, *get it right*!"

"I—I'm sorry Mom . . ."

"Don't sorry me, just *learn* the verses! You *need* to learn these!"

It was Monday, and Momma hated Mondays. There was a lot of Bible verses to memorize on Mondays. She dropped her head into her hands then raised it slowly, rolling her eyes dramatically.

"Okay, now, Hebrews 11:1. Do you know that one?"

"It's . . . I think it's, um. 'Hope is being sure of what we have faith in, and seeing what we are certain of.'"

Momma smacked her hand on the table creating a loud *whack*!

"No! No! No! No! No!"

She yelled and repeatedly slammed both of her palms on the table. Every smack caused me to jump, and I tried like the dickens to hold back the flood of tears. I pressed my privates against the seat of my chair and squeezed. I didn't know whether to pee, rub myself, or cry. She stopped hitting the table and glared at me.

"Nikki! You've been practicing all this time, and you can't even get it right? What is *wrong with you*? It's, *'Now faith is being sure of what we hope for and certain of what we do not see.'* Got that?"

I sat as still as a stone. It took every ounce of strength to open my mouth and begin again. Shaking, I repeated the verse to the best of my ability and silently prayed for Momma to stop banging her hands on the table. I don't think that God heard me; Momma realized that *picking up* the Bible and smacking it over my head would knock the most sense and learning skills into me, so that became her method of choice.

"Are you stupid?"

Whack!

"Why can't you ever . . ."

Whack!

"Ever!"

Whack!

"EVER!"

Whack, whack!

"GET IT RIGHT!"

Whack, whack, whack!

Blow after painful blow went against my head, neck, and back. I curled my body into a ball and threw my hands over my head, but they became jumbled in the attacks. Over time, I grew accustomed to her methods of teachings, and I excelled in Bible class. In fourth grade, I won almost all of the awards and became known as one of the top memorizers at school. Despite the beatings and verbal assaults, I knew Momma was proud. My mouth was as dry as a desert for any drops of her love; I was thirsty for her.

Soon, we changed houses again, and Nana moved in to help out with Momma's stress. She got her own suite on the bottom floor, and it was like our private world, where we could talk about whatever we wanted. I quickly forgot all about my sadness when I spent time with

Nana, but in the rest of the house, I felt afraid. Momma chased me a lot and hit me over the face with Christian's shoes.

Every day after school, I tried my best to dash straight into Nana's arms for a bear hug; she adjusted her apricot-colored glasses and smiled with her trademark, wide grin. When she hugged me, her ashen hair crinkled against my cheek, leaving behind the slightest traces of her beloved Rave hairspray.

She always listened as I droned on about my day, and regardless of *what* I had to say, she was interested. As I talked, she reclined in her plush chair and propped her feet up, then she poured over her trusted Bible and talked about God. My soul hurt less when she mentioned Jesus and his love. Her smell made me feel better, too; she liked to wear Old Charlie perfume, and although it was strong, it was comforting.

"I had a good day, yes ma'am,"

I always answered the same way, but, over time, she began to doubt my response. During one late afternoon, when the house was quiet, she came right out and asked me for the truth.

"Nikki, you don't look so good. What's going on?"

"How does she know that I'm not okay?" I thought.

"I'm okay."

"You know, you can talk to me about anything, darlin'."

She cradled my hand in hers and patted it gently.

"Sweetheart, I understand that life is not easy, but God has promised to be by our side *forever*. The verses in the Book of Psalms have always stuck with me. I want to share some of them with you, will that be okay, sugar?"

I jumped to my feet and sprawled across her bed. A gigantic knot lodged itself in my throat.

"Yes, ma'am."

"She'll never understand. She was never a bad child like me," I thought.

"All right now, here it is. This is Psalm twenty-three. It says, 'The Lord is my shepherd; I shall not want. He maketh me to lie down in green pastures: he leadeth me beside the still waters. He restoreth my soul: he leadeth me in the paths of righteousness for his name's sake. Yea, though I walk through the valley of the shadow of death, I will fear no evil: for thou art with me; thy rod and thy staff they comfort me. Thou preparest a table before me in the presence of mine enemies: thou anointest my head with oil; my cup runneth over. Surely goodness and mercy shall follow me all the days of my life: and I will dwell in the house of the Lord forever.'"

She set the Bible aside and looked at me with love.

"That psalm, Nikki, has helped me in more times than I can ever remember. When both of my husbands died, and whenever I have felt, you know, sad, these verses have brought me so much peace. I believe they will help you too, sugar. We are *never alone*. The world wants us to think that we are by ourselves, but with God, we always have a best friend."

I wanted to shrug off her words, but a warm feeling in my stomach pulled me toward the scriptures.

"Tha-thank you, Nana, I promise I'll read this."

I placed a kiss on her cheek and retreated to my room upstairs. As I plopped down on my bed, I mulled over everything she had said. I flipped to Psalm 23 in my pink Bible; I wanted to trust that God was my friend and that he loved me, but I had a broken soul and body. On top of my pain, the energy in the new house was dark and steadily drained me of hope. *"How can Nana be so happy all the time?"* I thought. I studied the verses and repeated the words.

". . . Yea, though I walk through the valley of the shadow of death, I will fear no evil: for thou art with me; thy rod and thy staff they comfort me . . ."

I let the words sink in, and then I looked out my bedroom window that overlooked the water; for once, I took in the scenery not in fear, but in admiration of the sun as it descended below the horizon. The setting of the sun was a reminder of the magnificence of creation. *"If God made the sun, surely he made me. He must love me, too. I'm going to believe that no matter what, God is with me. When I'm afraid, God is right by my side. I might not see Him physically, but I can see him with my soul; simply because I believe that God is with me, He is,"* I thought.

CHAPTER **3**

Binge Eating, Bulimia, & Momma's Demons

In the spring of 1993, the word "supper" began to take on a whole new meaning for me. Momma and Nana spent their days sweltering in the kitchen, whisking up new recipes. During classes, their cooking was all I could think about.

After school, nothing felt more comforting than helping myself to a loaf of bread, along with heaping spoonfuls of their creamy vegetable dishes and casseroles. I liked food before, but now, I felt passionate about every touch, every smell, every taste. Warmth and love filled my stomach and left me craving more after every bite; it was the same feeling that came from their gentle hands.

Sometimes Nana went out to eat with her church friends, and Momma and I turned supper into a party. Stephen worked late most nights to bring home more money, and that left time for Momma and me to be merrymaking fools. While the food simmered, Momma left Christian to play, and we spun around in circles all over the house to our favorite songs from *The Little Mermaid*.

"Ready?"

"Ready!"

We locked onto each other's arms, without a single understanding of life. Around we went, until our faces blended with the dizzying swirls of the room. Light brown locks flew in and out of my vision, but I caught glimpses of her beautiful black hair that kissed her face and tickled her teeth. Our souls awakened as we danced and flew; our love birthed magic, and the magic killed the bad memories.

Over time, suppers left me hungry for more. Soon I consumed snacks before supper and in-between all of my meals. Before I knew it, whenever I walked past the kitchen, which became increasingly often, I found myself opening the refrigerator and staring at the food, for no particular reason at all. I stood in front of the fridge, inspected every item, then closed it and walked away. I smacked my lips and twirled around the house, thrilled about all of the possible food combinations, *especially* with cheddar cheese; I rubbed the plastic slices together, over and over, and composed all kinds of incredible melodies with their ZIP, ZIP, and SWISH, SWISH.

One Sunday afternoon, however, an unpleasant sound interrupted my concert. Stephen arrived, and he started jiggling the front door handle furiously. I threw the cheese slices in the drawer and plopped down in the rigid dining room chair. Tiny beads of sweat rolled down my face; I threw my English homework open on the table and pretended to write.

"Where's everyone at?"

"Momma is with Christian, and Nana is with her friends at Piccadilly."

I peeked up from my homework as he stiffly ascended each stair. His black, leather loafers shone so brightly I could almost see his reflection in them. I heard his heavy footsteps trail down the hallway to their bedroom, but only detected muffled conversation. I tried to focus on my homework, but my mind was more interested in the intoxicating smell of beef casserole Momma had left simmering on the stove.

Waves of nervous energy swept throughout my body as I calculated the time it could take to scour for food again. I listened intently for any signs of life, then I removed my shoes and crept over to the refrigerator. I carefully opened the door to avoid any squeaks and began pouring over the contents. Nothing seemed to seduce my cravings, though; I peered up at the cabinets, and the thought suddenly struck me. *"That's where they keep the candy!"* I tiptoed to the dining room table and retrieved a chair, dragged it into the kitchen, and balanced on top of its wobbling seat.

I opened the cabinets and uncovered a world filled with colorful lollipops, dark chocolate bunnies, and miles and miles of truffles wrapped in shiny foil. Suddenly, I couldn't catch my breath.

With my heart racing, I grabbed handfuls of sweets and loaded them into my underwear. The wrappers crinkled loudly while I ran and checked for a human presence, then dragged the chair back to the dining room. All of a sudden, some of the candies dropped down my legs. I tried to catch them, but they landed on the carpet, spreading my guilt all over like a shattered, sugary rainbow. I scooped them up and plopped them in my mouth; the remaining sweets snapped against my bottom as I quickly sat down in the chair. I felt ashamed but thrilled at the same time, and I buried my head in my hand and giggled uncontrollably.

Momma and I routinely cuddled together on the couch, and being in her arms made me feel safe and secure. One Saturday evening in May was no exception; I made a home in her crevices, put my feet on top of her legs, and we started to watch the latest episode of *Frasier*. During the first commercial break, Christy Turlington appeared amidst the shimmering lights like a morning star. She showcased the latest mascara with her impeccably formed features and sultry expression. I admired Christy but felt self-conscious; her physical beauty greatly contradicted my bovine face, boyish hands, and tree-stump legs.

Slowly, the channel changed, and my imagination took over: there I was on stage, dressed in a beautiful gown. My hair was like spun copper, and as it tumbled from the crown of my head, it radiated endless vivacity, strength, and royalty. My eyes sparkled like dazzling gemstones, intensified by a forest of dark, lavish lashes. I quickly captured the world with my presence, and life was beautiful for me.

I looked out in the audience, and Momma was there, watching and cheering me on. I knew that one day I could be that fantasy woman, and I floated back to reality with a smile on my face. I changed the channel and turned to face her.

"Momma, do you think that one day, I can be a model, too?"

I anxiously waited for her to respond. I waited, and I waited. Finally, with her gaze still fixated on the television, she replied.

"There will *always* be someone prettier than you."

I cried that night when I went to bed, but I got over it within a couple of days. I figured that if I couldn't have Momma's admiration, at least I could have food. Over the next few weeks, I developed a serious love for eating cereal, especially Cheerios with sugar sprinkled on top. That took my mind off of Momma, and it gave me a big-time sugar high. Soon I was eating clumps of sugar from the sugar bag instead of the Cheerios.

It was a hit or miss with Momma. Some days she paid attention to me after school, and some days she didn't. Nana always looked after me, however; she let me eat cereal and read the comics at the dining room table. I felt important when I read at the table, like an adult. I sat a little taller and held the newspaper out wide while I searched for all the familiars: *Cathy*, *Garfield*, and *Peanuts*. If Stephen came home early and caught me, though, that was another matter. I was not allowed to read, put my elbows close to the table, or worse yet, make any noise as I ate.

Stephen started to watch me from upstairs, and he waited for me to make a mistake. When the spoon touched the sides of the bowl, and I made a noise, he beat my head, neck, and body severely until I remembered not to eat or read at the table. I learned fast not to make him mad, and I practiced in silence until I became invisible. I made sure that whenever I ate from a bowl, the spoon didn't touch the sides. This feat became difficult, though; I started to crave a few bowls at a time, and my stomach ached a lot. By the third or fourth bowl, I had sloppy coordination, but I could only think about eating more. Nana didn't like the way that Stephen was treating me, so she let him have it one day and continued to spoil me in secret. She slipped me goodies and gifts from her silver purse and took me out to eat at Ruby

Tuesday at least once a week. When summer rolled around, however, her gifts became fewer, and she directed all of her time and attention into a new love: Richard Simmons. I felt jealous, and I wanted to see what all of the hoopla was about. I popped in the tape, and instantly fell in love, too. My eyes became bigger and bigger as I observed Richard and his followers dancing wildly in their rainbow-colored shorts.

Richard looked like a televangelist. He wore a permanent, animated expression and spoke inspirational words to the audience—even his sweat motivated me to move. As the weeks passed, I daydreamed about dancing around the house; if Nana could easily follow Richard's commands and shimmy in unison to the music, then so could I.

One Sunday afternoon in August, Nana changed after church, pushed in one of the videos and began her routine. Just like all of the other times, I sat and watched in amazement while she started shaking and swaying around her bedroom. Suddenly, Richard began to shout over the music, and I heard him say that if his viewers repeated the routines faithfully, all of their fat would *melt off in a flash*. I now realized two things: I had fat and dancing would melt my fat away.

The next day after school, I wore my blue and gold polyester gym uniform and joined in on the videos with Nana. I felt in control as long as I did not miss a single step, but if I screwed up even the slightest bit, I immediately stopped the tape and asked Nana to repeat the movements. She laughed and gave me a weird look, but we made it through the routine.

We danced together a few more times, then Nana stopped participating. Instead, she sat and read from the latest *Readers Digest*, often pausing to watch and chuckle while I smiled and breathlessly hollered over the music about how much I loved Richard Simmons. She beamed at me, and I knew that *I* was the real starlet of the show.

Deep down, however, I felt like an imposter. Nana trusted me fully, yet I couldn't surrender an ounce of my authentic self. Every step, every smile, was beginning to feel like an act. I was leading her to believe that I was sane and that I deserved her love, when on the inside, I felt like a bad, crazed child.

The more I danced, the more obsessed I became with weight loss until I craved nothing but dancing in solitude. I tried to hide my obsession and did so for a year. Then summer came again, and my insanity got the best of me. It was June, on a humid Saturday morning, and Nana suggested that we go swimming at the county pool, but I pouted and insisted on staying inside the house. Shortly after breakfast, she fell asleep, and I slipped one of the cassettes into my denim shorts and crept upstairs. My heart hammered in my chest as my sweaty hands pulled my bedroom door to a crack—now I could escape into my world and dance forever. I inserted the tape into my video cassette player, and, as if in a trance, I walked over to the mirror and studied myself.

Suddenly, an angry male voice began to talk. *"That face. . .Look at it!"* I didn't question the voice. I leaned in until my eyes crossed and my nose touched the mirror. My glasses began to fog from my breath. The voice continued, and then another voice joined it: a giggly, female voice. *"Four eyes! Loser. No one will ever love you. What an ugly thing you are. I can't tell if you look like a girl or a boy. Get to work fatty! Change that face. Don't stop moving until it's done. You can win, you can be the winner!"*

"I can be the winner. Yes, yes I can. I can be the winner."

I pulled back from the mirror slowly. I swiveled my body from side to side, skimmed my hands over my belly and inhaled; the concave features, the disappearing waist—I *had* to possess them.

Once the mania began in isolation, I became a slave to my flesh. At all hours, I lived imprisoned in my imagination, unable to connect to reality and engage in life. On the outside, I seemed like an aloof nine-year-old, but at my core, I was an animal foaming at the mouth.

Every evening after supper, I looked for an opportunity to ditch my time with Nana; instead, I sneaked bags of candies and chips into my bedroom, then I binged and worked off the calories for hours on end. But no matter how much I exercised, I couldn't see a pretty girl in the mirror, only a freakish creature that deserved to die.

When the new school year started, I caged myself in from the world. I lied and told Momma and Stephen that I was doing home-work in my room when really, I binged and danced. The grueling routines left me exhausted, but a sinister force prompted me to press on; the evil voices controlled me, and they never let me turn my eyes away from the mirror. *"The fat isn't coming off fast enough, dumb ass. Hurry up!"* Although I was a hostage to my mind, I secretly loved it. Stephen and Momma didn't have to abuse me anymore, I could abuse myself.

By Christmas, I noticed the unattractive side effects caused by binging. Exercise couldn't hide my bulging facial cheeks, and I felt humiliated by their size. On Christmas Eve, I locked myself in my room and examined my face: massive glasses hung down my nose. I tilted my chin up slightly and stared. *"God, I hate myself,"* I thought.

The longer I stared, the more I wanted to storm into the kitchen and grab a knife. I began to fantasize about slicing off my face, and at the same time, I pranced back and forth on an invisible runway, pausing in the mirror to imitate the sunken pouts from the supermod-els on television. Momma didn't think of me as "super," but I wished that she did.

I knew that there wasn't a soul alive who could identify with my thoughts. Certainly, nobody fantasized about cutting their faultless faces—only a freak would do that. While all of humankind appeared rational, I was a child driven to the brink of madness.

January 23, 1995. The day after Momma's twenty-eighth birthday. On this day, sometime during the evening, it became clear that Momma was no longer one person, but four. Out of nowhere, the black clouds rolled over her honey eyes and her body stiffened. Different people entered her body, and I no longer communicated with Momma. She switched between Henrietta, Julie, and Betty. All three individuals had contrasting personalities, and none of them were fit to take care of Christian and me. Over time, I learned the hard way about each person inside of Momma.

Henrietta was the youngest: she acted immaturely and spoke in a little girl's voice. I felt helpless and wanted to run away when Henrietta started to babble. I longed to be the child, and when Henrietta showed up, I realized that I had to be the adult.

Julie was angry, violent, and talked in a deep voice. I feared for my life when Julie came around. She hurled objects at my face during her manic rages and trampled over my self-esteem with her fiery, verbal assaults. I believed that I deserved the pain and automatically accepted my depressive thoughts. *"Yes, I am a stupid idiot. I am. You stupid, stupid little girl. Why do you have to ruin everything?"*

Then there was Betty: she exposed me to the sexual side of life, like naked parades around the house and tickles on my chest. She looked and talked like Momma, but I couldn't trust her because she was wild and impulsive in her actions.

As the months passed, I agonized over how to fix Momma. For some strange reason, my mind told me that if I could just look pretty enough, Momma would become healthy again. I figured that starting with my hair was simple enough, and after my tenth birthday, I asked Momma if I could cut and color it. She said yes, but Stephen said no. He didn't want *his* little girl regarded in a sleazy light.

"No, you may *not* color your hair, Nikki! You are far too young! No child of mine is *ever* going to touch her hair. Pretty soon you'll be using *that makeup.* Then, before you know it you'll be out and foolin' around with boys!"

I binged to cope with the rejection, positive that Stephen had denied me a pleasurable experience for his sadistic thrills. For weeks, his words replayed in my head, and I found relief during lunch on Fridays. Every Friday was "pizza day" at school, and I took the liberty of ordering four platefuls worth. Afterward, I hid in the bathroom and stuffed slice after slice into my mouth and muddled over the conversation, letting the greasy cheese and bread numb my rage.

During the summer when I wasn't binging, I relied on my imagination, books, and drawings as an escape. In my bedroom, I read stacks of mystery and fantasy novels and drew pictures that depicted the medieval period.

When the house was quiet, I lifted my creativity right off of the pages, and made my own adventure. I always started at the top of the stairs, and as I descended, they transformed into marble and gold. Below in the living room, the citizens of my country beckoned me, and I reigned in my majestic robe of velvet. I was a noble, a fairy—anything I wanted to be.

After many weeks of play and peaceful reign, however, everything fell apart. A horrible sound from the Queen Mother's bedroom rang out through all of the dominion, and I recognized the noise: it was vile, putrid vomit cascading from Her Highness's mouth, into her golden throne.

On a late August afternoon, I sank back into my bitter reality and sauntered cautiously toward Momma's bedroom, half-hoping that she would not appear. An empty beer bottle rested on the console table at the end of the hallway; the sight was another rip in my dreams. Stephen usually had at least one glass of wine a night for "his heart," but Momma . . . Momma was rapidly becoming entangled in a scorching ménage à trois with bottles of wine and beer.

I knocked on the door, but there was no response. I tapped again and pushed it, and the door opened with little effort. The overwhelming stench of vomit validated that there was, in fact, life nearby.

"Mm—mom?"

I entered the powder room and saw that the bathroom door was wide open.

Momma sat on the lidded toilet, a fresh beer in her hand. Maybe she was Betty, Henrietta, or Julie, but I couldn't tell. A midriff-baring top and tight denim shorts barely covered her body; thick, black makeup and dark red lipstick coated her face.

"Mom, are you okay? I thought I heard you throwing up."

"I'm *fine*. I want my privacy dammit! Can't anyone have any privacy in this house?"

She looked away, took a sloppy swig of beer, and then smashed the door in my startled face. I raced down the hallway to my bedroom and fell into my pillows. I tried to breathe, but I couldn't, so I ransacked my closet for anything edible and sliced my palm on the metal hinge of the closet door. The pain didn't stop me, though, and I kept searching. The blood was nothing compared to the sadness in my soul.

Finally, my gaze rested on a bag of chocolate-chip cookies stuffed into one of my purses. I ripped into the bag like a lion, and in a few minutes, I slaughtered the cookies. I then picked and swallowed every single crumb off of the floor, and ate some of the carpet fuzz, for fear that Stephen might find out. I lurked down into the kitchen, hastily guzzled some milk and snatched another bag of cookies from the cupboard.

I crept upstairs, closed my bedroom door, and then mangled the second bag of cookies, barely breathing in the process. Hand over fist, I thrust them into my mouth. Then I remembered: *bread.* I tiptoed downstairs and shoved slice after slice of honey oat bread into my aching stomach; searing pain set in, and I grabbed a cup and headed to my bathroom. *"If Momma can do it, so can I,"* I thought. I filled the cup with water and switched on the shower and vent.

I purged in the toilet and then pushed the remaining chunks down the drain. The warm water felt soothing on my back, like loving hands. I rinsed, fell into bed and stared into my covers. Off in the distance, I could hear Momma choking in her shower, too.

The next morning, I asked Momma and Stephen if I could spend the rest of the summer and part of the new school year with Dad; secretly, I wanted to get away from Momma. They said yes as long as Dad agreed to take me to school. For a little while, Dad and I got along like a dream: I ate all day and purged while he worked. When school started back, however, my luck ran out quickly. I had nowhere to hide after supper and before long, he overheard me coughing and wheezing in the bathroom.

On Halloween, we went trick or treating, and I binged on a few bags of candy. Afterward, we went home, and I purged in the bathroom. I tiptoed out with bloodshot eyes and bits of vomit tangled in my hair. I was slick, but Dad was slicker, and I never made it past the window at the end of the hallway. He caught me, face-to-face; the toilet gurgled madly in the background, and all of the blood drained from my face, straight into the cracks of the wooden floorboard and cemented with the soil. I felt like dirt. *Sewage.* I wanted to die right then and there, break off one of those rusted floorboards and puncture my throat.

"What you're doin' in there is *wrong,* you hear me? You need to quit that, you understand?"

I burst into tears and promised in between sobs to stop throwing up. If only it were that easy, though; I don't think that either one of us knew what we were doing. Dad was trying to be a dad, and I—I was trying to be me. Afterward, I continued to binge and purge, and Dad never asked again.

I took advantage of the passive environment at Dad's house and manipulated the system in all sorts of ways. By age twelve, I was an expert, and I knew that running the water in the bathroom was the sure-fire way to conceal my purging. However, I never escaped the question, "How many showers are you going to take today, child?" I always laughed, or replied with a simple, "I like to take showers." Dad and Granny merely shook their heads and said, "You youngins' nowadays, I tell ya, ya'll can sure use the water now!"

The sound of running water allowed me to engage in my behaviors without any interference from the outside world. As it flowed into the rusty drain, I binged like an animal; I felt repulsive but liberated simultaneously. My stomach expanded, and my fat rolls folded over my clothes, but I fed myself more as punishment.

Purging brought on dizziness and fatigue, but out of fear, I got on my hands and knees and cleaned away any evidence the best I could. After the steam had faded from the shower, a dense vapor layered the bathroom, and a thick film coated the mirror.

One night, a few weeks after Halloween, I purged multiple times, and later started scrubbing every inch of the tiles. When the steam cleared a bit, I put a rag on the mirror, wiped, and froze: a hideous creature stared back, with lumpy skin and a rubber snout. I ran out of the bathroom, but the next night, it was still there. Over the following month, it appeared off and on, and slowly but surely, I became filled with a deep rage. When I looked into the mirror, I could no longer differentiate between my reflection and the creature's. I had a deep desire to smash my head into the glass.

I couldn't keep my angry thoughts and bad temper to myself for long, though. Dad and I shared similar temperaments, and in a short amount of time, we exploded in fits of fury. Mornings started off on the right foot, but by the evenings, we were throwing items and screaming obscenities. Our fights often centered on one issue, and that was Momma. Dad insisted on getting back together with her, and I felt powerless; their divorce placed me in the middle of their relationship.

No matter how upset we became, however, we made amends and promised to work on our relationship. The routine was always the same: Dad placed his hand on his heart and somberly expressed his commitment.

"Nikki, I swear to the good Lord in heaven, you can write it down. I will never hurt you again."

I nodded with the utmost sincerity as tears streamed down my face.

"Dad, I promise, I will never get mad again. I'm sorry."

But the mind is quick to forget, and in less than a hot second we lost our tempers and started a fussy quarrel. When my stubborn tendencies flared up, I turned to purging for comfort and support instead of reaching out. My lack of control in communication caused endless problems; whenever an important issue needed discussion, more often than not it ended in a heated argument and left me with feelings of resentment and powerlessness. In turn, I binged and purged to release the guilt I experienced for not being able to manage my emotions. It was a vicious cycle and one that quickly escalated.

After a while, my outbursts turned into something more than just bad tantrums. During our fights, I erupted in crying and screaming spells that lasted for hours. The terrible feelings and memories buried inside flew out of the deepest parts of my soul: Stephen and Momma as they beat me senseless, countless empty beer bottles, and remembering Uncle Robbie's hands on my thighs all made me want to kill myself.

When the images flooded, I shouted inaudible phrases, ran into my bedroom and smashed my head into the wall repeatedly, determined to obliterate myself. As I smacked my skull, I prayed for each hit to be my last. I wanted to die, and I wanted God to kill me swiftly.

"Nikki, stop! You're going to kill yourself!"

Dad always flew to my side and attempted to pry me off the wall with his brute strength, but the harder he tried, the harder I bashed my head, crying out for God to take my miserable, worthless life.

"I don't care! Kill me now, God, kill me now! I hate myself! I am NOTHING!"

My body rattled from the adrenaline and anger, and my mouth dripped with saliva. The blood vessels in my scalp threatened to pop, and my skull cracked under pounds of agony. The physical pain was nothing compared to the scars left on my soul, though. In some way, I enjoyed the suffering—it was the only time I felt anything.

CHAPTER 4

Teenage Years: BDD, Sexual Abuse & Domestic Violence

Stephen King's *Thinner* was a film about an obese lawyer named Billy Halleck: gypsies placed a curse on him, and slowly, he began to lose weight. Regardless of how much food Billy ate, he became thinner and thinner. I was obsessed; the movie triggered the notion that I could eat whatever I wanted and yet appear emaciated. During Christmas break, I moved back into the house with Momma and watched *Thinner* religiously with her, each time secretly squeezing my calf and thigh muscles underneath the couch pillows and wishing that they were shrinking like Billy's. The first of the new year, Momma caught me. She didn't act surprised, however, she just studied my thighs then rubbed hers.

"Well, we have big legs, sorry to tell you."

Big was a word I refused to accept. I couldn't stand to see my thick legs. After everything I had put my body through, they were still *big*. I kept visuals from *Thinner* in my mind for stimulation and vowed to myself to work harder than ever; really, I couldn't reach my goals soon enough.

Momma suggested that I join her on her daily walks around the neighborhood. They were part of her New Year's resolution to live healthier and lose weight, even though she was drinking more. I immediately said yes, and with every step, I imagined how my new legs were going to look.

Our walks lasted for a couple of hours, and they left me exhausted afterward. Momma never seemed tired, though; she said that a slim figure was one of the most valuable things a woman could ever own.

The obsessive thoughts about my legs grew, and I tried to push them aside, but there were other things clouding my mind: dark and strange things. As I tried to readjust to my room, I began to have night terrors and bizarre visions of the evil doll. I moved into Christian's room, terrified, but could still see shadows and hear voices during the day. To Momma and Stephen, the doll was a grand joke, a delightful conversation piece at the dinner table. I knew that what I was experiencing was real, but Stephen wrote me off as delusional.

After he returned home from work one Wednesday evening, he sat down at the table with the family and mocked my fears openly.

"Now come on, Nikki, you know a doll can't move around, that's plain common sense. But, come to think about it, I did see a little shadow move up the stairs a few minutes ago . . ."

Stephen flashed his teeth, and everyone turned to look at me. I desperately wanted to cry, to flood the house with my tears and swim away.

"Don't tease her!"

Momma swatted Stephen on the arm and gazed at me. Her rosy lips quivered for a couple of seconds before she gave way and released a long, loud laugh. She picked up her burgundy silk napkin and tried to cover her face, but her thoughts were visible. In fact, one glimpse around the dinner table made it clear: I was a loser.

Stephen said that I was acting like a baby, and he ordered me to sleep in my room for a week. The first night, I saw the shadow of a little girl with long, dark hair lurking in the corner. I told Stephen, but he didn't care; he did whatever he could to make my life a living hell. At different times during the week, he hid the doll in my closet and drawers where I was sure to find her and scream.

For months, the ghostly occurrences escalated and stalled, like a horrifying roller coaster that I couldn't get off of. When the summer came, the doll manifested into a presence, and I named her, *The Lady*

Without A Body. At first, she showed herself when Momma and Stephen argued; then, she appeared whenever I was by myself.

With her curtain of ebony hair and milky skin, she looked exactly like Momma. The entity never left my side; all day and night she breathed on my neck and made malicious faces. I debated whether or not to tell Momma. Then one Sunday morning as we cleaned the house, I summoned some courage and spilled the beans.

"Momma, I've been seeing something—somebody. If I tell you, please don't make fun of me."

"Now why would I do a thing like that?"

"Because ya'll always laugh at me, and it hurts my feelings."

"I'm sorry, baby. I won't laugh, just tell me."

"Well, there's a lady, in the house. She looks—she looks like you."

As I described the woman, Momma stopped sweeping and turned toward me.

"I've seen her, too. Not too long after we moved into this house, I started to see and hear lots of things, and she's one of them. I tell ya that's the devil now."

"Why didn't you tell me?"

"I didn't *want* to scare you, you understand? Now don't say anything to anyone. I don't want to scare your brother."

"But Momma —"

"That's enough."

The lady was now our secret, but it didn't change the fear that I felt, and it didn't stop the occurrences. The ghostly apparition continued to haunt me, striking terror into the deepest regions of my soul. I fell further into despair, feeling mad and worse, alone.

At thirteen, a foreign visitor invaded my body. Momma didn't take the time to educate me about my new friend. I learned at school and spent weeks pouring over whatever literature I could find at the library during lunch. Sometimes I hid in the bathroom stall with books, afraid and paranoid; I didn't want anyone to see what I was reading.

One day some girls rushed into the bathroom, blabbing about tissues and Tylenol. My ears perked up—Momma never mentioned those. Instead, she just bought wine, and I learned to shut my mouth.

I took an interest in makeup, hoping to feel closer to Momma and make myself beautiful like her. After school, I stopped studying as much and instead, poured perfume on my neck and painted my face for hours. The colors hid the hurt and the scars, but Momma never noticed my new appearance. Nana did; she said that I didn't need makeup, and that I was her pretty girl no matter what. Stephen, though, he was another case altogether. He didn't like me pretty. He caught me over Labor Day using Momma's makeup in the bathroom, and all hell broke loose.

"What's all this? Wipe your face and neck off!"

"But—"

"I mean it! Wipe that off. You smell like a French whore."

He walked away and gave the door a firm slam. I stood, numb, and turned my head to the mirror. I saw a cheap girl; cheap like the wine Momma bought. I saw a girl not worthy enough to use perfume; this girl in front of me was destined to be a whore. I scrubbed off the makeup with a washcloth and unmasked the ugly girl. Then I smacked the cloth against the sink and pinched my fat, nasty cheeks until they cracked.

"Dumb ass."

The tears flowed, and the pain pelted against my heart like a dull rain. But somehow, his words and my unsightly reflection reassured me and validated my deepest fear: I *was* a failure.

I tiptoed downstairs and quietly gathered food. The voices snickered and laughed as I choked myself. *"It doesn't matter. You're just going to throw it up, you stupid, stupid whore."*

My appearance constantly fluctuated. Sometimes when I looked in the mirror, I saw a worthless, disgusting freak, and other times, I resembled a man or a monster. I was never, ever a beauty, though. I preferred to live in an illusion. In there, I could be whomever I wanted. I usually chose Cindy, Naomi—and Momma. I still loved Momma, even though she chose the bottle most days over me.

In my imagination, I was an elegant woman. Everything about me sparkled beyond comparison, especially my long, beautiful hair. Curls cascaded down my back and reflected like diamonds when I twisted my perfectly manicured nails around them. Unfortunately, I passed a mirror far too often and discovered my true, wretched self: my nails were brittle and coated with white spots, and my strands were rough and haggard, not shiny.

I secretly envied the girls at school with the glossy hair, including Suzanne Brian, one of Northside's most popular cheerleaders. I sat behind Suzanne during Mr. O'Neil's math class first thing in the morning, and she didn't know that I stared at the back of her glistening, maple tresses. Most days I sat, lost in my obsessive thoughts, and watched her run her scrupulously maintained nails through her hair.

As the semester wore on, I decided that I *had* to have hair like Suzanne's; dying my hair was the only way I could have some sort of happiness. I pleaded with Stephen again and a month later, by some miracle, he agreed. Perhaps it was his way of trying to change and show me that he loved me after all. He even drove me to Sally Beauty Supply and purchased two boxes of bleach and four bottles of sandy blonde dye—just in case the first try didn't turn out right.

At the checkout line, he threw me a smile and a wink, and I felt warm inside. I wanted to reach over and hug him but then thought better about it. As I watched him joke with the cashier and hand over the money, I noted his sparkling blue eyes and dimples. He was a charming man.

On a Saturday, Momma worked both packets of bleach through my hair and poured the smelly dye on top. I sat on top of the toilet, cringing while the chemicals ate away at my raw scalp. An hour later, we had our results: it wasn't as golden as I had hoped, but rather, psychedelic. Layers of white, ash, and flaming orange melted into copper roots. Momma ran a comb through, but halfway down the middle an unseen, gummy force trapped and tangled it. She salvaged what she could, and turned the hairdryer on. Suddenly, a strange, burning smell came out, and my hair transformed into brittle straw.

The next morning, I woke up and ran into the bathroom to look at myself. In some alternate universe, I believed that I didn't look horrible and that my hair had returned to normal. But one glance confirmed my fear: my hair was an absolute disaster. I turned away and turned back again. Now, I was even more of a monster.

"I'm so ugly . . . I'm so fucking ugly! God, please help me!"

I sobbed uncontrollably. Shaking, I closed the door and lowered to my knees; as much as my appearance disgusted me, I wanted to stare, stare at my wretched self. All of a sudden, the voices started up. *"You can change it. You can change it until you're happy. Do it, do it bitch."*

I convinced Momma to take me back to the beauty supply store at once. She insisted that my color was all right, but I persisted. She didn't understand that I *needed* to change my color for the sake of my sanity. We purchased two bottles of dark blonde dye, but even after *that* change, I freaked out.

Over the following months, I used all of my allowance money and purchased bottle after bottle of color, from blonde to brown to red. I became a bottle-flipping machine, haunted by a vision of perfection. Every color was unsuitable. I tried another, then another and another.

I needed to get my fix; coloring my hair gave me a high unlike anything else. I started swindling money from Dad's wallet and hitched rides to the drugstore. While I paced up and down the aisles and shoved box after box of hair color into my basket, I slipped in bags of cookies and chips, too. My racing heart ruled my thoughts as I steered through the endless rows: *walk . . . sweat . . . food . . . sweat . . . grab . . . walk . . . paranoia.*

Stealing from Dad was not enough, though. Soon I began to pilfer money from Granny. Over Thanksgiving break I took a twenty-dollar bill from her wallet and bleached my hair, hoping to transform myself into a human Barbie doll. The thrill was electrifying; I could get what I wanted instantly. I never stopped to consider that Granny was wiser than me, though. When I came out of the bathroom with pale streaks, she questioned me about the missing money. I confessed tearfully, although I was only superficially ashamed; somewhere inside I felt the stings of pride. I vowed to God to never steal again and abandoned my hair-dying schemes—for a little while.

Stephen didn't let me forget about my messy hair. He beat my bottoms raw, and really, it was all just entertainment for him. I knew that I couldn't break free from his mind games, so I learned to adore him.

He didn't let Momma off the hook, either; he blamed her for my ugly looks, too. At night, I could hear him bashing her face in, so I starting sleeping with Nana. While she snored, I turned on the radio and twisted the knob to high. It was no use, however, for I could still hear Momma's cries.

The noises Momma made caused me to wince and rub my body all over Nana's sheets. Nana never woke up, though; she slept soundly while I stayed awake night after night. If I had to pee, I held it all in because I was afraid. Afraid like all the times when Uncle Robbie came into my bedroom. Afraid of everything.

♪♪♪

Christmas 1998. The moment Momma unwrapped the giant computer from its cardboard box, we became hypnotized. For days, Christian and I took turns exploring the bizarre universe known as the Internet; virtual card games and e-mails replaced movies and books. Our home rapidly became dependent on the mystery machine.

When school started back, the computer helped me write papers, research subjects for projects, and gain knowledge in the areas that I lacked such as science and math. Christian was only seven, but he was fascinated and spent hours after school studying the cords. Momma surprised him one afternoon with a discarded computer shell, and he taught himself how to pull it apart and put it back together. From then on, he spent all of his free time reading books on computer language and software.

This artificial brain seemed like an answer to our long-awaited prayers: not only was it a companion for our lonely, unsettled souls but it helped us run our lives more efficiently. Little by little, however, I noticed that Momma spent more and more time locked in her room with the computer. I didn't know *what* she was doing in there, only that she was doing it in secret.

On a Tuesday about half-past three in the afternoon, I received my answer. It was the beginning of January 1999, and the day was dreary, rainy. Nana picked Christian and me up from Northside and took us back to the house. I hurried upstairs to type a paper for English class, but when I reached the top, Momma's door was pulled to a crack, and some odd noises were coming from inside. I headed toward my room, stopped, and crept back over to Momma's door.

"Momma, are you okay? I heard some noises."

I held my breath.

"Ye-Yes honey, come in. I'm fine. I didn't know ya'll were back already. Come in, come in. I want to show you something anyway, but please lock the door."

I edged inside and scanned the room. Dressed in a satin, creamy robe, Betty sat perched on the edge of the computer chair with her legs slightly open, revealing her panties. My heart jumped. I didn't want to see Betty's panties, but before I could turn and walk out the door, she called out in a soft, childish voice.

"Baby, come here. Come sit down."

"Yes . . . yes, ma'am."

"I wanna show you somethin'."

She giggled, and her robe fell open, exposing her shoulders. I stepped back.

"Nikki, come here. I'm not gonna hurt you, silly!"

I had no desire to see her surprise, nor did I want to stay in that room another minute.

"Yes, ma'am."

"I said, I wanna show you somethin.' Now come here . . . Sit here, next to me."

She patted the bed, and I sat against my wishes. I couldn't help but notice the computer screen.

"What are you doing?"

"Shh. Don't tell Stephen, but I'm talkin' to a man I met online. Calls himself Levi. He sent me his pictures. He's pretty good lookin' now! I can talk to anyone, anywhere in the world in these chat rooms. It's unreal."

"So that's what she's been doing in here all this time," I thought.

My arms began to itch. I scratched them, but I couldn't reach the irritation. The sensation shifted to other parts of my body; the damn itch chewed at me like a mouse.

For a few weeks, Betty taught me all about life in the virtual world. The classroom was in her bedroom, and she conducted class when no one else was around. Dressed in nothing more than her robe and nightgown, she trained me how to be a mature woman.

In the beginning, I learned how to talk dirty to older men, and the sexy things to say to pique their interest. After the first week, Betty left me alone and instructed me to carry on without her. I knew why the men talked to me: like Betty said, I was only there to make their dicks hard. But there was something else alluring about conversing with faceless men behind a computer: it brought comfort and a sense of love to my lonely heart. Hell, they didn't know the real me, and I didn't know them, so I lived in a fantasy world and imagined that maybe, just maybe, there was a Prince Charming behind the next "JohnCums4U." It wasn't the kind of love that I used to draw and read about, but it was all that I could find, so I took it.

During the remaining weeks, Betty left her door open, and I watched her as she masturbated. Other times she held me close while she touched herself. She loved to walk around naked and tickle me. I knew that when I was in Betty's room, my breasts were hers to caress. Being with Betty was horrifying because I didn't know how to get away. When she pulled me in close, I had no idea whose eyes I was staring into, but I knew they weren't Momma's.

❧❧❧

The rain trickled down and landed on the skylight. I stared intensely until my eyes crossed into a blur. Suddenly, the room morphed into peaceful clouds, and I wanted to float in them forever.

"Hey girl, whatcha lookin' at? Get ya butt up! It's Valentine's and we goin' out tonight!"

My serenity was shattered by Betty's giddy voice and pokes in the chest. Covering my pitiful breasts, I turned to face her and adjusted my vision: thick makeup, a sleek ponytail, and a push-up bra made their way into my focus, and I struggled to hide my terror. When Betty pinched my nipples, my terror turned into shame and disgust; still, I couldn't deny that she was becoming like my best friend. She exploded in laughter and soon, I joined in. The rain beat down harder and melted with the sounds of our joy.

After supper, I primped in the bathroom with Betty. I put on my most adult outfit: a plaid skort and a white cotton shirt that slightly revealed my training bra. The skort exposed my chunky legs but Betty said they were beautiful, she said that they looked like hers. I spread blue shadow over my eyelids and dotted sticky glitter lip gloss across my dry lips. I hoped it was enough for men to take notice.

"We're gonna have fun, girl! Stephen is out of town, Christian is with your Nana, and we don't have any rules!"

She threw back her head, narrowed her eyes, and laughed. All of a sudden, the heavy odor of alcohol wafted in my direction. I excused myself and purged in my toilet. I brushed my teeth and joined Betty in her bathroom. As I reapplied my lip gloss and studied my reflection, I decided that I didn't look like a woman anymore, more like a woman of the night.

The drive downtown felt like an eternity. Stephen was in Columbia working, but secretly, I knew he was home, waiting for us with a butcher knife and a couple of body bags. I slipped down in the seat and tried to drown out my paranoid thoughts by listening to the pattering rain. Betty was neither paranoid nor shy about sipping a few beers in the van. By the time we reached the club, she was ready for an adventure.

We settled into the back row of The Farm, a notorious rock club in Charleston. The Farm looked like an old barn, and on any given night college kids and local indie rock bands filled its walls. When we entered, Betty slipped the security guard a fake license, and with my makeup and tight clothes, I passed for an adult. With a wink and a smile, I slid inside and took a moment to breathe in the air of filthy, sensual maturity.

A few minutes later, I leaned my elbows on top of the sticky bar and tried to relax. Hundreds of people began to jump and scream to the heavy metal music, and I looked over at Betty: she was bouncing and drinking a fresh bottle of beer, with an extra bottle in her other hand.

"Oh come on, Nikki—dance! I brought you all the way here, the least you can do for me is dance! Lighten up!"

I looked at Betty's beautiful, sloppy face. God, I wanted to smack her. I hated her for taking me to The Farm. I hated her for not being my mother.

I dove into the crowd of sticky bodies until Betty was no longer in sight. I jumped and pressed my body against sweaty strangers in the mosh pit; the music mixed with the heat was electrifying. Occasionally, I looked out into the crowd, but all I saw was a sea of empty faces. Underneath the dim, red lights, the club resembled Hell. *"It's not so bad here,"* I thought. *"At least I can do what I want."*

Some time later, I noticed a familiar form off in the distance by the bar. It was Betty, wrapped in the arms of a stranger. Whoever he was, he wasted no time tasting every inch of her neck. My heart sped up, and I pushed through the crowd to get to her.

"What are you doing?"

She casually stopped and turned to face me.

"Oh, hey! I was wo-wondering where you went."

"Who is this guy?"

I grabbed her arm and yanked her away.

"He's my friend, Josh! D-don't be such a baby. He brought his friend B-Brandon."

She giggled and wiped a string of drool from her mouth.

"I'll be back in a while. You stay here with Brandon!"

"Brandon? I don't want to stay with a stranger! Please don't leave me, Momma!"

For a moment she turned, and her eyes became soft. Then she swiveled around and walked away. Josh and Betty exited The Farm, laughing as they went. Just like that, she left me.

Out of the corner of my eye, I suddenly caught a flash of red, checkered cotton. I cautiously turned. A boy of about twenty-two was standing directly behind me. He was tall and wearing a Nike baseball cap.

"Hi, I'm Brandon. Don't worry, I won't bite. Unless you want me to."

Hearing his voice brought back memories of Uncle Robbie, painful memories that I wanted to forget. He was also a reflection of the men in the chat rooms—was he one of them? I couldn't trust a man anymore. I felt my temperature rising, and I started to back away.

Only one time had I allowed myself to feel close to a boy. It was recent, the past summer actually, and with the county lifeguard, Jacob. Jacob had sandy brown hair, freckles, and long eyelashes blacker than the night. He was my dream-come-true. I was confident that Jacob had loved me, and went swimming in the pool as often as possible, hoping to catch glimpses of him. Then one day Jacob cornered me. We went into the dimly lit storage room behind the pool and kissed heavily. I was in love, but he wasn't. After that day, he tried to have sex with me, in the same dirty storage room. I turned him down, in fear of his *thing*. He never talked to me again.

I was sure that Brandon wanted to show me his *thing*. Wanted me to grab it and do all sorts of tricks like Jacob and the men online. I plotted my escape. *"If I run out the side door and don't look back, I can make it. I don't know how to get home, but it doesn't matter. I can sleep outside as long as I don't have to touch him,"* I thought.

All of a sudden, Brandon waved his hand in front of my face.

"Hey, are you all right? I'm not going to hurt you. I'm sorry for what I said. . . I was only joking. Here, have this, it will make you feel better."

He passed a cold beer into my hand. I chugged it, hoping for one of us to disappear first.

"Whoa, slow down with that! Why don't we step outside? It's easier to talk there."

He grinned.

"I'll go, but, only if we stay on the steps."

"Deal."

We sat on the bottom of the concrete steps at The Farm. The air was thick with alcohol and urine. I clutched the railing just in case he tried to pull something funny.

"Honestly, you can trust me. Josh and I came down from Atlanta for the week. He has some business here to take care of. He met your mom online, and they decided they were going to meet up for Valentine's Day or some shit like that."

I looked down at the ground and played with my clogs.

"What's the matter?"

"Nothing. Well, it's just that, my mom's married . . ."

I peered up at Brandon's shocked expression.

"Oh, my God. I had no idea your mom was still married, dude! Man, I'm sorry. Sit down. Wait, how old *are* you?"

I shuffled my feet again.

"Thirteen. Almost fourteen, but. . ."

"What? No way. Your mom takes you out at *thirteen*? I'm sorry. I'm so, so sorry."

If only he knew that it wasn't my mom, but another person named Betty. I wanted to tell him, but I shut my mouth and sat in silence as the wind picked up and the rain beat in thick drops, ruining my makeup. Blue, black, and glittery magenta streamed down my face and collected in a prismatic pool, draining into the Ashley River. I shivered and pictured Betty having sex with Josh in a car. *"Why am I such an unlovable person?"* I thought.

"Hey!"

I turned and saw Betty wobbling down the cobblestone street with her new love, skirt twisted, and drunk as a sailor. I looked closer: Josh was stroking her stomach and playing with her belly button ring.

"Mom, please let's go home."

"Cut your whining, what's wrong with you?"

"Mom, I want to go home NOW!"

I grabbed her purse and pulled out her car keys.

"You're in no condition to drive."

She snatched her purse out of my hands and pouted.

"All right, okay, I—I'm coming."

Betty leaned in and gave Josh a long, hard kiss on the lips. I felt vomit rise in my throat; it made me gag, but it tasted like love. As they wrapped their tongues together like snakes, I had the strongest urge to heave myself into the river and sink into the murky bottom. She continued to kiss him with soft, twinkling eyes and smiled. I realized that I was nothing more than shit underneath her heels.

I suddenly caught my breath and noticed we were in the middle of a treacherous downpour. Josh and Brandon peeled out of the parking lot in their sporty red BMW, and I looked at Betty, who was fumbling in her purse for her keys.

"*I* have your keys, remember? You're in no condition to drive! You've had too much to drink."

"Oh p-please. I'm fine. Give me those keys. Get in the car. Now!"

She snatched the keys from my hand and laughed. I hesitated for a few moments before stepping into the van. Inside, Betty adjusted her contacts in the rearview mirror. She turned the radio on full blast, and I immediately felt a sense of déjà vu. Nirvana blared from the speakers, and she smashed the gas pedal so hard that my body gripped the seat.

"Don't worry, I've done this a million times."

I looked at her: she was both a sexual woman and a kid. At that moment, I felt like an adult, and I knew that I needed to be one for her and myself. I had to pay attention to save our lives.

As we tried to maneuver through the narrow downtown streets, the rain pummeled harder and faster. It was becoming increasingly difficult to see, and I quickly began to feel like a drowned rat in a labyrinth.

"Turn this way, yeah. This way, Mom."

"No, no, I know my way around. Do-don't te-tell me where to go. And call me, Betty."

"*Mom*, you're drunk! And you're driving. This is no time to negotiate. I'm not drunk. Some of these streets are one-way and tricky. *Please,* just listen to me!"

"I-I can see where I'm going, missy."

Her pointed brows and clenched teeth terrified me. All of a sudden, she swerved sharply. She stopped the van, squinted, and started rubbing the foggy windshield. Frantic, I rolled down the window and looked outside. To my horror, Betty had drifted into the wrong lane, and dozens of headlights headed straight for us. I screamed.

"MOM! YOU'RE IN THE WRONG LANE!"

I grabbed the steering wheel. She fought for control, but I smacked her and continued screaming until the wheel released in my hands. At the last second, the van rolled into the median, barely escaping a head-on collision. For a few moments, I sat, shaking. Then I peered at Betty, who seemed different now, more like my momma. Tears covered her face, and her sobs mixed with the thunder. She raised her head and gazed at me through those honey eyes.

"Don't—don't tell Stephen. Ever. Got it?"

I nodded.

"Yes, yes ma'am."

Momma slowly steered the van into a nearby gas station, and guzzled nearly a gallon of water in an attempt to sober up. The entire way home, I prayed for God to get us there safely, but I figured he wasn't listening. I knew Nana had said that God loved me *all the time*, but Nana didn't know anything about matters like this.

Around three in the morning, we returned home. When I got out, I noticed that Momma had parked the van crooked; it didn't line up with the other cars on our spotless street anymore. *"Maybe when the neighbors wake up in the morning, they'll see it and call the cops. I hope they do so they can finally take me out of here,"* I thought.

Momma stumbled as she tried to unlock the back door. I took the keys from her again, let her lean on me and opened it. I hunted for the light switch and stopped. A profound feeling of fear suddenly came over me.

Tap, tap, tap, tap.

I held my breath.

"Where the *hell* have you two been all night, huh? *Turn on the light.*"

I frantically searched for the switch and turned it on. Stephen stood before us, dressed in his neatly pressed work clothes. His skinny, chapped fingers beat impatiently against the kitchen counter. I could almost smell his anger, a raw smokiness that seethed deep within.

"Nikki, go upstairs . . . now, before I tear you up!"

He whacked the counter with an ear-splitting *smack*! I was familiar with that noise; pretty soon my face would be under his hand.

"And take off those clothes. You look like a whore. Just like your mother."

My eyes felt hot, and I moved my fat legs as hard as I could up the stairs. All of a sudden, the steps lengthened into a million, and I couldn't see the top.

Whack. Whack. Bang.

"No, Stephen, please stop!"

I could no longer see Momma, but I knew she was receiving a terrible beating. I pushed harder up the steps and finally reached the top. I hid in the corner of the hallway and listened. I could hear Stephen smashing her head against the wall, and Momma, as she fought back and smacked him in the face. The noises sent me into a silent rage; my body cracked with anger, and I crawled into my bedroom. If God was listening, he could mend my body and Momma's. I couldn't depend on God, though; I had to keep moving.

I crept over to the telephone. Maybe, just maybe, if I could call Dad the hell would stop. Slowly, I lifted the receiver until it was free in my hands. I cradled it up to my ear. There was no dial tone, however, only the sounds of my faint breath, followed by Stephen's voice.

"You think you're slick, huh? Well let me tell you something young lady, if you try to call *that man*, I will *kill you*, do you understand? You watch yourself when you go to bed tonight."

Click.

"Stephen, stop it! What is wrong with you?"

I heard Momma pleading downstairs. I wished for her sake to shut her mouth.

"Shut up, just shut up, Sandy!"

Whack, whack, whack.

"Ow! Stop it!"

Momma let out a long howl.

I curled into a ball and rocked back and forth, unable to feel anything except fear.

Sometime in the morning, I opened my eyes. Relieved to discover that I was still alive, I quietly tried to change from my smoky clothes. Stephen heard me, however, and yelled for me to come downstairs. I glanced at myself in the mirror first: baggy eyes, smeared makeup, and a bloated face. I sighed but knew that only ugly, stupid girls deserved the treatment I had received last night.

I stood up straight and walked carefully downstairs. When I turned the corner, I saw Stephen *and* Momma standing before me. Momma appeared amused, cheerful even; I couldn't tell if it was her, or one of the others. Stephen stuck out his arm and pointed with his finger.

"Sit down, on the next to the last step."

I sat immediately and gave him my full attention. He put his hands on his hips.

"What happened last night?"

Stephen had me, caught in a trap. I knew that I had to tell the whole truth. I glanced at Momma: she had a giant smile plastered on her face. What did that *mean?*

"Well, we—"

Whack.

Blackness. Total and utter darkness. I felt nothing but pain, like a thousand trains had smashed into my face. When I came to, the room looked blurry. I realized that someone had knocked my glasses off.

"What did you do that for?"

"She had a *stupid look* on her face!"

I felt sick all over. Sick in my brain. Tears came up and swirled with the sick. I wanted to die, die once and for all. *"God, please just finish me off,"* I thought.

Terrified, I knew that I had to do something. This man was going to find a way to kill me. Later that evening, while Stephen showered, I snuck into my room and called Dad. I didn't want to share our secrets, but I had to do something to save my life. Dad called the police immediately. They removed me from the house the next day and sent me to live with Dad. Fortunately, I was headed to a safer place, but unfortunately, the police said they couldn't do anything about the abuse because no one had called them the day it had happened.

I said goodbye to my life that February day in 1999; goodbye to Momma, Nana and Christian, private school and the house. Once I walked out the door, my soul broke free and started to run, and once it started running, it didn't stop.

Life is like a painting; our circumstances are the brushes that define which way the lines will flow and trickle. This endless mural reveals the contents of our souls through its unique colors, textures, and shades. As life develops, the mural shifts, taking on an infinite number of directions. During challenges and pain, our paintings smear, appearing with tears, splotches of black, and graffiti. In our culture, these strange arrangements of color resemble distorted images we've observed since childhood, such as our troublesome environments and the media. Deep longings to replace who we are with superficial guides may start out as innocent, but can end with severe, negative consequences.

I believe that our hearts alone, as hard as they may try, can never create the masterpieces our souls are capable of becoming. We need something greater to guide us, a Power higher than the things of this world. When the beautiful and mysterious energies of God guide our movements, our souls become the works of art they were always meant to be.

Throughout most of my life, my painting was a swirl of fragmented, blackened shadows. The tormented figures and idealized images I held in my mind were unattainable; they were lost and broken in storms of regret and confusion. The shadows lunged at me, laughing hideously and mocking everything I held dear. I was held captive in a prison of nightmares, and I thought that the only way to be happy was to numb myself. I lived under the pretense that at some undefined moment, something in the world would break me free and rid me of my inner anguish. I failed to understand that God was the key to my success, and I looked to things and others, expecting something that could never be. False prophets and selfish doctrines called to me, and I wandered endlessly searching for their promises through dark, forsaken tunnels.

Evil is distracting and destructive, and its objective is to break and damage our inner world. It wishes to extinguish our hopes and blot out the flames of joy and passion in our hearts. If it steals our happiness, it has managed to take away our strength. I repeatedly reinforced the evil that I received from others through harming and talking down to myself. I was unaware life could be different, yet I deeply longed for it to be. I believed that messages of inspiration and hope were based on lies, and I further isolated into my paranoid darkness.

CHAPTER 5

Sex, Suicide, Addiction, Bullying & Divorce

I unlocked the brass buckles from one of my leather suitcases and found Christian's yellow teddy bear, smashed atop a heap of wrinkled clothes. A day was not a long time to pack up my life, but at least I managed to grab a handful of good skirts and Ralph Lauren shirts from my closet. The teddy bear stared into my eyes with its arms spread open; it was cute, but a poor replacement for my brother. I picked it up and plucked the fuzz off of its belly. All of a sudden, I noticed the purple marks on my knuckles; they were scars from the purging. *"God, he's gonna hear me in the bathroom again,"* I thought.

Living with Dad was going to be a major adjustment. I wasn't a city girl anymore, but a youngin' in the country. I couldn't wear fancy clothes here. I had to buy jeans and shirts with no name on them— nameless, just like me. I imagined my first day at James Island High: the judging eyes and whispers about the new girl, the four eyes, the freak.

"What's her story, transferrin' in the middle of the school year?"

"I heard she has major problems. The police had to take her out of her own house."

"Looks like someone's crazy . . ."

"Not as crazy as her mother, apparently."

Momma called a couple of times and wished me good luck at school. She also told me that she wanted to work things out with Stephen and promised to stay in close touch. I decided to stop answering her calls. Momma was passionate about many things these days, and I wasn't one of them. I didn't call Nana or Christian, either; throwing up in the woods made me feel so much better.

During my first day at James Island High, I wandered aimlessly through the halls. Hundreds of students buzzed by, but I couldn't hear anything for the dark voices. *"Nobody will ever be your friend. You're a loser!"* I kept my head down toward the gum-spattered floors. I wanted to spare everyone from my hideous appearance. When the teachers called out my name during roll call, I didn't answer; instead, I sulked in the back of the class, afraid to utter a single word.

As the days passed on through March, I wanted to disappear. I was certain that if I stayed at James Island High much longer, everyone was going to out about my past. Deep down, I longed for others to understand, but I knew that no one could, so I avoided conversations at all costs.

During lunch, I anxiously raced through the lines and grabbed a couple of brown paper bags and desserts. I thought it best to dodge the noisy chatter at the tables and skipped straight ahead to the bathroom stalls. There I at least had silence. The crinkle noises my sandwiches made as I unwrapped them was all the friendship I needed. I had my food, and I had my thoughts. Although, I questioned my thoughts most of the time. I could only sit with my thoughts for a few minutes before purging; it seemed like the rational method to rid myself of the pain.

By April, I was at a mental breaking point. Trying to adjust to my new life was like trying to function with half a body. I had only one hope left, just one thing that could keep me from killing myself: the ability to change my looks. If I could alter my appearance, maybe I could feel better again.

On a Friday after school, I marched straight into the house and locked myself in the bathroom. I pulled out a box of dark brown hair dye from underneath the sink and went to work. I plucked my eyebrows and manipulated my face with bronzers and highlighters. Before I knew it, it was midnight; still, all I could do was stare at my reflection and critique my face and hair. Some time later, a knock came at the door.

Tap, tap, tap.

"Nikki? Are ya in there?"

It was Granny, and she sounded concerned.

I opened the door, and she jumped back, startled. I realized that my new look had power.

For a while, my appearance gave me a sense of entitlement. Before long, however, it drove me to binge. My obsession was ferocious: I couldn't stop thinking about my looks, even when family came over to visit. And when I thought about my looks, I thought about binging and purging—the cycle was never-ending.

I became the ultimate chameleon with the family, able to manipulate and blend in with any surrounding. I carried on full conversations while I binged in the kitchen. My heart pumped intensely, and I could barely hear, yet I pretended to know everything. While I shoved food into my mouth, I held up a mirror just to catch glimpses of my face.

Then the obsession to exercise kicked up again. For the entire summer, all I could think about was sweating off my fat. The long, wooded path beside the lake provided an easy escape. First, I began walking for thirty minutes; walking led to sprinting for an hour, then two, then four. Dad peeked outside occasionally to check on me, and I just waved and smiled. He always watched for a few minutes then shuffled back inside the creaky, old house. I was relieved to see him leave. Afterward, I erased the phony smile and ran a bit faster. I loved pushing myself to the limits. My body felt like it was falling apart; my muscles burned, and my knees cracked, all signs that I was one step closer to becoming truly beautiful, someone worthy of love.

Every day I attempted to run just a bit farther, and when I reached my goal, I binged on pizza or one of Granny's delicious suppers. I raced through the woods and sliced my legs on branches like an animal, bleeding into my socks and shoes. The sight of blood was soothing. Sometimes I tasted its metallic saltiness to keep myself motivated.

After exercising, I hid in the bathroom. While the sweat poured down my face and body, I scrutinized every inch of myself, and the voices talked down to me, too. *"You're hideous, absolutely hideous, bitch."* I showered, then blanketed every flaw with a mask of makeup until the voices faded into the background.

As I witnessed my face evolve, I felt my self-esteem soar. I stuffed my bra with toilet paper and turned the bathroom into a club. I brought in a radio, cranked the music up, and rubbed my ass against the wall. Even if it *was* all in my head, I was somebody special.

♪♪♪

With my new face, slightly slimmer body, and a bra brimming with toilet paper, the beginning of the sophomore year was less daunting. Dad had also taken me to get fitted for contacts, so now I was *really* a different person. In the lunchroom, I strutted past the tables instead of running to the bathroom. With my tray in hand, I arched my back and stuck out my fake chest. I no longer looked down at the floor and avoided eye contact; instead, I looked for an opportunity to talk to other students, from the cheerleaders to the goths.

One group at lunch, in particular, caught my eye: they were un-officially known as "The Untouchables." They were the students that everybody wanted to hang out with, but nobody could unless they had enough money and the right last name. Comprised of mostly blonde, junior girls and a couple of athletic, senior boys, they carried designer purses instead of book bags and wore expensive leather jackets. I wanted to be a part of their clique badly and went out of my way to get their attention.

The second week of the first semester, a girl from The Untouchables came over while I picked at my hamburger and introduced herself. I recognized her from my pre-calculus class. Her name was Lydia Sinclair, and she was one of the most respected girls in the entire school. Her hair was long and golden, and when she shook my hand, I caught the scent of vanilla flowers, like Momma. Instantly, I felt small inside and wished that I smelled like that; instead, a trace of vomit and filth from the morning lingered beneath my nose.

Within a few seconds, a swarm of boys surrounded her like bees. My theory was confirmed: in high school, achievements didn't matter, but having admirers did.

There was just one problem: even with my sexy look, not a single boy paid me any mind. So I clung to Lydia's side, hoping that I could attract a boyfriend through her status and beauty. For weeks we did everything together. She let me borrow her True Religion jeans and taught me how to style my hair into a high ponytail. She also educated me about high school boys, sex, and how to combine them. I wanted to tell her that I was already well versed in the opposite sex, but I thought better about it. I knew about men, but not in a real way.

Although Lydia made me feel happy, deep down I couldn't shake my insecurities. I compared myself to her constantly and wished that I had what she had and looked the way that she did. As I focused all my energy on Lydia and boys, my grades plummeted; academics had already taken a backseat to binging and purging, but now, I had no desire to succeed. I wanted everyone to want me, and I was willing to do anything to get their attention.

Little by little, Lydia and her friends started to invite me to a spot in the boonies known as Turkey Pin. It was a massive, open field in the middle of the woods where many of the popular kids gathered together and partied. I turned them down, afraid that Dad would blow his head.

One chilly October night, however, I answered the call to rebel. Dad and Granny drifted off to sleep a little after eleven, and I snuck out of my bedroom window, hopped in Lydia's Ford F250, and headed down to Turkey Pin.

On the way, Lydia gave me the run-down about "The Pin," as she called it: drinking was mandatory, and smoking marijuana was optional. When we arrived, I saw nothing but pickup truck after pickup truck parked neatly in a row. Loaded onto each bed were giant, heavy coolers. Lydia said that the coolers contained the good stuff: fruit peels, orange juice, and vodka.

The moment I stepped out of Lydia's Ford, my soul came alive. The loud, country music that played carried me back to the days when I was a little girl riding in the Cutlass with Dad.

I looked around and saw seniors and freshmen drinking and smoking together around a massive bonfire. Everyone seemed friendly enough, so I grabbed a cup of vodka, mixed it with fruit and drank it. Pretty soon, the world began to spin, and the faces melted into the stars. I felt warm inside and like I belonged. I realized that this, this *feeling* was what I had been missing all along. This was home.

Lydia walked over, poured me another drink, and we started dancing close to the bonfire. Time sped up, and the night became a blur. I smashed back cup after cup of vodka and took a few drags of marijuana from someone. Eventually, Lydia stopped me.

"Whoa, there! Someone likes her stuff!"

I wiped away the spit that poured from my mouth and exploded into an uproar of laughter. Lydia grabbed my arm, but I broke away and filled another cup from a truck with mostly vodka. I stumbled back to the bonfire and guzzled. I felt invincible, like a wild woman of the night.

The next thing I knew, I woke up in Lydia's bed with blurry eyes and a screaming headache. It was the following day, a Saturday, and by the shade of the light that came in through the windows, it was almost evening again.

Partying at Turkey Pin became a regular love affair and one that Dad eventually found out about. He forbid me to go, but I had my methods. I jumped from binging and purging to binge drinking and smoking marijuana every day. Lydia and her groupies began to suspect that I had problems. At parties, I ran off with food and purged in the woods. Lydia also couldn't account for all of the chips and cookies that went missing in her house.

By December, our relationship deteriorated, and I couldn't deal with the sadness and guilt that I felt. In a state of panic, I abandoned The Untouchables and befriended the alternative kids at school. When Lydia found out, she banned me from ever contacting her again and told everyone that I was a cunt.

Binging, purging and drinking provided a cushion, temporary relief to dull the sting. After all, I *knew* I was the ultimate badass; my false confidence was growing by leaps and bounds. The more I drank and smoked, the more sociable I felt, like I was floating on a constant cloud. Whatever the feeling was, I was hooked and took every opportunity I had to light up and drink.

I couldn't catch up with any of my homework over Christmas break, but I didn't associate my declining grades with the fact that I was partying all the time, either. I was focused solely on self-destruction, but I felt completely in control.

When school started back in January of 2000, I was a quiet student again, and all of my teachers commented on how shy I seemed. It was as if I had two personalities: in school I was soft-spoken and unsure of myself and at parties another side emerged, reckless and pretentious.

Dad continued to labor tirelessly as a sales manager for Krispy Kreme. He wasn't happy with my decisions, but he made two things clear: he loved and accepted me. Dad knew that he couldn't undo years of emotional damage, but he did his best to make our days together enjoyable. Having a full-time teenager in the house was a hefty adjustment, and he was learning many things. It was also a time for me to discover Dad all over again, and so, in spite of our differences, we became the best of friends.

And yet as it goes, when a parent tries to be a best friend and not a parent, more often than not there is heartache. I took advantage of situations repeatedly. I lied, manipulated, and stole money so that I could binge, purge, drink and smoke weed. I was caught up in a vicious web of deception.

♪♪♪

Nightmares occur on days when life seems to flow like a dream. The nightmare happened on a Tuesday afternoon around four in February, while the sun blazed brightly through my bedroom window and the flowers swayed in their beds to the honeybees like distinguished members of the choir. As I attempted to write an overdue English paper on my bed, Granny interrupted with a harsh knock on my door.

"Your stepdaddy's on the phone, child. Do ya want to speak to him?"

I hated it when she called me a *child*. Didn't she notice my huge stuffed breasts? I mouthed a giant *NO*.

"She just stepped out, went to the store. What is it ya wanted to tell her? Oh, okay then, I'll tell ya called."

She hung up the phone.

"He said it's important. It's about ya momma."

I groaned and rubbed my face. *"Why, God, why?"* This wasn't going to be good. I waited for a few minutes then dialed the familiar, disgusting numbers. My heart nearly stopped as I heard Stephen pick up.

"Hel—hello?"

"Hey Nikki, it's *your dad*. Listen, I need to talk to you. Can you go somewhere private?"

"Yes, sir. I'm alone."

"I don't know how else to say this, but your mom's gotten herself into trouble. She's really a very disturbed woman."

I wanted to stop him right there and dispute the word *Dad* with a fiery passion. But hearing Momma's name mixed with the word *trouble* made every hair stand on end. I couldn't speak, and an endless stream of horrible thoughts ran through my mind.

"Hello? Are you there?"

"Yes—yes, sir. I'm here . . ."

"*Why* didn't you answer me? Anyway, the police found her this morning by the ocean, in her van. Now I don't know how's best to tell you this, but she tried to kill herself."

The room became a swirl of ash and yellow dots, and the air left my body. I tumbled to the floor and dropped the phone. Somewhere in the distance, I could make out a familiar voice and the shuffling of feet. Suddenly, I felt a pair of strong arms lift me onto the bed, and I tried to regain my focus.

"What's wrong, child? What's the matter?"

"Momma! Momma!"

All I could muster between the tears and snot was Momma's name.

"She tried to kill—she tried to kill herself."

Granny sat beside me and picked up the phone.

"Go ahead now! We're listening."

She held it to my ear. Stephen delivered the details that I didn't want to hear but somehow couldn't stop myself from listening to.

"She left home early this morning while Christian was in school. It must have been around eight or so. I'm not sure. All I know is that she went out for a drive. While the police did their usual patrol around Folly Beach, they noticed a van with what looked to be a flimsy doll slumped inside the driver's seat. They got out and took a closer look. That's when they realized it was no doll, but rather, a grown woman. The officers broke the door open and discovered *your mom*, who appeared dead to the world. She had a faint heartbeat, however, and foam, lots of foam coming out of her mouth. There was a pile of wine bottles and scattered pills around her, and a piece of paper, a good-bye letter, addressed to you and Christian."

My heart stopped.

"Can I read the letter?"

"There's no way they will give it to you, Nikki. The letter is under the custody of the police now. Besides, you're too young, and your mom is in need of some serious psychological care. They took her down to Roper to get her stomach pumped and then will transfer her to Rayside Heights to get her evaluated. I assume she'll be staying there for a while."

Click.

Momma's private thoughts to us were in someone else's posses-sion. I had to get my hands on that letter.

For weeks, life was bitter. Why did Momma want to leave us? Trying to understand it only made me more vulnerable, more deranged.

Momma was assigned a social worker named Mrs. Mattie. She

explained that Momma could no longer understand her actions, but that didn't ease the pain, not one bit. I wanted her to be whole again, but with every passing, painstaking moment I knew that life would never be normal; I would never again be whole.

I wasn't allowed to visit her at Rayside Heights. I learned through different members of the family that she was evaluated and diagnosed with bipolar disorder and dissociative identity disorder. But there was one problem: she had to quit drinking before the doctors and staff could treat her properly.

She agreed to stop, and they sent her home in March, just before my fifteenth birthday. Stephen reported back every so often on her condition; she was adhering to the center's treatment plan and substantial trial medications. After a few rounds, however, she decided that they were not suited for her and threw the pills down the sink. She stopped seeing the doctors and declared that her home was her therapy. Apparently, so was the almighty bottle.

Momma and Stephen separated at the start of the summer, and they sold the house. The sale carried more than the house; it took many of our secrets with it. In my heart, I knew that moving on was meant to be, but telling my soul that was another story—the soul is no fool.

Nana moved into a tiny, rent-controlled apartment in West Ashley, about a half hour away. I promised to visit as often as I could, but something told me that these visitations wouldn't be joyful like the ones from childhood. Already I sensed a definite, deep sadness.

It didn't take long for Momma to begin a new chapter in her life. Christian moved in with Stephen, and the first of July, she rented a temporary apartment in Mount Pleasant and settled in as though nothing terrible had ever happened. Within a week or so, she embarked on a romantic relationship with a laid-back fellow who seemed to be the complete opposite of Stephen. George was originally from Puerto Rico and had moved to Charleston as a little boy. Closer to Momma's age, he was college educated and worked on computers in some of the premiere hotels downtown. They fell in love at once but kept their living arrangements separate.

I immediately warmed up to George, too. Here was someone who was eager to love and take care of Momma in spite of her past and troubles. We made many trips to the Isle of Palms over July and August; it was our way of becoming a patched-up family. During our many beach getaways, I sat and watched as George and Momma played like children on the sand and kissed like old lovers. Our mouths filled with grit as we ate spicy vegetable sandwiches by the ocean from the local deli, but we had no concerns. We were trying to love life again and keep our faces turned toward the sun. I figured if I kept mine away from the clouds long enough, my worries would fade away forever. After all, if I could hide my darkness from George, he would have no reason to leave.

♪♪♪

His name was Michael, and he loved The Doors. To Michael, life meant only one thing: getting high, fast and hard. Most days in September we left school early and went straight to his house. There we hid in his attic, smoked joints and talked deeply about nothing in particular. With each passing discussion, we teetered on the brink of a profound discovery; we not only believed our delusional reasonings, but we also lived by them. We kept our book bags packed, knowing that we could leave the shitty town of Charleston at any moment and embark on a grand excursion. Someday, somehow, we could even change the world.

Michael was my first love. From the moment our eyes met at school, we became inseparable. It was the beginning of my junior year, and I was late getting to homeroom. I was running through the hall and bumped smack into his chest. I had never seen him before; he was new and quite mysterious with his jet black hair, green eyes, and even darker, mysterious style. His clothing sense didn't extend beyond Dead Kennedy T-shirts and baggy satin pants, but there was an energy about him that was intense, almost magical.

Over the fall, we spent every single moment together, and we liked it that way. It was more than love and sex that bonded us, though, the drugs helped a lot. I wanted to please him sexually, yet couldn't do so unless I was high. Sex was an act, something that I did for his sake. Inside I felt like a dead horse but longed to do whatever it took to make him happy. We lit up every day at his house and fooled around, but the drugs became a distraction. He carried on continuously about acid, and its mind-altering trips seemed like a far better experience than sex.

Michael and I spent a considerable amount of time not only smoking but studying the buds and their colors. He taught me that the value of one plant was greater if it was one color, and how much the different plants cost. After smoking, we usually watched *Donnie Darko,* a film about a boy with paranoid schizophrenia. I always remarked that I experienced similar insanity when I smoked, then fell asleep, woke up, replayed the movie, and lit another joint.

Then came the day I tried acid. It was Thanksgiving break, and we drove to West Virginia to meet his mother. Out there in the mountains, I began to feel anxious and fearful. I figured a little acid could relieve my spirits; when it melted on my tongue, I discovered my immortality and tapped into a personality I didn't know existed. All the hopelessness and fear sailed away on luminous, rose-colored clouds. I felt confident and for the first time, truly alive.

When Christmas came, Michael began a job as a sous chef at a high-end restaurant on Folly Beach. Not only did his position make for raging parties with the staff, but it also allowed for incredible food that I binged on and expelled in the restaurant toilet or some random gas station during our drives back home.

But home was a fickle term, an ever-changing concept. Home meant love, and that was something I didn't have, especially for myself. I spent more nights over at Michael's house than anywhere else.

At the beginning of 2001, I experienced another side of acid. It spread throughout my soul, directly and magically. A mysterious light filled me with a sense of importance; the light exposed my true self, answering many questions I had buried inside. Behind the complexity and ethereal impact, though, something else dared to come to the surface: something heavyhearted and battered, like my lost, deeply damaged inner child.

At times over several weeks the light pulled me under, much further than I intended to go. Then piercing waves came, and they dragged me into a bitter darkness where stories from the past haunted my mind. I floated in the darkness for infinite amounts of time, and fought over and over to find the light, but the distorted images smothered me; the twisted illusions beckoned me to stray further. Although Michael was my faithful companion through these torturous hallucinations, I couldn't recognize his face. He stuck by my side, however, and together we traveled through obscure tunnels, convinced we had the ultimate answer to life. In the end, I always came out empty minded with suspicion, numbness, and hints of that familiar rage.

My self-control peeled away, and a tendency toward severe violence threatened to burst forth onto everything and everyone around me. My rage didn't faze Momma, though; she was certain that sedation was the answer. When I visited her and George one weekend in February, she slipped lithium into a glass of wine to soothe my anger. It blanketed my emotions instantly like a thick, warm quilt. The only problem, however, was that life was only truly tolerable with the quilt on.

⌂⌂⌂⌂

As the weeks passed, my perception of myself worsened. Most days, I spent hours staring in the mirror, worshipping the mask I had created, but I wanted to shatter the glass with my hands and pierce my worthless face. Life brought me temporary pleasure, and I yearned for something deeper; the voices inside started to crave things of a more sinister nature. *"Cut yourself. It's the only way to release the pain."*

Every few days, I dyed my hair a different color, and when I rinsed the dye out, I felt tempted to slit my wrists with the razor. Coloring my strands tempered my obsessive thoughts, but the craving for the sight of blood never left my mind.

One evening in March, I bleached my hair at Momma's apartment, and a patch fell off in the front. *"Why can't I ever be right?"* I thought. I showed Momma my disgusting hair, ran upstairs into the guest bathroom, and stabbed myself in the leg with a pencil. The pain was thrilling; it sent an electric charge throughout my entire body and confirmed that I was alive.

As I stood in front of the mirror with my bloody leg, all of time seemed to stop, and the air suddenly felt calm. But in the glass, my image shifted and changed. I slowly morphed into that familiar, repulsive creature: a beastly figure, a nightmarish version of my perceived, discarded self. I looked closer and noticed that firm, masculine features defined its face. How could I be both beast and a man? Desperate for help, I confided in Momma and Dad, but they just shook their heads and said that I was hormonal.

᠀᠀᠀᠊

Right before I turned sixteen, I started working with Dad at Krispy Kreme on Savannah Highway. Trying to juggle school, a boyfriend, and a job wasn't exactly a piece of cake, but Dad assured me that working hard and studying was the ticket to a better life. After the first paycheck, one concept sold me: the more money I raked in, the more valuable I was as a person. All of the drugs left me feeling like an insignificant shit, so I clung to my job like white on rice. In no time, I saved a substantial amount of cash and financed my first car, a turquoise Oldsmobile Supreme.

Working at Krispy Kreme allowed for precious father-daughter time. Soon, though, I started to stuff my face full of donuts when Dad wasn't around. Instead of money, my focus turned to how many sweets I could gorge on in any given day. I had the perfect job: I could eat whatever I wanted and purge in the customer bathroom.

Within a couple of months, though, I became increasingly lightheaded, unable to focus, and extremely irritable. During lunch breaks, I passed out in my car and sometimes didn't wake up for hours. But I couldn't let anyone know the truth; hell, I didn't even know the truth. No matter how sick I felt, I marched into work and made excuses. Lying was the only way to survive.

Momma and I tried to spend time together as the summer began, but it was evident that her demons were taking over again. Some days she was Momma, and other days she was one of the others. More often than not, her personalities shifted from moment to moment. During those times I realized she was never coming back. I longed for moments of genuine affection, but they were as fleeting as the passing rain. To make matters worse, she couldn't put down the bottle. I think the day she picked it up she died. As the sticky days lingered on, she cared less and less about our visits, and honestly, the interest departed from me as well.

Toward the end of the summer, Momma began sleeping at George's apartment; so often, that she practically moved in. But the longer she stayed, the more problems they started to have. George didn't succumb to her darkness, though. His persistent love for Momma was evident, and he was willing to take her, along with her mental torments. In some ways, the darkness helped him to understand her better.

♪♪♪♪

It was a Friday night in August. Dad and I sat down in the living room with a few sandwiches from Chick-fil-A and started watching *There's Something About Mary*. Just as Ben Stiller pulled the zipper over his crotch, the phone rang. *"Dammit,"* I thought. I hesitated to answer it. "Dad, I can't get up. This is just getting to the good part."

Dad laughed.

"Go on, get the phone!"

I dropped my sandwich and scooted my butt over toward the phone, praying that it would stop ringing. It didn't, and I answered it.

"Hello?"

"Nikki? It's George."

By the frantic tone of his voice, I knew that another nightmare had made its way into my life.

"Your momma . . ."

"Yes, what is it?"

"She locked herself in the bathroom and . . ."

"And what, George? Please, don't hold back."

He began to cry. *"Oh God, this is going to kill me,"* I thought.

"Oh no, George, please, no! Is she dead?"

The phone felt hot in my hands, and my heart couldn't take the pressure.

"She's not dead, but . . . Nikki, I'm so sorry. I came home earlier, and she had had another episode. Only this time she locked herself in the bathroom and sawed at her arms with a butcher knife. I tried to unlock the door, but I swear she was determined to kill herself. I broke it down and called 911. There was . . . blood everywhere. They came and took her away to Rayside Heights. I'm so sorry."

That was it. Momma was not on the other end of the line, telling me that she loved me. Instead, it was George explaining the gruesome details of her second suicide attempt.

This time around, I was permitted to visit Rayside Heights. I went down two days later and felt the rage bubbling underneath my skin as I passed through the security scanner. I wasn't allowed to bring anything, not even a toothbrush. Apparently, they had Momma locked away like a rabid, foaming creature, not to be trusted.

I walked through the halls and sensed the tension of tortured souls in the air. It was the feeling of people who had crossed a boundary deeper than any I had ever known, although many times I had danced along the border. When I finally approached Room 227, I saw a little girl lying in a stiff, narrow bed. She wore an agonized expression on her face and had white bandages wrapped around her tiny arms. I checked the name on the door: it matched Momma's name.

Certainly, this child wasn't *my momma*, the pristine beauty queen who crafted her hair so that not one strand stuck out of place. This child killed my momma.

I stepped inside, and the thought blinded me. *"Another suicide attempt."* The sick reality replayed over and over as I sat down next to her body on the white sheets. The color white was everywhere, but I knew that there was bloody red underneath her bandages. I reached out and touched her pale, clenched face. *"I love you, Momma,"* I thought.

Now, the whole family knew that her mental health was deteriorating; it had been for years, but no one had wanted to acknowledge it, including me. Every couple of days I went to Rayside Heights. On some visits, she muttered that she was sorry and that she needed help, but I couldn't conjure the strength to believe her words anymore.

Life oozed by like a slimy, bad dream, and gloomy, anxious thoughts continually clouded my mind. Her suicide attempt haunted me in many ways, especially the dark voices. *"Stick your hand down your throat, you little bitch, yeah that's it. Just one hit. One more drink, just another won't hurt you."* But the voices also became my savior, my way to cope with the pressure. Every time I walked through the doors at the ward, my strength drained away. I needed something to motivate me back to life.

Eventually, I couldn't handle the voices anymore, so I started a journal and scribbled my thoughts there. In the pages, I pondered how our lives had gone awry. Where was God in all this? Did I do something to deserve all of this pain? Countless questions flowed from my pen, and I contemplated if I were to blame for her hatred of life. Dissociative identity . . . bipolar disorder . . . Hell, did she always have those? I didn't know *why* she didn't love us enough . . . Love herself enough to hang on and build something better.

After August, I stopped visiting Momma as often and focused more on the upcoming school year and work. I caught word from George that they had sent her home, but I couldn't bring myself to see her just yet. Working at Krispy Kreme was an escape from thinking about Momma so much, but once school started again, I was still miserable. I needed to get my mind off of things; perhaps if I made even more money somehow, I could forget about the pain altogether.

I didn't know what to do to make money, though. I didn't consider myself to be a talented person, and God only knows I saw an ugly fuck when I looked in the mirror, but I was desperate to make some money. I considered trying my dream - modeling - although I was sure that Momma would have some choice words to say about it. On a boiling Tuesday afternoon in September, I mustered the courage and walked up the steps to the most esteemed modeling school in Charleston. Vandershall School of Modeling had placed an ad in the *Post and Courier* the previous week, stating that their modeling classes would start soon. I had nothing to lose; being denied by Momma had to be the worst rejection possible.

Tap, tap, tap.

I knocked on the door. I never noticed how chubby my hands were until that moment.

A captivating, brown-haired girl with sapphire eyes as big as saucers answered. Her smile made me feel welcome, but I was intimidated by her beauty. At 5 feet, 9 inches tall and 140 pounds, I looked like a gnome next to her statuesque and narrow frame. What the hell. My life was already a wreck; being turned away at this point wouldn't make much of a difference in my destiny.

"Why, hello. May I help you?"

I had about two seconds to run away.

"Yes, y-yes ma'am."

"Oh, God. Why did I just call her ma'am? She can't be that much older than me! I'm so stupid," I thought. She looked me up and down so fast I wasn't sure if my eyes were playing tricks on me. She stepped to the side and motioned for me to come in.

"My name is Julia Pierpont. It's nice to meet you. And your name is?"

"Nikki. DuBose—my name is Nikki DuBose."

My voice squeaked at the end, and I tugged on my shirt to pull it over my stomach. I could only imagine what she was thinking. Suddenly, the voices chimed in. *"I'll tell you what she's thinking. That you're a fat, fucking monster, that's what!"*

Perfect Miss Julia Pierpont led me into a sophisticated office. On the desk was a stack of portfolios embossed with a giant letter: "V."

Standing behind the stack was an older lady, adorned with red lips and a tweed Chanel suit. I recognized her pointed face immediately from the newspaper: it was the owner, Mrs. Vandershall, in the flesh.

"Come here, please."

I didn't hesitate.

"Yes, ma'am."

"How *old* are you?"

"Sixteen."

"Good. Although with all that makeup on you look years older. Always have a clean face."

I rubbed my cheeks.

"*Why* are you here exactly?

"I—well, Mrs. Vandershall, modeling has always been a dream of mine. I would love the opportunity to come here."

"I see. Darling, *Vandershall* is the best in this state, and we are noted for our excellence all over the nation. If you make it here, you'll have access to some of the top agents later. Now, I don't want to hurt your feelings, but our acceptance rate is not that high. It depends on many factors. For starters, dear, where are your parents? Normally, girls make an appointment with their mother or father. *You* just showed up out of nowhere. Listen, Julia will have you fill out a form with your information. Then we'll take your measurements."

She stared directly at my hips and legs. Now I was confident I did not imagine things.

I filled out the form, all the while dreading her bony fingers coming anywhere near my hips. I thought seriously hard about running away again after I finished the paperwork, but realized I was out of luck.

"*Shit. I'm trapped,*" I thought. Mrs. Vandershall was watching me like a hawk, and her minion Julia was right by her side, measuring tape in hand. "*Don't they have anything better to do?*" I thought.

"Done? Bring it here, please. Let's collect your measurements."

Julia wrapped the tape around my chest, stomach, and finally, hips. *God, I hated that.* I felt her hatred toward my meaty thighs and enormous butt. She looked at the number, shook her head and measured again.

"No, that can't be right."

Still, her fingers landed on the same place, and she twisted her lips and held up the tape for Mrs. Vandershall to see.

"Thirty-seven and a half. Dear is there any chance . . . Well, how can I say this? We prefer to work with girls who are at a thirty-six. Of course, we would *rather* you be at a thirty-five or a thirty-four because that's what the agencies like, but with *you* . . ."

"Oh, God . . ." I thought.

"Well, classes start in a few weeks, and they cost five hundred dollars. Can you get down to a thirty-six-inch hip?"

Surely, I could do anything if it meant getting accepted into this school.

"Of course, I can."

"Now, this doesn't mean you're in. We have to review all of the other applicants, and there are *many*, but I need to know that you are dedicated. Modeling is a career, and it's one to be taken seriously, you understand?"

"Yes, ma'am, I'll do my best."

"Good. Julia will see you out."

I walked through the door confident that I would never hear from Mrs. Vandershall again. Perhaps working at a bakery was my destiny; it suited a girl who obviously enjoyed her food like I did.

A couple of weeks passed. It was Tuesday afternoon again. I was lost in thought, ringing up Mr. Bogart, an elderly gentleman who came into the bakery daily for a glazed donut and a hot, black coffee with two sugars. All of a sudden, I felt a tug on my back. I turned around: it was Chivonn, my feisty co-worker, who ran the shop like a tight ship.

"What's wrong?"

"Nothin' child! Why do you always think somethin's wrong? Whatchu tryin' to hide, hmm? You have a phone call, ma'am. Go on, ansa it. I'll take over fuya."

I glanced at Mr. Bogart, who was fiddling with stacks of quarters as usual. He laid them out ever so precisely on the counter and counted them aloud.

I walked briskly to the back and almost slipped on patches of jelly and custard.

"Hello?"

"Hello, Nikki."

The smooth voice could only belong to one person. Still, I couldn't believe that she would call me herself—and at work!

"Mrs. *Vandershall?*"

"Yes, yes it's me. I am calling about your recent application to Vandershall School of Modeling. We can only pick twenty girls out of the hundred or so who applied. Unfortunately—"

I prepared to keel over.

"Unfortunately, we cannot choose everyone, but we see potential in every girl. However, I want to let you know that you are one of the twenty picked!"

Whatever she said after that was a dizzying blur of nonsense. *I was accepted.* I was *somebody*, a *real somebody*, and soon everyone would know it. *"I've finally done something worthwhile with my pathetic life!"* I thought.

"Mrs. Vandershall, I'll be there!"

"Great, I've always believed in you. I'll be sending a packet to your address, and *do have* your mother or father come with you to classes. Oh, and there is one more, vital issue. It's five hundred dollars for the runway training. You *must* pay it before the start of the first class in November, or we will have to give your spot to someone . . . *else.*"

"Shit. I'll have to ask Dad! Hopefully, he can lend me the money," I thought. I could get the money, but there was no chance in hell that Momma or Dad would accompany me to classes. And how could Mrs. Vandershall possibly say that she had always believed in me? Only a couple of weeks ago I left her school feeling like the bottom of the barrel.

"No problem, I'll get everything situated at once!"

But I didn't have time to wonder about her intentions—I was flying. I was an instant supermodel, and almost just as quickly lost my appetite. For the next four weeks, I shrugged off the hunger pains and told everyone who asked that models didn't eat as if it were a fact taught in school. As far as I was concerned, they consumed mostly diet pills to maintain their slender physiques because it seemed to be all the rage on television, so I went to the drugstore and armed myself with a bottle of the strongest ephedrine-based pills. I couldn't avoid food for long, though; even with my belly full of pills, I raced to Jack's Place Bar and Grill and binged on burgers and fish tacos every other night. The purge sessions left my cheeks puffy, which sent my anxiety into overdrive.

I couldn't let the class see me as anything less than absolute perfection; Vandershall was going to launch me into fame and fortune. I needed extra bottles of ephedrine to compensate for my swollen face. If I took extra, I could lean out, and no one would ever suspect that I was binging and purging.

The first week of November, on the morning of the first class, I changed clothes at least ten times and struggled between wearing makeup and going au naturel. Although I knew Mrs. Vandershall wanted a clean, youthful glow, I couldn't bear to see myself in the mirror without paint. *"One glance at me like this and they'll kick me right out of there,"* I thought. Finally, I settled on tight black pants with flared bottoms and a white polo shirt. I patted on foundation, mascara, and nude lipstick and took another look at myself.

"Ugh, Nikki, you look like a freak."

I dug into my makeup bag and slathered on a darker shade of blush and lipstick.

"There we go. And while I'm at it, a bit of eyeshadow wouldn't hurt either . . ."

Within seconds I transformed my minimal look to the full-fledged oversexed Nikki I was so fond of seeing.

I stood back as far as I could and surveyed my body.

"There's no turning back now."

Suddenly, the thought struck me. *"God, I miss momma. I wish she were here to help me."* For a brief moment, I pondered what she was doing and if she even knew about my important day. Maybe Dad told her, maybe not. I could have said something, but I was too busy fantasizing about becoming an international superstar. Secretly I wished for Momma's guidance, love, and support, but I was not about to let her know that.

At half past nine, I walked through the door of Vandershall for the second time and looked around: everything seemed much more daunting. I made my way through the narrow, old-fashioned hallway into the last door on the right with a paper sign taped to it that read, "Runway Training 101." I opened the door carefully.

Inside a long, makeshift runway awaited me, and a handful of naturally beautiful girls buzzed about. I adjusted my eyes and noticed that most of the girls didn't look older than thirteen, and they were all with their mothers. I slipped quietly towards the back of the room and sat down on the floor; my mind went into a raging battle. *"Why in the hell did I come here? I'll never measure up. I need to think of a way to get out of this fast. Nikki, get a hold of yourself! You can do this. No, I can't!"*

"Girls! Gather 'round please, it's time to get started. We have much to go over."

Mrs. Vandershall waltzed in, dressed in black leggings and a matching spandex top. Her hair was pulled tightly into a bun, but somehow she appeared chicer than ever. Sweat began to seep through my pores, and I peeked at myself in the floor-length mirrors. Compared to everyone else I was a foul swine; even the mothers didn't look a day over twenty-five. Couldn't they see? Surely Mrs. Vandershall noticed. She was keeping a close eye on me, even though I sat in the back. Perhaps it was my vile smell, the unmistakable odor of a pig.

I was terrified to walk down that runway; on that runway, a thousand eyes could judge me. I was nowhere near as tall as the other girls. I was not a long and lean giraffe like all the other supermodels.

I was a stumpy pig whose sole purpose was to provide entertainment for the giraffes.

Immediately I wanted to grab my purse, duck, roll across the room and crash through the window; it could be my James Bond moment, however awkward. But I hesitated, terrified and unsure of what to do. Suddenly, Mrs. Vandershall clapped her hands together loudly like thunder. Julia was now by her side, also looking effortlessly elegant. My self-esteem plummeted through the floor. I had never walked down a runway in my life. Sure, I had tried to prance fiercely in a semi-straight line in my room about a million times to the likes of Chaka Khan and Rupaul, but *this*, this was *it*. It was now or never.

"Now, I want you all to stand up straight in a single file line over by the mirror."

Julia loaded "Simply Irresistible" while Mrs. Vandershall directed us over to a spot by the mirror. I made sure to remain in the back of the line so that I could study how each girl walked. I noticed that they all wore leggings, fitness tops, ponytails, and no makeup. *"Crap. There must be some secret modeling society that I am not aware of,"* I thought. *"I'm clearly not up to their standards."* One by one the hopeful models sashayed down the shortened catwalk; ever so slightly my turn inched closer. As each girl exited, Mrs. Vandershall approved with a curled smile.

"Yes, darling, YES! That was gorgeous!"

Sweat trickled down my back, and I suddenly wished I hadn't binged and purged earlier. All of a sudden, Julia called my name, and I felt faint. I nearly stumbled my way onto the runway, and I watched as everyone stared, waiting for me to strut.

I arched my back and put one foot in front of the other. The room turned foggy, but I kept walking and faked my way down the unsteady platform with my head held high and my knees shaking. At the end, I attempted the infamous "S" pose. I heard bits of snickering and shuffling in the background, and I knew this was it; I was going to fall, vomit, and die of embarrassment. But I didn't. I turned, walked back and basked in my glory.

"Excuse me, Miss DuBoise, is it?"

The sound of her creamy voice snapped me back to reality and made me cringe.

"Um, my name is DuBose, not DuB—"

"Ahh, *DuBose*, yes I see. Could you come back here, please? I would like to show you something."

Dammit. What did Mrs. Vandershall want now?

"Okay, Miss DuBose, I am going to show you how to walk down a runway properly."

She turned me around and positioned my body in various ways.

"Stand up straight, tuck your tailbone in, pretend your head is being held up by a string, and tighten up your abs."

My abs? My abs felt like a jelly roll.

She then rolled up my shirt, showcasing my bare stomach in front of the class. A sharp, disapproving look formed on her face.

"Nikki, what exercises do you do? Your body is clearly out of shape! See their stomachs?"

She pointed to the girls and their tummy-baring shirts.

"They have the *stomachs of models*, tight and flat, and this is what *you* need to have. *Tighten your body up!*"

She patted my stomach, sealing my doom. I made up my mind right then and there to get the hell out of Dodge. I dropped out of Mrs. Vandershall's class and decided to focus on school and my job at Krispy Kreme, an ex-model before I was ever even a model.

⁑⁑⁑

At Christmas, Michael and I broke up. Really, the relationship had been holding on by a string for a while, but I finally ended it. I then jumped from one relationship to another without any thought. Maybe it was my way of getting over our breakup; maybe it was my way of getting my mind off of life. I had a lot of sex, with a lot of guys, but it never felt good. I wasn't looking for sex anyway, I was just searching for love.

I dreamed for my love to come, to come shining down on my

ugly face. I dreamed for my prince to wipe the tears from my eyes. In my dreams, we passionately kissed until our lips ached, and never let each other go.

But that love never came, only sex and pain; pain and sex. All the guys I had sex with complained that I was the only girl they had ever known who not only despised pleasure but couldn't seem to experience it. I just ignored their words; they had no idea what it was like to ward off family members and devious adults from their bed as a child.

Sex also helped me get through school, and as the end of the senior year approached, I mulled over the big changes ahead. Soon I was going to be out of high school and transitioning into the phase known as *adulthood*. What did adulthood mean? I had felt like an adult since childhood, but something about it now terrified me. I longed for something *different*, but I wondered if passing through the next phase would suddenly transform my life. In so-called adulthood, was I going to be someone who I could finally face in the mirror and accept?

In February, I decided to take my attention away from sex and give school my last bit of energy. I signed up for the newspaper, the *Odyssey*. Although I was late getting into the class, the teacher, Mrs. Gott, encouraged me. She taught me how to craft articles and interview subjects in the community, from CEOs of non-profits to dozens of students on campus. Within a month my confidence grew, and I realized that I could truly accomplish something that had nothing to do with my body. My dreams evolved, too. I told Dad that I was going to go to college to become a news anchor, even though I was ill-prepared. My published articles became my obsession; seeing my name in print somehow made me feel validated as a person. I had a mind and a voice of my own. I was *somebody*.

I started visiting Momma again in March. I thought that my articles would make her proud, but they seemed to excite her about as much as a bowl of ice on a winter's day. I tried to push her disapproval aside, but as the month hurried on, her negative spirit was always on my mind. By the end of March, my grades slipped, and depression swallowed my brain like a dark fog.

The first week of April, I made my decision: I decided that I couldn't manage anything, anymore. It was a Thursday after school, and as I drove down the long, dusty road to Dad's house, reality punched me square in the face. I realized that all of the years of school didn't mean shit. They couldn't help when you were a dummy. I pulled into the driveway, slammed on the brakes, and raced into the house.

"I'm quitting."

Dad blinked hard and put his coffee down.

"You're what?"

"*I said* . . . I'm quitting. Dad, I can't do it anymore. I decided today that I'm not going back."

"Nikki, now *come on*. You're weeks away from graduation. Don't do this. Think about what you're saying!"

"*Oh*, I've thought about it. I've thought about it *hard*. And I just . . . I just don't want to. I'm going out for a drive. I'll be back later."

I hopped in the car and peeled out of the driveway. I didn't care where I was headed, just as long as I could get the hell out of there. I drove to the nearest ATM and checked my balance. The screen read just above fifty dollars; perhaps that could take me some place where no one could find me. I pulled out forty, stashed the passenger seat with junk food, and drove around Kiawah and Seabrook for a few hours. Every thirty minutes or so, I stopped at a random spot and purged, then cranked the car up and started all over again. Sometime in the evening, my joyride ended, and I headed back to Dad's house. I dragged my body to bed and passed out in a daze, sick from all the purging.

The next day, I announced to my English teacher, Mr. McCauley, that I was leaving school. He was sorely disappointed at my announcement. I sensed the common tragedy felt by educators when they believe that their good will and efforts have gone to waste. He knew my family had struggles, but he also believed I had endless potential. As well, my classmates at the *Odyssey* were crushed. Taylor Strudors, the senior editor, said that I was smart and talented and that I had proven so with my articles.

Their positivity wore on me, but I couldn't bring myself to graduate with the class. I left school and went back to work at the bakery. I couldn't keep my mind off of the fact that I had quit, though. A couple of months later, I broke down and made a pact with Dad: I promised to work hard and finish school at night.

In September, I enrolled at West Ashley High and in October, I graduated. I didn't get the chance to walk across the stage with the rest of my friends, but I couldn't feel sorry for myself. I had chosen this path, and I had to accept whatever consequences came with it.

On my final day at West Ashley High, there was no phone call from Momma, no celebration or hug waiting for me outside of the school. Instead, I got into my car and headed off into the darkness, with my paper diploma and Rage Against the Machine to keep me company.

I had no clue what my next step was going to be. Having a diploma didn't grant clarity or security; if anything, I felt more lost than before. I drove around the city in the evenings, not knowing where I would end up. Every song on the radio seemed to be filled with anxiety and dread. Driving to nowhere was pointless, but I couldn't stop. Life couldn't get to me as long as I kept moving.

꩜꩜꩜

November 2002. Love came, just not in the way I expected. Benjamin was a strapping young man from Florida studying nuclear engineering at the Nuclear Power School in Goose Creek, which was managed by the United States Navy. I served him one day at the bakery, and he kept coming back. With piercing blue eyes, bulging muscles, and about a zillion tattoos, he was the epitome of someone who could send Dad into a blazing panic. I sized up Benjamin and figured that he was perfect, if only for a little while.

With no clear direction, I was looking for a concoction to transform my life and burn away the suffering. I was certain that Benjamin was this magical potion, but I was far too broken to handle it. We began dating, and I unfairly attacked him with guilt and shame and demanded perfection with no room for error. I refused to let him into the vulnerable parts of myself; food, alcohol, and diet pills covered those up. A few weeks into the relationship, I really let the beasts out. Instead of communicating, I hit my head against the wall and worse, locked myself away and proceeded to cut or rip my hair out.

Benjamin and I fought more than we got along, and yet, we couldn't live without one another. Less than two months from our first date, we moved into an apartment together. Ironically, the apartment was not far from the Hubba Bubba house, and as soon as we unpacked, memories of Uncle Robbie came flooding back. I became aloof and held on to a quiet rage. In my mind, Benjamin was responsible for the injustices caused not only by Uncle Robbie but by every person who had ever hurt me.

While Benjamin went to school every day, I binged and purged until I could no longer stand. I didn't care about the crippling headaches and nausea that lingered afterward, though; they were nothing compared to the fact that no matter how hard I tried, I couldn't kill the monster in the mirror. I knew that eventually Benjamin would discover it, and would either throw me to the streets or try to murder me while I slept.

But he didn't. He loved me and only saw my good qualities. I, however, couldn't see anything positive about myself and continued to binge and purge. After my eighteenth birthday, the pain and anger became too much to handle. On a Friday morning, I sat in bed and thought about Uncle Robbie. I thought about him long and hard, until the walls washed over in a flaming scarlet.

Suddenly, I wanted to leave, not only our apartment but life itself. The light within me began to fade, and it was clear, so remarkably clear, that I wanted out. The only permanent happiness was in death. I now understood how Momma felt.

I headed into the bathroom and fumbled for an unopened bottle of diet pills underneath the sink. As I broke the seal, the dark voices beckoned. *"This is it. Are you ready?"* One by one, I slipped the capsules in and washed them down with water. Some of the pills broke open or dissolved, and I tasted the ephedrine in my mouth. Tears began to drip from the corners of my eyes.

The room slowly melted into a milky pool. My throat and stomach burned and an intense sickness surged through my body. I fell to the floor and closed my eyes; my mind went to a different place. I stood inside an old house. It was Christmas, and I was searching, searching for something that I desperately wanted but couldn't find. I touched a cobblestone fireplace, and it fell to ashes, leaving my body saturated in thick smoke.

Hands touched my face, and I gasped for air. A hollow voice called out: was it, God? Ever so slightly I opened my eyes. Benjamin was standing over me. He dragged me over to the toilet and helped me purge the pills. I knew he was my savior, but secretly I despised him.

After that day, I vowed never to attempt against my life again. I refused to talk about my dark thoughts, though, and swept them under the rug with the rest of my demons.

I figured that carrying on with our lives was the only way to mend our relationship. Benjamin agreed, and in April, we got engaged. Momma was not happy when we told her; she was unwilling to help throughout the planning process. I decided that I didn't need her help. I purchased an off-white wedding gown from eBay with my money and combined my jewelry with some cubic zirconia pieces from bargain stores. Momma was unimpressed by the dress and jewelry and cited that we were far too young to marry. At the rehearsal she refused to come; instead, Julie showed up and cornered Benjamin's mother, who was visiting from Florida.

"Honestly, I don't know what he sees in Nikki. She has nothing to offer."

While old and new family members ran around the church and chatted about the wedding, Julie sat in the corner, cold and distant. I couldn't participate in anyone's happiness. Deep down, I was fearful that her words reflected the truth.

June 12, 2003. The day of my wedding. As Dad walked me down

the aisle, I felt Stephen's gaze from among the crowd, and I wondered if he wished it was his hand holding mine instead of Dad's. When our hands slipped away, and my face met Benjamin's, I knew I was making a decision I already regretted. My smile was as artificial as paint, and if we stayed underneath the bright lights of the church long enough, it would melt down my cheap dress and expose my true feelings.

I didn't love Benjamin. I only loved my addictions, my obsessions. I looked out at the mass of people, and a cruel and merciless realization crept into my mind: our new family could never fill my emptiness. I already felt cheated and longed for a different life, but I sensed that it didn't matter how badly I wanted to escape, I couldn't. Was this how Momma had felt in her marriages? I glanced over in her direction. By the size of her grimace, I knew that Julie was still present.

A few hours later, we drove off into the picturesque sunset while the rain lightly drizzled. I forced myself to believe that God was honoring our marriage and that all of my problems were fading away, but they didn't, they only became worse. A few days later, I lashed out at Benjamin, and clung to the distorted ideals of love. Benjamin was determined to fix me, however, and stressed that a move to San Diego was going to paint a beautiful, new chapter in both of our lives. Distance couldn't cover my sickness, though. Within a year of our move, I cheated on Benjamin, and we divorced soon after.

CHAPTER **6**

Name Your Price, Snort Some More

Fall 2004. The scenery in San Diego was different than Charleston, but the pain was all the same. I was living in a private hell without a way to escape. Bit by bit my heart, soul, and sanity eroded with every trip to the toilet and swig of the bottle. Purging and drinking brought temporary comfort and fired an old sadness through my veins simultaneously.

Despite this, I fantasized that life was moving towards a state in which I could finally be in control of my destiny. In this imagined utopia, I was going to find the happiness and love I had always searched for. I didn't anticipate, however, that I was going to look for this happiness in the arms of Oriol, my Latin lover. Once Benjamin started the divorce process, Oriol and I embarked on a torrid relationship for a year that ended dozens of times. Although what we had for one another was merely lust, I mistook it for love, desperately needing something to fill the emptiness inside.

Immediately after our relationship ended for good in the fall of 2005, I threw myself into countless affairs and one-night stands. With every new lover came the false belief that they could provide some dream world, an illusionary realm where pain didn't exist. Sex was a tool to mimic love and desire, but like always, it was a sport. I wanted the satisfaction of knowing that I could please my lovers, yet I couldn't feel a thing.

Starting a genuine relationship was impossible. When the sex

101 ❧

ended, The Monster emerged from its hiding spot. Burning rage took over, and I could no longer hide the binging, purging, and drinking. I loved the things that destroyed me, and a man was merely someone to take the punches when the pain became too much to bear.

When October came around, I started to get itchy and wanted to do something besides have sex. I decided to enroll in Southwestern, the nearby community college; it seemed like the logical step to take.

The second Tuesday in October, I walked into the registrar's office. The counselor asked me if I knew what major I wanted to pursue. I thought about it for a minute and boldly pronounced biology with an emphasis on pre-med. I figured there was no way anyone could look down on me as a doctor. I could already envision it: Dr. DuBose, the first physician of the family, a star in the medical field with a legion of awards and admirers to back up her name. I signed up for twenty-three credits. She shook her head, pushed a giant folder full of papers across the counter and sent me on my way.

During the first semester, I dove into my classes with focus and passion. I stayed up most nights until two or three in the morning to ensure that I typed every assignment perfectly. The continuous flow of "A's" reflected my determination to succeed, and I binged and purged through every one of them.

As the end of the semester neared, however, the need for success at any cost backfired. I lost focus, and my grades reflected it. Out of desperation, I bought diet pills, hoping that they would sharpen my mental skills.

I squeezed in a few hours of sleep a week at best and somehow pushed through. Pill-popping, binging and purging was a small price to pay to prove to everyone what a big success I was. I just had to pass finals then I could rest and recharge my brain.

My strategy worked, until the morning my biology professor, Dr. Searle, handed back my final exam. The letter was a big, fat "F"—a failure, just like me. The room turned a bloody red, and I felt the glares, waiting for me to crumble. I ran out the door and never returned.

ﾠﾠﾠﾠ

The start of 2006, San Diego was an ugly reflection of two things: my infidelity and my stupidity. Charleston swung in front of me like a silver pendulum; a part of me longed to return home, yet if I admitted it I had to surrender to my pride, and I didn't want to do that.

I lived in dreadful conditions, and I didn't have two cents to my name, but I couldn't bear the idea of seeing Stephen's face. If he saw me again, he would curl his thin lips, and happily utter the sickening phrase, the one that would make me want to cut my wrists and bleed out onto the floor.

"You are a failure."

I didn't want to face him, but I didn't want to live in my apartment any longer, either. There was no lock on the front door, and the wood was rotted and cracked. Worn, ripped furniture sprinkled the dingy living room, and it reeked of a decaying matter that I couldn't quite trace. In the bedroom was a simple, soiled mattress; during most nights, I slept on it and shivered underneath a borrowed thin sheet with my eyes clamped tightly shut.

I had abandoned my family, but I felt like the forgotten one. It was a struggle to pick up the telephone and call them, let alone return to Charleston. I had deserted them with no intention of ever coming back, but now I was desperate for love, the one thing that a family could provide.

By the time the first of February came, I had exhausted all of my resources in San Diego. I had blown every last penny on food and alcohol; hell, it had all wound up in disgusting pools of vomit in the toilet and shower.

On the evening of the fourth, I swallowed my pride, picked up my prepaid phone, and dialed Dad's cell. My mind was blurry from a recent purge; I could barely recall the numbers as I pressed down with slippery fingers. Nevertheless, I was determined to get out of this hellhole. Dad was clueless as to how I was living. He was also unaware that I had quit school and I was not paying the loans.

After a few rings, he picked up.

"Hello?"

"Hey, Dad. Is this a bad time?"

"Are you kidding? Not for my favorite daughter! You are my only daughter, but you know what I mean, knucklehead. What's going on?"

"I don't really have time to get into too many details. Dad . . . I want to move back home."

The conversation ended there, no questions asked. In less than a week, Dad landed in San Diego. He didn't say much, only offered hugs and a shoulder to lean on. Together, we crammed the back of my Volkswagen Beetle with trash bags full of clothes, a few books, some photographs, and left that stained mattress behind in the dust. I felt hopeful that the Big Man Upstairs had something positive waiting for me on the other side of the country.

For five days, Dad and I transformed into rugged explorers. We drove through the rough, rocky hills and mountains of California, coasted through the painted desert of Arizona, and raced through the dry, flat lands of Texas. I confidently took control of the wheel while Dad stared in wide-eyed wonder at the ever-changing scenery, but his company and the breathtaking landscapes weren't enough to distract my attention from food; we had stocked the car with snacks, and he seemed oblivious as I shoved bags of sweets into my mouth. I pulled over frequently for bathroom breaks and took every opportunity to purge and purchase more crap to binge on.

Dad drove dozens of times. Every time he asked to switch seats, I went through the same obsessive ritual. I binged, curled up in the passenger seat and tried to sleep, but the feeling of food sitting in my stomach kept me awake. I gazed up at the sky, and I prayed. *"God, help me."* I closed my eyes and fought the deranged thoughts, but they became stronger, so I asked Dad to pull over to the nearest station and purged. Afterward, I experienced peace—for a little while.

We arrived in Charleston on the sixteenth of February, just after noon. The heat was stifling; it was absolutely suffocating. I stepped one foot outside the car and onto the damp soil, and then I knew,

I knew I was home. That thick, Charleston air was the same, and in many ways, so was I.

But the heat was overwhelming, and it caused my brain to swell with paranoid thoughts. My journey with Dad was over, and reality was setting in. In only a year, my marriage had exploded into a fiery train wreck, just as Momma had predicted, and Stephen had judged my character well: I was a *whore*. Perhaps, just perhaps it was best for everyone if I ended my life and spared them all the embarrassment.

Stephen made sure that I couldn't have a moment to myself, however; that evening he organized a family dinner. Around six Dad and I headed downtown to one of the oldest seafood restaurants in Charleston, The Lighthouse. When we pulled up, the headlights shone in the window, and they illuminated what appeared to be Nana and Momma sitting inside. My nerves began to twitch; I imagined the contrast between Stephen's fake smile and Nana's real one. Then there was Momma; which face was she going to wear? The unknowns about sent me straight into a frenzy.

I walked through the front door of The Lighthouse. Instantly, my eyes met Momma's and I smiled, but she didn't smile back. I realized I was staring into Julie's darkness, not Momma's beautiful eyes. Stone-faced and rigid, Julie barely uttered a word. I turned to Nana and gave her a long, heartfelt hug.

"Oh, I'm so happy to see my baby! Give me some sugar, darling. Please, come sit beside your nana!"

She squeezed me tightly and kissed my cheeks; distance and time hadn't stopped her from loving me. I moved in next to her at the table, and she patted my leg. Dad sat down next to Julie, who was too preoccupied staring at the ceiling to notice. *"At least we're all familiar strangers,"* I thought. Soon Stephen and Christian arrived. We ordered, and began to eat.

I stared at Christian. He was a foot taller at least, but he was still my baby brother. Stephen kept a wide grin plastered on his face as he chewed on a piece of chicken and cracked jokes about Hitler. It was evident by his behavior that Dr. Jekyll was amongst us. As the evening wore on, I was careful not to scrape my fork against the plate; if I did, Mr. Hyde would show up, and his smile would certainly turn into a deadly one.

No one mentioned my divorce, but they insisted that I return to the buffet for seconds and thirds. Most of all, everyone was careful to avoid Julie; she stabbed her peas with her fork and kept her lips tight. If anyone even looked at her the wrong way, she exploded. I filled my stomach to the brim, and then, as Julie watched with laser-like focus, I excused myself to the bathroom.

"She'll never understand me," I thought, as I wiped the vomit from my mouth with the back of my hand. *"Even if she did, there's no way to make her care."*

✦✦✦

Somewhere inside, I knew I wasn't a failure, but the result of years of trauma that needed healing. I was trapped in a destructive cycle, a sea of demons that I couldn't escape. Still, inner strength and courage pushed me forward. I didn't know where I was heading, and I could barely swim, but I kept putting one arm in front of the other. Underneath my mask was a girl fighting for her life.

The day after our family gathering at The Lighthouse, I called Nana and asked her if I could stay with her for a while; maybe living with Nana could fix my problems. She had always been my rock, and now I had a chance to rebuild our relationship. That evening, I hauled my stuff into her cramped apartment in West Ashley. She didn't seem to mind, so I didn't care about the mess, either.

The next day she cooked the familiar dishes from my childhood, and life felt simple and happy again. In spite of the joy that I felt, though, I purged everything in her teeny bathroom and ran the water. I knew that she could hear me, but I couldn't stop. After a week, I felt depressed and *needed* to release the food to feel normal. We tried to bond over reruns of *Murder She Wrote* and the *Andy Griffith Show* in the evenings, but I couldn't get my mind off of binging. And although she read scriptures from the Psalms and brought me to church, God was a stranger to me; nothing took away the pain, except more pain.

A month passed. I binged and purged multiple times every day for thirty days before I realized that I needed to try and take control of my life; I couldn't expect Nana to mend my broken soul. I enrolled in the Matthew Haywood Real Estate Program, run by Mr. Haywood himself, one of Charleston's most successful agents, and in three months I graduated and started assisting one of his best brokers. Day and night I worked, and soon the money poured in. For the first time, I was making a substantial living as an adult, but the job also provided an escape from Momma and Stephen.

Money was my ticket to freedom and bliss. In July, I applied for a loan to purchase a modest townhouse in Summerville, about forty-five minutes outside of Charleston. To my surprise, the bank approved me on a Wednesday afternoon, and on the following Tuesday morning, I hauled my things into trash bags from Nana's apartment and drove them to my new place. It was hard to leave her, and I promised to visit often. Inside, however, something told me that I wasn't going to.

The townhouse sat in a quiet, family neighborhood. That evening, I looked around the inside and thought, *"Hell, this is a far cry from living on a mattress."* I moved my bags around and settled on the rented sofa. I gazed at the classic furniture and freshly painted walls and tried to reflect on my recent accomplishments.

But, something was different. I closed my eyes and tried to figure out what the feeling was. All of a sudden, I opened my eyes, and the tears started falling. I understood: Charleston didn't seem as menacing anymore. No shadows lurked around the corner. I was free to roam as I pleased.

I walked upstairs into the bedroom, wrapped some sheets around my body and sat on the floor. I tried to drift off to sleep, but an old desire came stirring: in the midst of the peaceful, tree-lined street, the obsession to drink and binge found me again. I hurried downstairs, dug through the trash bags and found a black minidress. An hour later, I was downtown partying. The following night and every night for weeks, I hopped around bar after bar and guzzled as much liquor as I could. Somehow, I managed to wake up on my couch every morning.

Before work, I always checked myself in the mirror and splashed icy water on my face to reduce the swelling. One morning in August, however, as I prepared to leave home for the office, I noticed a shocking change in my appearance.

My face was melting off. I skipped work, raced to CVS, and purchased cosmetics, tanning supplies, and hair dye to cover the hideousness. I returned home and spent hours in the bathroom, but it was no use: my skin was still sliding off. Reluctantly, I went into the office the next day, with pounds of makeup covering my face. Menacing thoughts replayed in my mind constantly. *"You're a freak, a faceless freak."* Over the following week, I noticed that Becky, the secretary, stopped making eye contact with me, but when I turned my back, I heard her chanting in a dark, sinister voice:

"Freak, freak, freak. That's what you are, you're a freak, freak, freak."

It was all too much to handle, and I needed relief. I figured that alcohol and food could quench my insanity, so I continued in my nighttime rampages—no one could see my ghastly face in the darkness. I piled more makeup on The Beast than ever, but at the clubs, the obsession wouldn't leave me alone. I drank, danced, drank, scrutinized my face in the mirror, and drank some more. In the back of my mind, I knew it was only a matter of time before the music died and the lights came on. At least when The Monster was exposed, I was always unconscious.

In the rare quiet moments, when I was sober and alone, I peered out my bedroom window and questioned the value of my life. Who was I? I couldn't reach myself through the internal noise and fast lifestyle. The more money I made at work, the more I wasted on liquor and junk food to binge and purge on.

When October arrived, I couldn't make my mortgage payment. Desperate to make ends meet, I searched for another job, one where the money was fast and easy. I heard from an older lady named Jaime Soto, a party friend I had recently met at one of the bars, that Club

Paragon was searching for a shadow dancer. Club Paragon was the hottest bar downtown, so I went the first week on a Friday evening and applied. The owner, Dominic, was slick-talking and smart with money. He told me that if I could dance behind a box for six hours a night, I could make a few hundred dollars; it was a few hundred dollars I needed to keep my house, so I signed on without a second thought. The job came with another perk besides money: free drinks. As long as I could keep the blackouts from happening until *after* working hours, I could make some serious cash.

To the hundreds of strangers who filled Club Paragon nightly, I was a shadowy silhouette, a mysterious temptress who mesmerized the room with the flick of her hair and twist of her hips. In the box, I transformed into whatever I wanted and let my inhibitions run wild, but it was another facade, another way to disguise and distract from my true feelings. The box couldn't hide everything, and within a few weeks, I began to slip shots behind the screen. By November, I danced completely intoxicated.

Christmas came. Now, it was normal behavior to blackout at work. I was no longer an enchantress, but a sloppy, high dancer carried off the stage night after night. Nevertheless, I continued relentlessly. I made friends with the bartenders and club hoppers; they encouraged my lifestyle, and I loved it. I was dubbed the "hot, exotic girl in Charleston," and commended for my ability to drink more than any man, but behind closed doors, I couldn't see any traces of hot or exotic in the mirror, only a freakish fiend who deserved to die. Carnal pleasures and the desire for physical beauty and acceptance ruled my life.

☽☽☽

After months of shaking my ass at the club, I was tired. Tired of making dollars that could never compensate for my weary, bruised soul, and every night after dancing, I came home and scrubbed my skin mercilessly to unmask two different faces: a used-up, filthy *whore* and a misshapen swine. To make matters worse, I was a *fat whore*;

constant binge drinking and binge eating had packed on a hefty amount of pounds.

Dancing and real estate weren't an option in the new year. I blew away both opportunities, and it was time to search for a different job, something that paid well but didn't require a college education. Wallowing in my despondency didn't leave for many options, so I spent the first couple of weeks in January looking online for anything easy; although in the virtual world, *easy* opened the gate for all sorts of wacky jobs, including those reminiscent of Betty's taste, like strange men during my adolescence.

I found a slew of advertisements in the online classifieds screaming for girls—always pretty, always naïve. I didn't think I was either, but I *was* desperate for money. Most of the men seemed to request the same: eighteen to twenty-five and slender. However, they always exposed some bizarre fantasy at the end which caused me to continue hunting. I wasn't desperate enough to become some old guy's slave just yet.

Right before I gave up my search, I came across a listing that read, "WANTED: AMATEUR MODELS FOR PAID PHOTOSHOOT." I clicked on it and skimmed the description. It seemed harmless enough, just an artsy guy who liked to take photographs in exchange for a couple hundred dollars pay per session. After my past experiences with the modeling business, I felt uneasy, but I had to be optimistic. This was an advertisement for pictures, not a runway show.

I called the number, half-hoping to get a voicemail, but on the second ring, a man named Tom picked up. His voice was slow and by the tone of it, I sensed that he did this often. He asked me if I had ever taken pictures before, and I responded: "once or twice." I *was* lying, but he was already making me nervous. I decided to get straight to the point and asked Tom if there was going to be nudity on the shoot. He insisted that there wasn't going to be if I didn't want any. Less than a minute later, I agreed to the shoot that evening and began searching my closet for the most provocative outfits I could find.

I looked for clothes, and I thought about Tom. I tried on outfits, and I thought about Tom some more, and the more I thought about Tom, the more terror coursed through my veins. What was going to happen if I showed up and he didn't find me attractive? If I didn't show enough skin or pose nude, the probability was high that he wasn't going to pay me.

I piled trash bags full of clothes into my trunk and drove to the address he had given me. Tom lived in a good part of town, so I felt safe driving late. When I finally arrived, it was well after eight at night. I parked my car in the driveway and stepped out. Something inside switched as I walked toward his house with the bags of clothes; I intentionally made every move as sensual as possible. I knocked on the door, and Tom answered immediately. He looked me up and down, smiled, and led me inside.

Earlier, I was scared to undress, but now, the thought of baring my soul for the camera was somehow tempting, downright stimulating. Here was my chance to expose a different side of myself, without anyone to stop me. I went into the bathroom and changed into jeans and a jewel-studded halter top. I piled on thick layers of make-up complete with dark red lipstick and smoky eye shadow, then I stepped back and took a look at myself in the mirror. All of a sudden, I transformed into a divine being. I wasn't The Freak anymore; I left It inside the Volkswagen.

Tom noticed my exotic appearance as soon as I stepped out of the bathroom. He looked me up and down and immediately commanded me to sit on the backdrop paper. I did, and without any further explanation, I began to move like a snake. Something needed to be released, and it escaped as soon as the camera and lights turned on.

Tom clicked away furiously for hours, capturing my body at endless angles. We shot well into midnight and stopped to review the images in his computer room. He sat down in his chair and offered me a spare, but I settled on the floor instead. He paused, placed his hand on my shoulder and smiled. Then he turned to the computer screen and started reviewing each photo. Suddenly, I no longer felt like a divine creature; if anything, I was surprised at how ugly I appeared in the pictures, like a beast in heat. I shut my mouth, though; I didn't want Tom to fly off the handle if I said anything against his work. After a while, he turned off the computer, sat back in the chair and nodded his head.

"These are incredible. You really have a natural talent for modeling."

I hesitated.

"I do?"

"Yes, yes you do. Hey, I have an idea."

He leaned over and placed his hand on my shoulder again. I looked at it, and I looked at him.

"Now that you're comfortable, how about we do this again, but with less clothing."

I wanted to rip his sweaty, pale hand off of my shoulder, but I didn't. I couldn't. I was frozen; frozen in fear, like all the times Uncle Robbie had held me down on my bed. *Frozen.* A voice inside screamed, *"Run away, child! Run away and don't look back!"* But I couldn't. I felt oddly trapped. One part of my soul longed to stay and please him, but another part wanted to fly away like a bat out of Hell. I felt like a child, and the longer I stayed and stared into his beady brown eyes, the more power he gained.

All of a sudden, I came to my senses and tried to pull away, but he leaned in even closer. His gaze became intense, his smile, warmer. I gave in and agreed to the second round of photos, and Tom wasted no time grabbing the camera again. It was after one in the morning, and I felt tired, but I dropped my clothes, exposed myself on the floor and didn't look back. I knew I was selling my soul for a couple hundred dollars, but I needed the cash.

And with every click of the camera, the voices inside directed my next move on the cold, hard floor. *"Yeah, act like you like it. You know you really do. Lean back, that's it. Now, bend over, show him what you're made of."* For two hours, I smiled and gave Tom what he wanted. Two more hours all for a grand total of two hundred dollars. *Two hundred lousy dollars.* At least I had an idea of my worth.

We finally finished at half past three in the morning. Tom wiped his forehead with his T-shirt and asked if I wanted to review the pictures. I wanted to do nothing of the sort, but I agreed. While we looked at the photographs, I noticed something interesting. My gaze gravitated toward my face, not my body, and I didn't see the face of a beast anymore, but a lost, lonely girl. Tom didn't appear to see that; he was ecstatic and carried on about my supposed beautiful thighs for ten minutes. I saw only tree stumps with waves of cellulite that resembled cottage cheese and made a note to self: *"At first chance, kill yourself, you ugly bitch."*

Suddenly, his enthusiasm changed. He pointed at my breasts and asked if I would ever consider implants. I couldn't take it anymore. I excused myself to the bathroom and began to put on my crumpled clothes. As the shirt slipped over my head, it became stuck below my eyes. I searched in the mirror for help, but I could only see the eyes of a desperate girl, a *slut*. Rage boiled until my body trembled uncontrollably; the weight of my tears and anger overwhelmed me, and I collapsed onto the floor. The voices hissed at me. *"You are a worthless nobody, you know that?"* I tried to breathe, but I could only muster a gasp here and there. I smashed my fist against my head repeatedly until I could no longer see or hear anything.

Time crawled by as I sobbed on the floor. A while later, I stood up and cleaned off my face. The pain was over; it was time to collect my money and go home. I walked into the computer room where Tom was sitting in the same spot, staring at the photos.

"What do you say we schedule another shoot?"

"I'll let you know."

He handed over the cash. I collected my trash bags and stormed out of the house without a shred of dignity.

꙳꙳꙳

February 2007. The bank was threatening to take away my townhouse because I had spent months blowing the mortgage payments on booze and food. I told them to take it and packed my car once again. California seemed like the only suitable place to head to—it was tainted, but familiar. I secured a cheap apartment in San Diego, said goodbye to the family and promised to keep in touch.

Being broke, frustrated, and uncertain about the future wasn't such a bad thing. The ball was in my corner; I could start over clean on the West Coast. I left Charleston on a Saturday morning around nine and hightailed it through the states. The next day, Sunday evening, I rolled up to my new place in Mission Valley. It was a little after eleven; I lugged all of my trash bags into the shared apartment and fell asleep on the couch.

On Monday, I took my remaining money, and on a whim, enrolled in another school. Southern California Esthetics Institute was a four-month-long, intensive esthetician program, and it started the next day. On the way back to the apartment, I called Dad from the car and told him about my new plan. He was impressed by my persistence to obtain a degree and wired me money to help with the expenses. I felt ridden with guilt; I knew he couldn't afford to pay my way through school, so I looked for a job right away.

A week later, I started working at Benny's, a local bar and restaurant. The manager hired me as a hostess, but I made plans to move up to a waitress position quickly. Within a few days, however, my efforts demonstrated to be futile; at the end of every night, after the last customer left, I found myself in the women's bathroom, staring into my vomit. If only my classmates knew the truth: I was caressing their faces during the day with filthy hands.

I left Benny's after a month and bounced between several different waitressing jobs, but I couldn't seem to scrape together enough money for my compounding bills. Previous loans from school and various debts piled up. However, I always covered my food and alcohol. As long as I could numb myself for the day, I felt happy.

I felt like esthetician school was going great at least. It was halfway over, and everything was flowing by easily. My almost perfect grades gave me the confidence that I could finally make something worthwhile out of my life. But when March rolled into April, and

April turned into May, the thought of having to pass a final exam for licensure became terrifying; it was enough to send me down a week-long spiral of binging and purging. So I did what I had always done: I quit. No explanation, no calling. I simply stopped going.

Mid-May, I was back to square one, and I wasn't learning a thing, either. Instead of building a life and planning for the future, I continuously set myself up for failure by putting all of my energy into destructive behaviors. Life didn't exist, only the desire to live impulsively. But a reckless attitude wasn't going to pay my rent and bills, it was going to destroy everything I had.

I was in a dilemma again. I needed to make a lot of money, but who was going to offer a college dropout tons of cash? A couple of days after I quit school, I powered on the computer and hunted through the classifieds. In less than five minutes, however, it became crystal clear that there were no miracles waiting in the shadows of the Internet.

I sat for a bit and thought. Could I possibly return to the one job I had sworn off? Amateur modeling had proven to be a dead-end career, but the money flowed like water. *If* I could ignore the greasy photographers and survive the shoots without having constant meltdowns, perhaps I could rake in enough money to make ends meet.

I returned to the classifieds and answered the first post that advertised for an amateur nude model. My hands shook as I sent an email with my height, weight, and a few candids, but I was willing to do what I needed to do.

For the summer and into the fall, I flashed my flesh to any photographer who threw dollars my way, cash preferred. The money was modest at best, but it covered the rent, and more importantly, the lifestyle I wanted. It gave me food and alcohol to binge on, and more clothes, makeup, and hair dye than I knew what to do with. As time went by I felt empowered by my ability to negotiate my body for money. It was all too simple; I wasn't a fool anymore. At the end of every day, I was the winner because I had the money.

⫘⫘⫘

Tonight, Carl and I met up at seven sharp. On this brisk November night, like most, we shared a bottle of fine wine, an elegant dinner at La Rive Gauche, and dancing at the Four Seasons. The glittering scene was a far cry from a couple of months earlier when I spent my days scraping together nude shoots and my nights groveling over the toilet in agony. Mr. Carl Balatorri was my boyfriend; he was short, balding, and forty-six, but he was a gentleman, kind and sensitive to my needs. I met Carl one day through an amateur photographer named Gary, who promised to pay me four hundred dollars a day for pictures of my breasts. Although the work with Gary was sleazy, I figured that a date with his friend couldn't be any worse.

From our first conversation, I knew Carl was different. He listened to everything I said. He liked to hear me talk about my childhood and about how much I enjoyed reading. I fibbed terribly, though; how could I have told Carl the truth about life back in Charleston? He would have left me on the first date.

My world turned around for the better when I started dating Carl, but there was just one problem: he was a married man. According to him, *things were complicated*, but I apparently brought elements of laughter and beauty into his universe. To show his undying affection, he offered to pay my bills and lavished me with gifts. To put it frankly, Mr. Carl Balatorri asked to be my "sugar daddy."

I continued to model for Gary and some of his fellow, amateur photographers to collect some holiday cash. Whenever one of the "guys" asked to shoot a picture of a random body part, I volunteered, but I never allowed anyone to photograph my *face*. I didn't want them to capture The Beast on film.

After Christmas, Gary introduced me to another gentleman named Emilio. He was from Italy and came to San Diego often for work, although he never disclosed what *kind* of work he was involved in. I fell in love with Emilio's dark eyes and dimples immediately, which was a massive mistake. His story was similar to Carl's as well: his wife lived in Naples, and she never questioned him about his adventures overseas. Our attraction was intense and passionate, and he showered me with gifts and money. However, the longer I stayed with Emilio, the more jealous he became. In February, I stopped amateur modeling to please him but continued dating Carl in secret.

For a few weeks, I remained both Carl and Emilio's girlfriend. Our affairs took us on wild trips all over the states together, but deep inside, I felt invisible. I was the other woman, and I didn't have a voice. Even if I spoke up, who was going to listen? I was the homewrecker, *the whore*. The voices took advantage of every opportunity to torment and remind me, too. *"You've become what I always knew you would. You're a whore just like your mother."*

The guilt became too much to handle, and I moved on in March. My trysts with Emilio and Carl, however, had expanded my social circle to include men and women of wealth and prestige. I wasn't attracted to guys my age anymore, only older, powerful men.

I started dating immediately. San Diego was brimming with financially stable, capable lovers, and I wanted in. Every week, I slept with a different man, or two, or three, and I gave them exactly what they wanted—sex.

I delivered like a perfectly trained actress every time, but if they could have undressed my skin and uncovered my soul, they could have seen that I was an eight-year-old child acting like a vamp. I wasn't after the sex; I was looking for love, the light to satisfy me internally and guide me out of the darkness. The only problem was, I couldn't find it anywhere.

During sex, I turned the lights off because I didn't want to see my lovers, or worse yet, have them see me. After all, I was covering a monster. And sometimes, even in the dark, even when I shut my eyes and gave the bastards what they wanted, I saw one face looking back at me—the face of Uncle Robbie.

For weeks, the sex and glitz entertained me, but after a while, I needed a change. I started to venture downtown during the weekends and listened to blues and jazz music in random bars. It was then on a Saturday night in April that I met Allison Crane. Allison was a spunky girl with long blonde hair and bright, blue eyes that hooked me immediately. We began chatting by the bar, and within ten minutes, we started dancing in the middle of the room like kids. I felt free; she was a change from the rich stiffs I normally hung out with. We shook our ass for an hour then ran off to The Mellow Rose, where we bonded over margaritas and shrimp tacos. In that hole-in-the-wall on Clover Street, we became instant friends. We found out that we enjoyed similar tastes in music, clothes, movies, and even the same funky shade of lipstick. Allison knew when to stop ordering margaritas, though—I didn't.

After that night, Allison and I spent every minute together. We wasted away the spring afternoons underneath the sun and cruised all over San Diego in her midnight blue Mustang convertible. We set the radio permanently on Delilah, a national host who played romantic songs and talked to callers about their love lives. We imitated their longings and heartbreaks and giggled uncontrollably as we imagined guys dedicating songs to us.

I felt fine around Allison as long as we joked and talked about hypothetical love, but that's where I drew the line; I didn't have any love for myself. Inside, obsessions about food and my body controlled my mind. She was slim, and I secretly envied her figure. As the weeks passed, I ate less and less around her, but in my apartment, I binged and purged until my throat burned.

One of the major things that attracted me to Allison was that she was a fashion designer for an accessories company, and her job granted exclusive access into the industry that had rejected me. The more time we spent together, the more I became curious about the glowing models in her company's catalogs; before long, all I could think about was my face covering their faces. Allison sensed my obsession. Our talks became less about boys and music and more about the models.

The first week of May, on a sunny Tuesday afternoon, I mustered up the courage at The Mellow Rose and asked her if she thought I could actually *be* one of the models. I pointed at a blonde on page twelve, and my finger shook. Inside I felt like my child self, shy and afraid, but bursting with excitement. Allison quickly replied that yes, in fact, not only could I, but it was a mystery to her as to why I wasn't already a top model, soaring with the greatest of the greats.

I took a harder look at the girl. Had I been misled all this time? Why wasn't I able to see what Allison saw? Deep down I wanted to be admired like a model, but I couldn't see anything beautiful in the mirror. Surely she could never understand that I saw a monster.

From that moment, Allison made it a point to invite me into her private world, and every Saturday night, we attended a party for the local fashionistas in San Diego at Club Republic. I was swimming in my heart's delight; not only was I meeting trendy designers, but I was rubbing elbows with the models, too.

Then on the last Saturday of May, Club Republic held a party for the fashion magazine *Isabelle*, the standard for local trendsetters. Allison grabbed me by the arm and led me straight to the editor-in-chief, Stephanie Marsak, a quick-witted girl from New York who also happened to be her friend. As we shook hands, her dark brown eyes wasted no time in tracing the lines of my body. She ended on my face and paused. Then she leaned in and stared directly into my eyes. I wanted to look away, but I was hypnotized, unable to move a muscle.

"You're gorgeous! Allison told me you were pretty, but I didn't realize you were *this* pretty."

I wasn't sure I heard her correctly. Perhaps I was hallucinating again.

"I—I'm sorry?"

She threw her head back and laughed loudly.

"Darling, didn't you hear me? I said you're *gorgeous*. Hasn't anyone ever told you that before? With that face and body, you should model for my magazine. You have curves, and *curves are in*. I would love to have you in the next issue."

Had she and Allison lost their minds? If I was hallucinating, I didn't want to stop. I fell in love a little with Stephanie Marsak at that moment, and as she handed me her business card and sauntered away, I knew my life would never be the same.

❧❧❧

Ten bikinis. Ten candy-colored bikinis spilled out of my hands and onto the bathroom sink. While I attempted to shut the door with my back and save the swimsuits from getting drenched, I caught a glimpse of something. I stopped and looked. There, in the mirror, was the deformed swine, watching me. I blinked and looked again, but it was gone.

I saw only my face, red and puffy, ruining the fresh work of the make-up artist, and heard the voices reminding me of what an ugly piece of work I was. *"You've screwed it up now! Look at your fucking face. And take a look at your thighs while you're at it! How on earth are you going to fit into those tiny suits? Hurry up, fatty, hurry up and change before she comes in here."*

I tore off my jeans and squeezed into a silver, Brazilian-cut swimsuit. The bottoms wedged tightly between my thighs, and I checked the size tag: *small*. The voices laughed. *"How embarrassing. You don't fit! Wait until Stephanie sees you, fat ass."* My legs began to tingle, and a familiar, sharp anger rose as I struggled to fix the suit. Amidst the building rage was an impending desire to smash my face in the mirror. I closed my eyes and inhaled deeply. Tears poured down my face, ruining my makeup.

"I can't do this . . . not right now. Pull yourself together, Nikki," I thought.

I opened my eyes, patted my face, and stepped away from the mirror. I tried to get a good look at myself, but I couldn't beneath the teased, curled hair and pounds of bronzer. I recognized my thighs, though; they burst through the bikini like swollen sausages. I squeezed the fat around them and pulled them back, trying to imagine what my new thighs would look like if I starved.

Bam, bam, bam.

Suddenly, Stephanie rushed through the door.

"Why hello, my lady! Are you ready? Jack is ready for you honey, and we need to get moving because of the sunlight. If we want to get an iconic cover shot, we have to have everything photographed *now*. The light is our best friend! Uh, wait a minute. Turn the other way, please. Let me check your butt."

I spun around, and she let out a low, purring sound.

"That looks . . . well. Gloria! Will you come in here for a second?"

Gloria, the assistant, came running in. She had a tool belt wrapped around her waist, filled with safety pins and clips.

"Do you think this is too much ass? No, no right, of course not. Never too much ass. Okay, thank you, Gloria."

Gloria hurried out. Stephanie twisted my body back around and noticed my ruined face.

"Oh, what happened? Boyfriend trouble?"

"No, I—"

"Don't worry, they come and go *like flies* in this business. Let's go into makeup again and get you touched up. You have to understand one thing, and one thing only. You look perfect. And because you look perfect, you *are* perfect. Now, are you ready to go make some magic?"

ﮩﮩﮩ

"I told you, you're a star! Two covers of *Isabelle* in three months, *how* do you like that?"

Stephanie slapped the glossy magazines on her posh desk and smiled while she studied her scarlet manicure. I held my copies tightly in my hands and slowly nodded. I looked glamorous; the girl on the covers was a sexpot, a symbol of the thousands of models and actresses I had always idolized. Still, as I flipped through and inspected the photographs, I couldn't help but notice that my stomach was narrower, my legs longer and slimmer. This girl was me, but different. I searched for the words to say so.

"It's something! Honestly, I always wanted to be a real model, just never thought it would happen. Thank you, Stephanie."

"You've always had it in you, Nik—."

I stopped her.

"Just one thing, though. My body . . . It looks like I've lost weight in the pictures."

"Oh, that's just some retouching we decided to do at the last minute. You know, it's normal. Photographers retouch like crazy."

My gaze drifted to the wall, and I felt my spirit sink. What happened to her love of curves? Although I disliked my body, her original praise had given me hope; now I was questioning myself all over again. I wanted to remind her of our first meeting at Club Republic, but fear kept me from opening my mouth. Stephanie was powerful, and she had the ability to put me on the cover as much as she wanted. I didn't want to ruin my chances of success and happiness. That night, when I returned to my apartment, however, I let her know who was *really* in control. I purged in the shower and pretended she was the drain. I released my frustrations all over her metal face.

The two covers of *Isabelle* launched my career successfully in a short amount of time. In the fall, other local designers called and asked if I could walk in their shows and star in their print campaigns. The pay was low, but I didn't care; my long-awaited dream was becoming a reality.

According to the designers, the unique shape of my body was something to be celebrated; it could start a revolution amid the malnourished girls who usually ruled the spotlight. I impressed the clients and photographers, too. My ability to bring sensuality to fashion was a feat that most models couldn't accomplish.

Day after day, as they dressed me in couture and painted my face, I grew into who I was always meant to be—anyone, anyone but me. Nikki DuBose from Charleston was dead. The scared girl from the South would have never lasted under the bright lights anyway, but I thrived off of it. I needed the glitter-filled air to survive.

When the bulbs flashed, I looked into the camera with an unmatched intensity. The camera was my lover; it brought out my raw sexuality. The love affair between us was electrifying. Really, I had never felt so aroused in all my life.

After a few weeks, however, I began to melt underneath the lights. The bulbs burst and blistered my skin, and the makeup artists ripped and picked my flesh at every given chance. I heard the whispers and snide comments, too. The clients flung those freely at my heart like daggers.

"Don't eat the muffins, honey. What size are you again? A six?"

"*Your hair.* Christ, where are all the girls with suitable hair? We'll be here all day at this rate."

"Is that her *hip? Oh, God.* Photoshop that out, please."

"She's just too big for this shoot. Replace her. Put Sofia in, instead."

Their words destroyed my self-esteem. I stopped modeling before the winter arrived and locked myself in my bedroom with a stack of my editorials. I wanted to figure out how I could alter myself to win their approval. Above everything, I wanted nothing more than to be loved.

Every day for a week, I studied my photos. I examined them from every angle, and then I looked at them some more. When the weekend came, I finally left my bedroom. I walked into the bathroom, took a long, hard look at myself, and realized that I had become obsessed. I wasn't eating or sleeping, and all I cared about was The Nikki in the magazines. The Nikki in the magazines, however, was an illusion.

The girl seductively gazing back at me boasted an ample chest, plush, cherry lips and a thin nose. She was supposed to be me, but the real me wasn't good enough to be her. Really, the real me had never been good enough to be me.

As the winter approached, modeling lost its appeal, and I spiraled into self-criticism, sadness, and anger. Time melted together, and I cycled through self-harm, drinking, binging, and purging. On some days, I stared blankly out the bedroom window and watched as life drifted by my eyes; the deadness felt soothing, like a blanket for my cold, lonely soul. Given the strength, though, I would have crawled into the kitchen and stabbed myself in the stomach. Allison and Stephanie called relentlessly, but I never picked up the phone; I just let it roll to voicemail. Truthfully, I couldn't let them see *what* I was becoming, or what I had always been.

Finally, in December, a bit of light broke through my clouds. I began to crave the madness of life again, someone or something that could drive me into a blissful state. Modeling was a dreamland, one that I deeply longed to play in, but the forces within had made it clear that I didn't belong—my freakish appearance was too appalling. I needed to find a world where I could exist freely and be loved unconditionally.

I didn't waste any time in searching, and before Christmas, I called up old lovers and arranged to party the holidays away. I felt relieved. Sex was my friend, and I could always rely on it. When sex was around, so was company, and when company was around, so was alcohol. The alcohol brought music, laughter, and freedom. Most of all, the sex brought love, or fair imitations anyway. It didn't matter who the sex was with: one night Sabrina, the next evening, Stan. Some nights it was with Sabrina, Stan, and a curious-looking stranger.

In the new year, Allison and Stephanie introduced me to yet another world, one where I met a group of kids—young and rich as sin. They made their money in real estate and finance, and they spent it loudly, too. The king of the bunch, Max Allen, held a swanky dinner at his Mediterranean-style mansion every weekend. Max was a well-known banker in Del Mar, and the topic of conversation always led to how much money he had raked in that particular week. After dessert, his devout proteges gathered together to indulge in their other interest: cocaine. They disappeared into the back of the house and retrieved bags of white powder. I usually sat and watched as they snorted lines across the marble and gold dining room table, tempted but fearful. The more I watched, however, the more I began to crave the pale dust.

It only took a couple of weeks for me to crack. One evening in January, after the usual pompous discussions Chase Perry, a successful day trader, poured out a mound of coke on the table. I felt like I was in a scene from *Scarface*. Max and Chase snorted a few lines, then summoned me over. Like all the other times, I declined; then, I hesitated, and for no real reason at all, I bolted over to the table.

"Wait a minute. I want to try."

Max lifted his head.

"I knew you had it in you. Come over here already, let me show you how."

He didn't have to demonstrate. I figured it out on my own, and from the first snort, it hooked me. The cocaine flew up my nose and transported me to a place I had never been before. In this world, there was no love or happiness, but I had something better: I was indestructible, and I felt like I could fly. One hit turned into a line, and one line turned into five.

I snorted with Max and Chase every weekend for a month, but severe crashes came, and when they did, I snorted more cocaine to lift higher and higher. The more I snorted, the more I needed to sustain my superhero status. I couldn't get my hands on powder fast enough.

The coke had its drawbacks. I became aggressive, my nose bled, and migraines with chest pains became routine occurrences. Attempting to function with a foggy mind also felt impossible, but I kept going.

After lines, I advanced to plates. I could have more coke on plates. Soon, that wasn't even enough, so my buddies happily supplied me with ecstasy and unmarked pills. I didn't care what was in the pills; I just wanted the pills inside of me. My life consisted of sleeping for a couple of hours every few days to the rhythm of my trembling heart, and then I woke up, stayed up for days, and *pop, pop, popped* pills like candy. I felt my brain disintegrating as each rainbow-colored pill raced down my throat, but I didn't want to stop; I wanted to disconnect permanently from everyone and everything.

By March, I practically lived at a supplier's house. I met him through different party friends who came and hung out at Max's mansion. One thing led to another, and I left the original group and stayed with my new friend, the direct source. He granted me unlimited access to cocaine, ecstasy, pills, and alcohol.

Allison was a true friend, though. She bailed me out of that house every weekend. Usually, she found me stashed away in the corner of the living room, unable to speak or move. She then lifted me up and carried me in her arms, placed me in my car and drove me home. It always took my body a week to recover, but I wasn't grateful; I resented her for caring for me. Really, I just wanted more drugs. Allison and I fought, and I swore that I didn't have a problem.

A few weeks passed, and when Spring Break arrived, I flew in Jamie Soto for a weeklong visit from Charleston. Although Jamie was a party woman and enjoyed barhopping, she despised drugs. I stashed away the powder and pills in my bedroom drawer before her flight landed, and I cleaned myself up and put on a smile. For the first few days we shopped, dined, and traveled up the Pacific Coast Highway, but at every available opportunity, I found myself on my knees, snorting lines and purging in the bathroom. Jamie was no fool; she caught on quickly. She said that my leaky nose was a pretty obvious sign, although I had no idea what I looked like. After a long, heartfelt conversation she packed her bags and left San Diego early. I cried for hours, and finally, I took every last bit of coke and pills into my bathroom and flushed them all down the toilet.

CHAPTER 7

My Life as a Twenty-Something-Year-Old Model

A few days after Jaime left, I decided to leave San Diego. The city was making me sick. I jammed my belongings into trash bags again and moved to Los Angeles. The evening after I arrived, I immediately hit the clubs; I figured that as long as I avoided the white stuff, I was good. After many nights of partying, I met Larry Black at the Chateau Marmont. Larry was one hell of a crackerjack. He promised to manage my career as a television host, and he made the job seem exciting and lucrative. After chatting with Larry over several glasses of vodka, I knew that my life was solved.

In less than two weeks, I was hired to work for an Internet television network, and life began to advance at a supersonic pace. Not only was I plunged into a new line of work filled with Hollywood celebrities, but also back into the obscure realm of extravagant parties and superficial friends. While I learned the ropes of the business and mingled with luminaries, however, I struggled to maintain my poise. Rabid thoughts of food and the bottle seized my mind during all hours.

As time passed, I grew comfortable with putting on an act and fighting with my mind, but there was something unsettling about the business. I heard the whispers and noticed the prolonged stares from the crew; it was enough to make me want to rip apart my flesh. *What was wrong with me?* Finally, I unloaded during a swanky dinner one late spring afternoon at Spago in Beverly Hills. Jason Espinoza, the head producer, was sitting next to me at the fancy table. While the waiter brought plate after plate of pasta and steaks, I noticed that Jason was giving me that *look*. I turned to Larry, who was sitting on the other side of me.

"Fuck, Larry. Is something *wrong* with me? Jason is always giving me that weird look like I have something on my face."

Larry leaned in.

"I need to get straight to the point here, Nikki. There're no hard feelings. Jason loves you on camera. Every time we watch the playbacks together, he says you look great."

I watched his eyes. He wasn't looking at me. He was staring at my plate of buttered pasta.

But, there is another thing I've been meaning to tell you. Jason doesn't . . . well, there's just something about your face."

My feet began to sweat.

"Wh-what's that?"

"It's your nose. Jason and a couple of other producers said that they think it's too big."

Bang. I couldn't keep my shit together, and according to my manager, I was ugly and unwanted in this godforsaken town. From that moment on, whenever I saw myself on camera, all I could see was a nose that looked about twice the size of my face. Over the following weeks, I screwed random guys, drank, binged and purged to try and boost my confidence, but it was no use; my nose was only growing larger, my face more horrid and grotesque.

The desire to escape Los Angeles was growing faster than my nose, and after a couple of months, I decided to give one last shot at life and work in California. Larry negotiated me out of my hosting gig, and I signed on with a boutique modeling agency. I booked small jobs for catalogs and print campaigns rather quickly, but the nose issue came up again, and I canceled my contract. I fired Larry and planned my next move. Larry was an idiot, I figured, and maybe California wasn't the place for me. Really, there was only one place for me to go: Miami.

Weeks passed. I waited to hear back from the agencies in Miami, and then the emails began to trickle in. Mixed in with a handful of dismissive one-liners was a message from a scout named Charles at Danellas Model Management, one of the most successful agencies in Miami. The feedback was different—sort of.

Dear Ms. DuBose,

We would like to meet you. Can you come before the fall?

Also, some areas need attention on your body. The thighs and hips, in particular, have to be reduced. Competition here is intense!

My mind went racing. I was accepted, but I needed to change—again. No biggie. Whatever Charles asked, I could handle it. I was determined to be who he wanted me to be. God knows I didn't like who *I* saw when I looked in the mirror.

I replied to Charles and told him that I was coming. I spent the remaining summer in Los Angeles trying to whittle my body down, and I slipped to more desperate measures than normal. Every day I exercised for three to four hours then binged and purged. Afterward, I locked myself in the bathroom and scrutinized my face and body.

I left the house, but only to purchase more food and diet pills to fuel my obsessions. I took photograph after photograph so that I could measure my weight loss. In my mind, the more pounds I lost, the more I achieved, and the more I achieved, the more valuable I was, to myself and the agency.

It was fall, but the Miami weather raged on as if the summer had no end. I was overwhelmed by the move into my new house, the excitement of being in a different city, and the fact that I was finally going to become a bona fide model. This was no small agency shit here; I was playing in the big leagues.

The morning of the third of September, I headed to Danellas Model Management. The scenery on the way was a sharp change from Los Angeles; it was not going to be easy to hide. Girls and guys buzzed about on the white sandy beach in barely-there bathing suits, roller-blading and confidently participating in everything from volleyball to basketball. I watched, walked and fussed at my form-fitting skirt. Charles had informed me the day before that I should wear something body-hugging, but now I was regretting it. I could feel a thousand unwanted eyes ripping off my spandex as I passed by the endless row of restaurants on Rio Drive, and I walked faster.

Finally, I reached the steps of the sleek, two-story building that faced the crystal Atlantic. I entered the office, quietly took a seat and soaked in the moment.

I was the only person in the waiting area. All around me, large framed photographs of supermodels hung on the walls. I recognized every single one of them from the '80s and '90s. I was in awe. I wondered if I was going to be a supermodel, too. In my heart, I hoped so. I clutched my portfolio tightly and noticed a tall wall filled with rows of composite cards. Each card displayed a beautiful model from the agency. My eyes skimmed over the boys but rested on the girls.

"Wow," I thought. *"I wish I could look like her. I wonder what it's like to be her, to be like that."* All of a sudden, I became lost in the sea of faces and felt myself drowning in anxiety. Did I lose enough weight? What if they didn't accept me? My foot shook uncontrollably, but I tried to appear calm. I glanced up. On the second level behind a glass enclosure, a few agents stayed glued to their computers and telephones; they didn't acknowledge my presence. I checked my phone: 9:49. The appointment was at 9:30. I bit my breath and quietly sat.

"Yes, how can I help you?"

Suddenly, a tall, shapely woman with silky raven hair stuck her head out of the door and curiously met my eyes. The voices immediately attacked. *"Turn back now before it's too late, dummy. You don't belong here."*

"H-hi, my name is Nikki, and I have an appointment with...with Charles."

I looked down at my phone to double-check the appointment details. My delicate voice struggled to find its confidence. By the woman's somewhat perplexed expression, I assumed that she didn't know about my meeting. I started to sweat.

"Um, I was picked. I flew here, from Los Angeles. Charles told me to come and sign the paperwork. He said I was already accepted."

She briskly walked over, plopped down, and crossed her stiletto boots in the creamy plush chair.

"I didn't know anything about you coming. Do you have pictures already?"

I handed over my book of photos. The portfolio was modest at best; it was a collection compiled from the small print campaigns in California and old editorials from *Isabelle*. She rapidly flipped through the pictures. Then she closed the book, smacked her gum and breathed a heavy sigh.

"Okay. Fill out some paperwork for me and then we will take measurements and polaroids. I'm Celia, by the way."

Celia grabbed a stack of paperwork from the filing cabinet in the corner and smacked it down on the table next to my chair. She walked back up to the second level, sat down and began clicking away on the computer again. *"Measurements and polaroids,"* I thought. *"Measurements . . . and polaroids."* I grabbed my oversized purse and rummaged through piles of candy wrappers and sticky garbage bits. Finally, I uncovered my beloved enemy: my mirror. I removed it, pulled it toward my face and stared.

"Fuck. Fuck, I hate my face," I thought. I felt numb, disgusted by my reflection. What was Celia going to think when she reviewed the polaroids and discovered that I wasn't even a human, but a slobbering animal? I looked at the giant window that faced the ocean; I

madly wanted to jump out and drown myself in the briny deep. I felt incredibly worthless. What in the hell was I doing here?

Suddenly, a seagull flew in front of the window. Then I realized: the paperwork. I peered at the stack of papers next to me. On top, was a sheet with the questions I feared most.

Age:
Height:
Weight:

Raging thoughts sprinted around my mental track with no end in sight. *"If I just bend the truth, I will look better,"* I thought.

Age: 20
Height: 5'9.5."
Weight: 115

I didn't just bend the truth; I fibbed badly. I shortened my age by three years. If they knew that I was twenty-three, then that was *it*; I was outta there. I didn't want to be viewed as too short or too *fat*, either. I remembered that various gossip sites had reported famous models as weighing 115 pounds, so I stuck with that.

⁓⁓⁓

In the end, it wasn't hard getting past Charles, not hard at all. Celia, however, proved to be a different apple. The casting process around Miami was hell, and I wasn't booking any jobs. As late September arrived, clients began to trickle into the agency to cast shows instead of at remote locations, and Celia watched me like a hawk.

After an audition for Chloe on Thursday afternoon, Celia took another round of polaroids and asked me to stay in the office. I sat for an endless time, hot and anxious, thinking about the comments that she had thrown around about my body like yesterday's trash.

"Move your hips the other way. Yeah. Your legs are too big to photograph like that."

"Are you dieting? No? Hmmmm."

"Some implants will go a long way with you."

The voices started up. *"Of course, she noticed your weight! That's what happens when you eat before you take pictures. You better starve from now on, like the other girls. They're the ones making all the money. With some nice boobs too, you'll finally be somewhat attractive."* I glanced over at the other composite wall and searched for my face amidst the beautiful of the beautiful. I searched, and I searched, and finally, I found myself, tucked away in the bottom right-hand corner. I was still on a paper card and didn't have my permanent card yet. The voices continued, louder. *"You'll NEVER be like them. NEVER!"*

"Nikki?"

Celia's firm hand on my shoulder brought me back to the present moment.

"Yes, I—I'm ready. What is it you wanted to see me for?"

"Oh, not me. Helena wants to see you in her office."

Helena's office. The large, glass office that loomed over all the agency; a place that few ever ventured. Helena, the owner, practically lived there. I learned about Helena's office the second day when a couple of terrified models came running out of it, and every day after, as I passed through the main entrance, she was somehow always aware of me, yet engrossed in her affairs. Helena intimidated the hell out of me and knew it, too. A well-known figure, she had guided the careers of some of the world's most recognizable faces for over twenty years. For a brief second, I wondered if she wanted to help me, as well.

I crept up the stairs toward her office and stopped. I adjusted my white cut-offs for a solid five minutes, took a deep breath, and continued up the stairs. When I reached her door, I hesitated, and knocked as lightly as I could.

Within a few seconds, I heard her voice.

"Come in and sit down, please."

I quietly walked in and sat in the chair across from her. The office was even more elaborate than what I had imagined. On the dark hardwood floor a beige fur rug was spread wide. Fancy candles and framed articles highlighted jewel tones and animal prints throughout the room. Photographs of famous supermodels coated a massive wooden desk; I felt about as big and important as a discarded peanut shell.

Helena took in a long breath and searched my body with a neutral face, but her eyes pierced right through me. She opened her mouth.

"It has come to my attention that, that there is a . . . a problem darling with some things. Some things that need . . . fixing."

As she spoke, she twitched her hand in the air and rolled her eyes from side to side. *"Fixing? Oh, my God. What did I do that's so bad?"* I thought. In an instant, I traveled back to my childhood. I was in the presence of Momma, waiting to show her my grades, and waiting to get a giant, fucking smack across my face and head. I snapped back to Helena's office and felt the wetness collect in a thick puddle between my legs.

"It's your nose, darling. It's the shape . . . and the width. It's *too big*. One of the agents brought it to my attention in the polaroids that you took. At first, I didn't notice. Then she showed it to me again, and I thought . . .*no big deal*, you can just cover it up with makeup, but it's going to be a problem for clients. It's already *been* a problem, do you understand what I'm saying?"

I did understand. I did *so fucking understand* what Helena was saying, and it took all my strength not to melt onto the floor in a puddle of tears. Momma was right all along—I was ugly. And it wasn't just Momma. It was Jason and Stephen, too. Hell, it was the whole world. I couldn't disappoint Helena, not when I was just getting started. I straightened my back and smiled.

"O-Okay. Yeah, sure. I understand. You are just looking out for my best interests."

"Good. I'm glad you understand, and if you want, I have an excellent plastic surgeon that I've sent other girls to. He's *the best* in Miami. You'll love him."

"What the hell did she just say?" I thought. I smiled even bigger.

"Yes, ma'am, thank you for telling me."

"Think of it as an investment in your career, and in your life."

She stared at me.

"That's really about all I needed to say to you."

She turned, looked out the window, and motioned me out the door with her sharp crimson nail. Change my face? Change my life. As I walked away, I could feel the heat from her blistering flames, threatening to singe me.

※※※

The Miami palm trees swayed to the rhythms of the salty, ocean air. I sat inside Dr. Melbourne's office at half past one on a Saturday and detected two noises: the frail beating of my heart and the maniacal ticking of the clock that hung on his pasty wall. As I listened to both sounds, the smell of sterilization fluids filled my lungs and brought me to a nauseating reality.

I was trapped. To escape, I needed to dash down the long hall-way and face one eerily altered nurse after another, explaining why I didn't want to get my breasts enhanced. *Enhanced* sounded so . . . so innocent, as if putting on a padded bra could have sealed the deal. But no, I was fully aware that soon I was going to be under the knife again, and Dr. Melbourne, Miami's finest, was going to slice and stuff giant balloons of potentially harmful substances into my chest.

But those giant balloons were going to bring me success—if not for me, for everyone else. I wanted to please my agents and make money, lots of cold, hard cash. I couldn't feel good about myself unless the agents and clients loved me. My body was a disgrace, a shameful representation of what a woman should look like, and my lack of jobs proved it.

I was finally going to have a new lease on life. I was finally going to be a woman, and maybe, one step closer to a *beautiful woman,* not a stupid, little child or a pig. After the surgery, I was going to be, above all, good enough.

Just a few months ago, I had entered through Dr. Melbourne's office for the first time for rhinoplasty. He was Helena's favorite, and I had borrowed the money from an old friend to get the surgery. I was terrified, but Dr. Melbourne replaced any fears when he outlined my face with a likeness of my improved self. He held up the mirror, and I was pleasantly shocked. The Freak was not there anymore—just a perfectly formed image.

I turned my head from side to side and realized that this surgery could put me in a position of power. Not only could I book more jobs, but I was never going to be looked at as ugly again. It was the ultimate payback.

After weeks of lying in bed with bandages, I uncovered my new face. Dr. Melbourne removed the layers and brought the mirror over. I saw a petite nose, and more importantly, a Nikki who was finally worthy and desirable.

Once I returned home, however, I became sick with anxiety. I spent hours in the bathroom obsessing over every little detail of my face, from my bones to the amount of hairs jutting out from my eyebrows; there were just too many of those, so I plucked away until my head turned into a bloody mess.

Stephen's unrelenting voice mocked me while I recovered. *"You're a whore, Nikki, just like your mother!"* I tried to ignore it, but it came back, and for the rest of my rehabilitation, I plotted to kill myself. I failed miserably.

Now, a hard knock on the door brought me back to Dr. Melbourne's chalky walls. I looked over as a life-sized doll dressed in a tight nurse's uniform entered the room.

"Hello, I'm Theresa. Ms. DuBoise? DeBase?"

"DuBose."

"Oh. Okay, Ms. DuBose, please come back with me. We need to take your vitals, check your weight, et cetera."

"God, my weight," I thought. Theresa left, and I stood up and

placed my feet together. I had to check and see if my thighs touched because I hadn't eaten a single crumb for days in preparation for this moment. To my relief, they didn't.

I slipped down the hall and caught up with Theresa, who was waiting by a scale. I took off my shoes and stepped onto the platform, then I shut my eyes and balled my hands into fists. As I squeezed them, I felt like my body might burst into flames. *"Please God, please don't let her tell me the number. Please God, please don't let her tell me the number,"* I thought.

"123."

Too late. Theresa scribbled some notes on her pad. *"Oh well. 123, that's not that bad!"* I thought. Not my goal, but not enough to send me into a tailspin at the moment, either. I lifted my flat chest a little higher and repeated the number all the way back to the room.

"123, 123, 123, 123 . . ."

Theresa closed the door. She looked at me and smiled.

"123 . . . that's a lot for a model, isn't it?"

❧❧❧

My breast surgery was set and scheduled with Dr. Melbourne. Right before the day, however, I hit a wall. Danellas Model Management closed suddenly—no explanation given. I found myself stranded in Miami without an agency *and* my paycheck. Charles didn't desert me, though; he emailed a couple of days later and said that I was a good fit for Hurst Model Management, one of the most exclusive modeling agencies in the world. That weekend, the director of the agency was holding a casting to choose a few girls from Danellas, and Charles asked me if I wanted to go. I agreed without much thought. Hurst was supposed to be the best, and I wanted to be, too.

At noon on a sizzling, golden Saturday, I followed Charles's directions and arrived on a private, luxurious island a few miles from Miami Beach. I drove a bit farther and pulled up to what appeared to be a mansion on top of the water—I was *impressed*. Soon, several young, strikingly beautiful girls and their mothers showed up, and I noticed that we had all dressed in our best ensembles of stilettos and sundresses with delicate lace trim.

I walked up to the door and rang the bell. A lanky girl with miles of silky blonde hair opened. She threw us a glance, grabbed a red dog leash from the key rack and retreated into the house. I turned and looked at the others, dumbfounded. All of a sudden, I heard a booming voice with a Latin accent.

"Welcome, welcome."

I swiveled around. An older man with dark, curly hair and deep brown eyes stood before me. He wore tight jeans and a dress shirt, slightly unbuttoned.

"I'm Marcos. Yes, hello. I'm so happy you could all make it. Please, come to the back and relax for a bit before we get started."

He gave us all kisses on the cheeks, then signaled and led us to the back of the mansion onto a spacious veranda.

My body followed, but I couldn't get my head to; it was still at the front of the house with that kiss. *That kiss.* His lips had only brushed my cheek, but it stirred old feelings. I couldn't place it, but I had seen Marcos's eyes before and felt his kiss. An uneasiness began to grow in my belly, but somehow, it drew my attention closer to him.

Suddenly, I became aware of my loneliness, and I thought about Momma. Of all the times to miss her, I missed her now. The girls found seats at the table with their moms, and I settled on an empty spot next to Marcos, who was quick to offer it. He looked around with twinkling eyes and offered everyone water. I politely and nervously declined.

In less than an hour, Marcos had everyone nearly salivating at the mere mention of the word *Hurst.* I watched him carefully; with his grand gestures and confident smile, Marcos seemed aware of his charm. Then it hit me. He reminded me of Stephen.

He finished his speech about the agency and asked us to give our best runway walk. I cringed as each girl stood up and sauntered past the table. Marcos flipped through the portfolios, scrutinizing their bodies and silently passing his pleasure or distaste with his dark eyes.

When my turn rolled around, I gave my best runway walk, but

couldn't shake off his stare. He looked through my portfolio and wasted no time in getting straight to the point.

"I think you have great potential, Nikki. With the right guidance, I mean people who know what they are doing in this business, you can go as far as you want."

I paused, and my heart started to beat fast.

"Really?"

"Of course! It's easy. You come in on Monday. I'll change around the pictures in your book, send you off to a couple of photographers, and you'll be working with the best in no time."

I wasn't so sure about Marcos, but I agreed immediately. With Hurst, my career was sure to soar higher than the stars.

☽☽☽

The following Monday, I entered through Hurst's ultra sleek doors. My knees rattled with every step, but I ignored my nervous feelings and pushed ahead. *"Do whatever it takes to impress them,"* I thought. I walked up to the front desk.

"Hi, I'm here to see Marcos?"

The receptionist flipped through two separate appointment books. She didn't stop to look up.

"And who invited you?"

"Fuck my life," I thought. I knew it had all been too good to be true. Underneath my dress, my inner thighs became wet with sweat and the skin started to stick together. I dropped my purse on the floor.

"Well, Marcos did."

She peered at me.

"Oh, okay. I'm Pavla, sorry for my rudeness. It's just that . . . there are so many people coming in and out of here all day. *Everybody* wants to be a model, but that doesn't mean they can be. Know what I'm saying?"

She raised her right eyebrow and smirked.

"You can have a seat in accounting. Danielle will have you sorted out with your paperwork before Marcos sees you."

I picked up my purse and walked into the accounting room; it was a little room off to the side with light pouring in from a generous window. One chair rested against the wall. I sat in it and began thumbing through the collection of shitty photos in my portfolio. Suddenly, a blonde girl about six feet tall rushed in.

"Hi, I'm Danielle. You must be Nikki. It's nice to meet you."

She genuinely smiled, passed me a stack of papers, a pen, and sat down at her desk.

"It's nice to meet you, too."

"Finally, someone around here is real," I thought. I clicked the pen and began to fill out a paper asking for my general information. All of a sudden, I heard an awkward, angry sound—like a screeching hawk. It was a voice, and it belonged to a woman.

"What? Well, *what* do we have here? Oh, no you don't. Marcos! No way."

I winced. The sound of her voice scared the shit out of me.

"Come here, please. Look at her! Just *look* at her."

I dreaded confronting the face that claimed those words, but I bent my head until a short, blonde woman came into my frame. I relaxed a bit. She looked harmless enough. Marcos entered the room, laughing, and she suddenly lunged at me, picked up my hair and held it in the air like a rancid animal.

"Look at her hair! *This* . . . This will never do! And I saw her pictures already. She's too sexy, Marcos, really, *what* were you thinking? Well, I know what you were thinking, obviously!"

Marcos tried to conceal his amusement, but his face was bright red, like a tomato. He removed my strands out of her grip.

"Sofia, relax! There's nothing wrong with her hair that an appointment at the salon can't fix. We'll send her over to Roscoe and get her straightened out. You'll love him, Nikki. He's straight to the point, and he gives you the best service."

He winked and grinned. Sofia threw her hands up in the air and stormed out. Danielle, who had been staring the entire time, turned back to her desk.

"Just take those papers home and bring them back to me by the end of the week."

I returned home, signed my contract, and headed off to see Roscoe in his private salon a few days later. My wavy, black hair was cut and lifted into a chocolate shade; I felt like a new person and decided to keep going with the trend. The next day, I scheduled my breast surgery with Dr. Melbourne again.

A couple of months passed, and I recovered from the surgery. I went back to the agency with a burning confidence and a sore and ample chest. At first, Marcos and Sofia applauded my new look, but three weeks into castings, Sofia changed her tune. Every day, I heard the same comments.

"We go for a more natural approach at Hurst. Not so much for the big boobs up to here, okay?"

"I don't understand. Why are your arms so skinny? Your legs are big . . . I don't get it."

"The clients booked you, but I told them that if they wanted Holly they had to book Nikki, too. It was a package deal. This is what I'm going to tell the clients from now on. If they want a particular girl they have to use you, too."

"I couldn't get you in to see them. Your legs are just too large for what they're looking for. I'm sorry, but what they like is what they like."

Her words sent me into a mental hell. I went back into my obsessive rituals to numb the agony; before and after castings every day, I scrutinized my face, hair, and body for hours.

"Fuck. Fuck. Fuck! What kind of exercises do you do? I'll fucking show her. Hell, I'll show everyone. I'll never fucking eat again!"

Sofia frightened me. She was Momma and Stephen, all wrapped up together. One moment she was nice to me, the next, she was rude and downright mean. I wanted to please her, I truly did, but I wanted to please her because she scared the living piss out of me. I thought about Sofia while I went to castings and worked, and the more I thought about her, the more desperate I became to change myself and make her happy. I ate diet pills and yogurt for a while, but nothing worked. Sofia and I still hated each other, and more than anything, I hated myself.

In some way, my obsessions brought peace to my chaotic soul and helped me to cope with the stress at the agency. Life outside their arms terrified me, and I couldn't recognize myself without them. In Miami, if I wanted to be accepted and valued, I *had* to continue my behaviors; I was a slave to them.

I could handle it, though. As time went on, I learned to ignore Sofia's psychological tactics and played along with her games. Uncle Robbie was right all along. Life is all about games, and you can decide how far you want to go.

As the months passed, I decided that I wanted to go all the way. I let the bastards mold me into their image, and I watched while, after shoots, the photographers altered my pictures and laughed about it to my face. I listened to the disparaging comments that they made about my body; I was nothing more than an animal that they could butcher over and over again.

You know what they say about keeping your friends close and your enemies closer; in the modeling business, I couldn't have friends, only enemies, but my enemies became my friends, so truly, I was screwed in every way. However, many people in the industry are a bit deranged. They liked to be screwed and to screw others.

In the fall, Marcos and I started to get well-acquainted. I was dating, but that didn't seem to matter to either one of us. Marcos hosted dinners almost every night. On some nights, at the trendiest restaurants in Miami, and on other nights, at his mansion. During these dinners, a select group of models gathered together with him and his influential friends, usually the owner of Hurst and other millionaires, over swanky meals topped with wine and liquor. He began to invite me to these dinners, and I felt obligated to come. I didn't trust Marcos, but he was my boss, and in my eyes, he mirrored Stephen.

But wait a minute: *his girlfriend,* Corina. I couldn't help but wonder if she knew or cared about his playboyish ways. Marcos spared no expense when it came to having fun, and he seemed to like to mix personal and professional life. He drove exotic cars, lavished his home with some of the finest art, and spoiled his girlfriend rotten: his girlfriend, the top model at Hurst. She worked constantly, and it didn't take a rocket scientist to figure out that he sent her away so that he could have his pick from the litter during the "model dinners." The ones that he invited me to.

Before long a pattern began to emerge. When I accepted Marcos's dinner requests, I worked, and I worked a lot. Campaigns and coveted covers poured in. Some of the best photographers captured my face for Perry Ellis Swim, *Glamour, FHM,* and *Maxim*—the jobs seemed just to land in my lap. I loved the attention and success, but, secretly, I assumed that I was not the only pig sweating under the weight of Marcos's influence.

In a game, there comes a time when it's clear who is the winner and who is the loser. I knew that eventually, Marcos and I could reach that moment. Someone was going to be the winner, but I felt like it wasn't going to be me. Marcos's eyes shined too brightly; his smile lingered far too long after dinner was over. He didn't just want to stare at my face; he wanted to fuck me.

When Thanksgiving season arrived, many of the models returned to their respective hometowns, but I stayed in Miami. My boyfriend and I moved into a new residence together in a quiet area of Miami Beach; going back to Charleston wasn't a high priority on my list.

One evening, the owner of Hurst decided to sponsor a feast at Mr. Chow, the happening restaurant of the moment. I agreed to go and spent hours curling my hair and pounding on the makeup. I decided on a black dress—always a black dress and always tight, to keep the jobs coming.

Around nine I walked into Mr. Chow. Marcos was sitting at a big table in the middle of the room, with the owner of Hurst and a few, giggly models. I noticed that Corina was missing, and I took a seat across from him and ordered a glass of water. During the meal, Marcos thundered with his buddies and photographers and ordered bottle after bottle of wine. Our eyes met each time we raised our glasses, and as always, I drank one too many. At the end of the meal, I ordered champagne and chased everything down with a couple of shots of limoncello. Afterward, everyone exited Mr. Chow separately. I nearly reached my car when Marcos stopped me in the parking lot.

"You are a woman of few words. You've hardly spoken anything tonight."

I hesitated, and my heart began to flutter. I felt aroused but afraid. Still, what did I expect to happen?

"I don't know . . . These things intimidate me, I guess."

He kept his distance, but his eyes narrowed.

"Come back with me tonight. Corina's not here . . . We can go back to my place and talk for a bit."

I didn't want to get into his Lamborghini, but I did. The entire way, Marcos raced dangerously through the streets of Miami Beach, and I gripped my seat. When we turned into his neighborhood, he placed his hand on my left thigh. I looked at his face. He wasn't smiling. He pushed the pedal to the floor, and the car sped up. It was my moment. If I turned him down, I could lose everything I had worked so hard for. My lips curled into a soft smile, and I let him run his fingers up my thigh.

"You're a slut, Nikki. A bitch slut, like your mother." The voices taunted me while Marcos rubbed on the inner meat of my thigh. We arrived at his driveway, and he leaned over the seat and brushed all over my neck with his lips and tongue.

We continued inside his mansion: inside the walls, colored with gold. He didn't ask for what he wanted. He simply took my hands and placed them on his crotch. I tried to slow down, but that just turned him on even more. He became aggressive, and secretly, I liked it. Still, I hated it at the same time; he was like Uncle Robbie.

He led me into the bedroom, and we played around with our mouths. Then he pinned me to the bed with his massive strength. I closed my eyes and opened them—once, twice. His face switched between Uncle Robbie's as he held me there and groped my breasts and vagina. I liked it and I didn't. *Fuck*, I wanted to break away from his heaviness, but finally, I relented. I was scared out of my mind, but my privates felt wet.

♩♩♩♩

Marcos was well aware of his influence, as were the models. No one spoke a word about what was *really* going on behind the scenes, however; a model was a toy, there to do as Marcos pleased. As long as the money and fame rolled in, did anything else matter? The only real price seemed to be sex, and wasn't sex supposed to be fun? If one girl didn't want to have sex, she was easily exchangeable for another. The modeling industry was a breeding ground for girls willing to do whatever it took to be successful, and I was one of them.

During the holidays, the nightlife in Miami was like breathing speed, and I inhaled every second of it. I ditched my boyfriend and spent all of my time at the clubs. In my eyes, everyone saw me as a sexual goddess, a top model, and therefore I had the upper hand.

When the new year came, and the spring turned into summer, the jobs became few and far between. Most of the hopefuls jetted off to Europe to shoot high fashion editorials, but I stayed because Marcos insisted that I develop my image in Miami and focus all of my attention on local clients. I wanted to grow, but Hurst wasn't giving me the opportunity. Sofia was no longer in charge of my career, only Marcos, and whatever Marcos wanted, Marcos got.

After several weeks worth of mediocre castings and odd jobs, I was growing reluctant and expressed my feelings to Marcos. He told me not to worry, and a few days later, an important casting suddenly popped up for the following Saturday. He said that this casting was crucial for my career, and if I impressed the photographer, I could make *lots* of money. The casting was happening at his mansion; I thought that sounded a little odd, but I agreed to go. Then Marcos told me that it was going to be just us four: him and Corina, the photographer, and me. My stomach felt a tickle, but I shrugged it off.

On Saturday, I woke up and changed into my favorite, black two-piece with a tunic, grabbed my portfolio and headed out the door. When I arrived at Marcos's mansion the weather was luminous; not a trace of a cloud lingered in the bright sky, and a soft, pleasant wind blew across the water.

I rang the doorbell and Marcos answered. He winked and led me inside to the living room where I met Adrian, the photographer. Adrian looked to be about thirty at best, and scrawny. I smiled and waited for either one of them to say something about the casting, but they just turned and headed out the back door to the veranda, so I followed behind.

Outside, the table held a massive display of lobster, pizza, and salad. I glanced at Marcos, and he nodded at Adrian. Corina walked by and threw a half-grin. I realized that this wasn't a casting.

"Shit. I can't leave," I thought. I took a deep breath and sat down. Corina and Adrian joined me; Adrian settled across, and Corina, on my left. Marcos went into the house and returned with bottles of champagne. He sat, poured us all glasses, cracked open a few lobster tails and placed a portion on our plates. We toasted with the champagne and Adrian began firing rounds of questions.

"So, where did you grow up?"

"How long have you lived in Miami? It's nice here, huh?"

"What kind of movies do you like?"

"I love this cheese. We have all sorts of amazing cheeses back home in Sweden. Perhaps you should try them sometimes, you'd like it there."

I answered his questions, and I answered them with a smile, but with every response, my stomach felt tighter and tighter—I wanted to throw up. Sweden sounded nice, but not with Adrian. Something about him reminded me of Tom. I half-expected him to offer me two hundred bucks for pictures of my privates.

Marcos watched us talk for a little while, then he slapped my shoulder and joined in on the conversation. He instructed me to drink and soon, the discussion picked up the pace. Marcos and

Adrian went back and forth like kids and chatted about everything from work to the weather to sports. After thirty minutes of listening to them talk, I couldn't take it anymore; their mannerisms reminded me of Uncle Robbie and Stephen. I stood up and walked into the kitchen.

Corina and Marcos quickly followed. Marcos stopped me, looked me square in the face and lowered his voice.

"Nikki, Adrian is an important person. Really, go back."

I froze. He cocked his head and motioned for me to go outside. Corina stood by, emotionless, and I forced a phony smile.

"Sure. No biggie."

I stepped outside and sat down. Next to my plate was a fresh glass of champagne. Adrian sat back in his chair with his hands behind his head, and his faced tilted towards the sky. I lifted the glass to my mouth and took a giant swig.

Darkness. I opened my eyes and saw Corina sitting next to me on a little space near the kitchen. Suddenly everything went dark again, and then I saw light. I laughed but couldn't feel anything. My vision went dark once more, and then I saw Marcos and Adrian. They were standing above me, smirking and shaking their heads. The room tilted, and it went dark.

At some point, my eyes opened. Hands; I felt hands removing my bottoms on a bed. I heard a voice, saw a face: it was Adrian's face. I wanted to move and scream, but I couldn't. I felt paralyzed. The darkness came again, and time drifted as the cycle continued: *awake, silence, darkness.* So much darkness.

Nausea woke me up. I opened my eyes and saw black, all around. I slowly raised my body and touched next to me, but felt nothing. I hobbled off the bed, felt around for the wall, and found the light switch; the brightness burned my eyes. Nausea blistered my belly and my head—like fucking knives! I clutched my stomach and slid down. That's when I felt it; my vagina touched the floor.

"Oh, my God."

My head pounded, harder and harder. I hadn't been . . . *raped.*

Trembling, I stood up and scanned the room for my bottoms. I tore the sheets apart, and flipped the mattress upside down, but I couldn't find them anywhere.

"Fuck!"

My hands shook, and I tried to put the bed back together. I tiptoed over to Marcos's room, my legs trembling with every step. I knocked on the door, and Marcos opened.

"I have to tell you something."

"What is it?"

I started to ramble.

"Marcos, I—have you seen my bathing suit bottoms? I had them on at lunch and then when I woke up, they were gone. Hold up, how did I get drunk off two drinks? It was weird! I swear I felt someone taking off my bottoms. Actually, I saw someone too, but . . ."

"But what?"

"All I know is that my bikini bottoms are gone. Don't you find that odd? And I feel sick to my stomach like I want to vomit but I can't."

Marcos fluttered his eyes and folded his arms.

"Nikki, Nikki, what exactly are you trying to say here, huh? I don't know *what* you're talking about. You fell asleep, and we carried you to bed earlier. Corina and I have been in bed this whole time. Adrian is in his room resting. You just had too much to drink. . .it happens with the hot sun."

"But what about my bottoms?"

"I *don't know* what you are talking about. I'm sure your bottoms are here somewhere. Corina has a drawer full of bathing suits, do you want me to grab you something?"

I couldn't believe what he was saying. I bit my lips.

"No, I don't. I'm going to go home."

He looked at me with a cold stare; one that shot through my heart. I had lost already, and it was going to be my word against his.

I grabbed my portfolio and purse and ran out the door. The vomit threatened to come up my throat, and I swallowed hard to push it down. I jumped in my car and hightailed it out of the driveway; the faster I could get home, the faster I could clean my vagina. I wanted to wash away the filth, and my entire life.

My boyfriend was fast asleep when I arrived. It was after midnight, and I crept into the shower. I turned the faucet on high, let the water flow onto my back, and began scrubbing with a sponge. The rough fibers slowly ate away at my skin, but I liked it; scrubbing over and over was the only way to cleanse my dirty body. I rubbed harder until tears and blood spilled into the drain, and I heard the voices. *"Little girls need to mind their manners."*

I didn't say a word to my boyfriend. Instead, I shoved my feelings down with food and brought them up all over again. The following Wednesday, I questioned Marcos once more in his office about the missing bottoms, but he immediately shut me down. He told me that I was crazy, and I should forget about everything.

I was insane. Marcos could see it, and if someone knew about the situation, they didn't say a word. Adrian disappeared, and I shut my mouth and returned to castings. Hallucinations and haunting memories of his face, however, resurfaced over and over again.

As the weeks rolled on and the season kicked into high gear, I attended the extravagant parties and acted as though nothing had happened. Inside, though, something shifted. I felt overly suspicious and bitter; the darkness and greed of humanity had destroyed another vestige of my innocence. The sinister voices that once occupied space inside now sucked the breath from my lungs—they controlled everything.

Deep-seated rage burst within, and to quiet it, I screamed and threatened myself with butcher knives. I smashed my head into walls and doors. Really, I just wanted to see my blood.

The police came after nearly every episode. When I saw their blue lights pull up, I feared to go to jail, but they just wrote a report and called me crazy, too.

For the rest of the summer, my affair with Marcos continued. My career climbed higher, but my relationship with my boyfriend fell apart. I was a cheater. I hadn't learned anything from my divorce.

I constantly struggled with the voices; they demanded that I persist with the fling, while my conflicted heart commanded me to leave my career behind for the sake of loyalty.

Flirting with Marcos and having mindless sex allowed me to feel alive. Deep inside, though, I knew I was a fraud. Our rendezvous always left me with a sense that I was living on top of the world, but it was an obsession, and I needed to see him over and over again to feel good about myself.

In August, after a fashion show for Fredericks, Marcos introduced me to his friend, Pio Catanni. Pio was another fifty-something millionaire with an affinity for dating models. Pio and I clicked over drinks back at his even bigger mansion, and he offered to fly me all over the world. He made life seem easy and appealing, a little too quickly. I didn't care, though; I just wanted love and sex. I stopped dating Marcos, ended the relationship with my boyfriend and moved into Pio's estate.

Over the fall, Pio spoiled me with gifts and took me to the French Polynesian Islands. I was impressed by his ability to sweep me off at the drop of the hat. I focused all of my attention on Pio and as a result worked less and less. As we spent more and more time together, however, his real side came out. During sex, he slapped me on the face. At first, I became aroused, and asked Pio to choke and smack me hard, but after awhile, I couldn't become turned on unless he hurt me. He was Stephen and Uncle Robbie, and I was drowning in the twisted world of perverted pleasure. Pio, however, didn't stop in the bedroom; he began to slap me in public, too. The longer I stayed with him, the farther away I drifted from myself.

꘎꘎꘎

Pio and I continued to play dangerous sex games for a little while, but before the winter, I decided to leave Miami for good and take life into my hands. I canceled my contract with Hurst, packed my bags, and headed to Manhattan.

I arrived in New York in October. I'm not sure *what* I was expecting to find, but life in New York City wasn't it. The weather was harsh and chilly, the streets smelled of piss, and my apartment was more cramped than a can of sardines. I signed a contract with New Directions Model Management, a boutique, hip agency close to Union Square, and they moved me into a two-bedroom unit on Roosevelt Island with seven other girls; it was a fifteen-minute trip into Manhattan on a *very* good day. Each bedroom in the apartment contained four bunk beds; not exactly the glamorous life I imagined from watching *Sex and the City.*

Only a week after moving in, I ran out of money, so I asked Dad for some change, but he was also short on funds. Jessica, a junior agent at New Directions, gave me a bit of pocket money and sent me to dozens of castings, but the pocket money lasted for a couple of days, and I didn't book any jobs. I stole food from the kitchen cabinets, binged, and purged in the shower, knowing that some of the girls could hear, but I couldn't stop.

On Friday the following week, the head booker at New Directions, Carol, confronted me about my eating habits. I was pissed, fucking flaming. I knew that one of the models had told her, but I didn't know who; hell, I had swindled practically everyone's food. I lied to Carol's face and assured her that I was going to quit.

Within a day, however, I was back to stealing, binging, and purging. I was in denial; I felt sure that I didn't have a problem with food. Still, I couldn't keep my head out of the fridge and toilet.

Later that night, I settled into bed. The sheets felt cool on my skin as I slithered around and tried to grasp the reason behind my obsessions. I gazed at the ceiling for a little while and finally closed my eyes. Suddenly, one name came to mind: Momma. We tried to reconnect in Miami a few times, but it never panned out. Now I felt more distant from Momma than ever. Sometimes she seemed like herself, other times, like one of her other personas. During our conversations, Momma talked about many things, most of them absurd. Lately, though, she had the craziest idea of them all: she wanted to be my manager. I dismissed her. I couldn't have a drunk as a manager!

But now in my crowded apartment, I felt depressed, and I missed Momma. The next afternoon, on a Monday, I called her.

She brought up the word "manager" within a few minutes, and I decided to take a chance. If Momma wanted to be my manager, she was going to be my manager; I just hoped that it was *her* reaching out. I rented a spare apartment, purchased her flight ticket, and arranged for a limo to pick her up from Kennedy Airport. I didn't have the cash, but I charged the expenses to my agency account and asked for some more pocket money.

Momma flew directly from Charleston to New York City that Saturday. I passed the time by pretending to shop for new clothes and rummaged through racks of jeans at Macy's. Thirty minutes after her flight arrived, I called her phone. She assured me that she was gathering her luggage and was heading to Macy's shortly. An hour passed, then two. I dialed her number a few times, but it went straight to voicemail.

The sun began to set, and darkness swallowed the last colors of the sky. I was becoming quite familiar with Gail, the sales representative in the women's department. She asked me for the tenth time if I needed help, but I shook my head and acted like I was going to buy a couple of cashmere sweaters. Suddenly, my phone vibrated in my pocket; it was Momma. She apologized for not calling sooner and asked me to meet her on Avenue B in an hour. I hopped in a taxi and made the trip across town. When the car pulled up, I saw her standing outside.

I squinted. Momma was deep in conversation with a scruffy-looking gentleman. I hurried out of the taxi and pulled her aside into a corner. She tried to look at my face, but her eyes wobbled. I questioned her about how many drinks she had had, and she laughed. She demanded that we eat next door at the little Italian restaurant.

I didn't want to believe that Momma was drunk, so I arched my back, braced her arm and waltzed into the restaurant. As soon as we sat down, Momma picked up the wine list and ordered a bottle of Cabernet Sauvignon. I grabbed the waiter's arm and tried to stop him, but Momma raised her voice and began to shout—it was her way or no way.

Later, our plates arrived. Delicious creamy linguine spilled over the sides, but Momma hardly touched a bite of hers. She did, however, drain two bottles of Cabernet. I binged on a few breadbaskets, polished off the linguine, and ordered a generous portion of tiramisu. I asked Momma if she wanted some, but she slowly closed her eyes, lowered her head into her plate full of pasta, and began to snore loudly. I paid the bill, propped her upright, and carried her out as demurely as possible.

I helped her into the apartment and tucked her into bed. She slept soundly, and I studied her red, swollen face. My heart sank into my stomach; I *had* to leave the apartment. I wrapped a scarf around my neck and hopped the train to Times Square. The frosty air outside nipped my skin, and I breathed it in.

I walked around the streets with no real purpose, only a pain in my soul until I passed a neon Ruby's Diner sign. I stopped and stared as the hot pink flashed before my eyes like a parade of Johns in rainbow trench coats. I couldn't resist the temptation. I headed inside and binged on a couple of Philly cheesesteaks, fries, and milkshakes. The shake came up easy in the teeny bathroom, but the rest didn't. I punched my stomach and stuck a pen down my throat to force the rough bits out. I needed to get *all* of that shit out.

I headed back outside into the cool night air, and I felt it—the obsession was still there. To my left, was the Hershey's store. I quickly walked inside and froze. Children rushed about, dragging their parents from one oversized candy display to the next. Suddenly, I wanted to set fire to the damned place and wipe out every happy family. Instead, I continued in, purchased forty dollars worth of chocolates, and binged all the way back to Momma's apartment.

Momma was awake when I arrived, sitting on the bed and *quite* unhappy. She began to throw a fit and demanded to return home. New York City was never for her, she insisted, and who was I to bring her there? I left her in her madness, locked the bathroom door, and showered until the scalding water turned to ice. I purged and watched the vomit swirl into the drain; sorrow and rage left my body. Who was I to be fooled by my own mother? *"She'll never make a good manager anyway,"* I thought. I fell asleep in the spare bedroom, relishing the salty tears as they dribbled into the corners of my mouth.

The next day all was forgotten, and the sun blazed brightly in Momma's sky. At ten in the morning, we arrived at the agency with smiles painted on our faces. I felt happy; for once, Momma was by my side.

Momma kept herself composed during the meeting. As I watched her grill Carol about the future of my career, I reconsidered her becoming my manager. She exuded tact, grace, and most importantly, business sense.

We left and walked around the city, and for a little while, I felt four years old again. I stood next to Momma on the bustling streets and held her hand softly. I felt unaffected by the chaos; she was all I wanted, all I needed.

An hour later, we headed up Twenty-third Street and passed the window of Blick Art Materials. Her eyes lit up, and I grinned and motioned to head inside. She drew back, however, and a look came over her face—like a child. I realized that Henrietta was before me. Droves of people hurried around, and I tried to coax her into sharing lunch instead. Her body shook profusely, and I grabbed her hand and led her down a block into a tiny Asian restaurant.

I ordered, and Henrietta stayed glued to my hip. We sat and devoured dumplings, salad, and brown rice without saying a word. For a while, Henrietta peered sheepishly over a cup of water and stared out the window. All of a sudden, depth returned to her eyes, and I knew that Momma was back.

"You know, I like this place. Thank you for bringing me . . . I don't remember how we got here."

"I'll show you when we leave."

Her eyes lowered, and she studied the mini ripples in her water.

"I'm happy you ate all of your food. This brings me a lot of joy . . . bein' with you here, in this city. I can't remember the last time I got to sit down and eat a healthy meal with you."

"Mom—"

"I'm serious! Do you know how happy it makes me to see you eating? I know we don't talk about this, but I think we should. I want you to take care of yourself, all right? You know, I used to struggle with some of the same issues, too. Of course, I was younger, but I threw up and did all sorts of crazy things to try and control my weight. I eventually had to give all of that up and learn to be happy with the way I looked."

"What about the alcohol?" I thought. I nodded.

A little time passed. We sat on the creaky stools and carried on about nothing in particular. I didn't want to run to the bathroom and purge; all that mattered was this moment.

The next day Momma flew back to Charleston, and immediately, the obsessions returned. I stumbled around the city and binged on bags of chips as I made the journey to my apartment. *"Yesterday was such a nice day. Why can't it be like that all the time?"* I thought. I stuffed my face, and I thought. I thought, and I stuffed my face. I paced down the busy streets, determined to make it home in time to purge.

❧❧❧

The message was loud and clear—I was *fat*. Everyone inside Manhattan's fashion circle thought so, and I had the lack of jobs for months to prove it. The only logical thing to do at this point was to take a break. If I left for a couple of weeks, no one was going to miss me. I certainly wasn't going to book a life-altering campaign. On Tuesday, I told Carol that I needed time off, and headed to the apartment. At least this place was *mine*; a couple of months ago, Dad had sent me money from his savings, and I had moved into a townhouse in East Harlem.

Unretouched photos from a shoot in NYC by Federico Peltretti. Playing pretend was just another day at the office, yet this was when I felt my most comfortable: when I could be someone else.

Two golden weeks of bliss were all mine. The idea was almost too much to handle. I locked myself in my bedroom, sat my portfolio on the floor, and looked around. Suddenly, I felt itchy, and I wanted to eat—a lot. That afternoon and every afternoon after, I walked swiftly down the street to the pizzeria, purchased a couple of extra-large pies with all the toppings, and headed back to my apartment. I tore them apart in the silence of my room until I choked, and each time I purged, it became harder to bring the food back up. The pain was motivating, though; it talked to me and pressed me to purge harder. *"That's a good little bitch."*

Afterward, I hit the streets for another round and wandered aimlessly with a pounding headache and twitching legs. I felt the suspicious eyes and whispers revealing my secrets as I tried to cover the bleeding sores on my mouth.

On the inside, I envied the successful models, and that kept me locked in my room, day after day with my food. I longed to be free from the jealousy and enjoy life's precious moments, but I needed to be normal to enjoy life—no one could understand my insanity. Clearly, I was the only one riddled with pain. The other girls couldn't comprehend what it was like to feel lost and rejected. The sheer mass of my misery formed a wall so large that it divided me from the entire world.

When I returned to work two weeks later on a Tuesday, my mind was fuzzy, and my energy was low, but all I could think about was food. The next evening, after an agency dinner, I purged in the bathroom stall. Some models overheard and told Carol again. I could lie for a little while, but not forever.

⟩⟩⟩

It was early on this Sunday morning. So early, that the birds weren't even awake, and that was early considering the birds began chirping outside my window before the crack of dawn. But Momma was relentless in calling me even before the birds did. That's how I knew she was either angry or drunk; I wished it was the first. I pulled the covers tightly over my head and tried to fall back asleep, but it was no use; my cell phone continued to ring. I sighed and removed the covers. "H-Hello?"

"Now I know what you think. Carol called me the other day and told me what happened. I'm not mad . . . I'm *not* mad. Listen—"

"You're *not* upset with me?"

"No! Do you remember the conversation we had in New York?"

"Yes . . ."

"Well! Why would you think I'd be upset with ya? I'm *concerned*, more than anything. I hear you haven't left your apartment for weeks . . . I also heard about you throwing up at that dinner."

My blood turned hot.

"I'm sorry, okay? I didn't mean to! You think I wanted to do that?"

"No, I don't. But honey, Carol and I think that you need to get some help. Take a break for a while. A real break. Why don't you see about checking in to see a doctor, huh? It might do you some good. I think that getting away from all of this modeling business and taking care of your health could give your mind the peace that it desperately needs."

"Mom . . .I'll call you back."

I threw my phone on the floor and cried until I couldn't cry anymore. Momma was right, but I didn't want to admit it. If I didn't seek help, I was going to lose my career, maybe even my life. I picked the phone off of the floor and dialed the agency. Shit, I didn't want to do it, but I did. Carol answered, and I almost hung up. I stuttered the whole way through and vowed not to return to the agency until I was healthy.

I hung up and stared at the phone. There was another call I needed to make, and my inner battle began.

"There's nothing to think about, just do it!"

"I'm trying!"

I made a tight, right fist and pummeled it against my forehead.

"Do it, just fucking do it, stupid!"

"But I'm scared!"

I crawled into a ball and gazed into the distance. My left eye throbbed something terrible. I sat up and inhaled from down deep in my belly. *"I can do this,"* I thought. I dragged the laptop over and scoured the online directory. After a while, I found a therapist by the name of Dr. Kelly who specialized in abuse. Every number terrified me, but I dialed them all into my phone.

The next afternoon, I met with Dr. Kelly at her private office on the Upper East Side. She was a no-nonsense type of therapist and got straight to the point within the first thirty minutes. She said she could see me twice a week for my trauma-related issues as long as I took responsibility for my eating disorder first. Everything else faded into the background after I heard the words *eating disorder*. Did an official diagnosis mean that I was in danger of dying? Life seemed much more fragile somehow. I liked my life before talking to Dr. Kelly; if I didn't know that I had an eating disorder, then I didn't have to take responsibility for it. Still, I had agreed to take control of my life, even though I had no idea how to go about doing so.

She told me about a twelve-step group that met daily in the city at St. Thomas Church on West Fifty-third Street. If meetings didn't help alleviate my behaviors, she explained, I had to check myself into outpatient therapy. I vehemently disagreed to the conventional care route and agreed to attend the twelve-step meetings. When our first session ended, I trekked more than thirty blocks to the church.

When I reached the grand, Gothic-style church, I paused; inside these walls, was my answer. I walked up the concrete stairs and entered inside. It was almost seven, and the meeting was about to begin. To the right, was a piece of paper taped to the wall. I looked closer: "Recovery Meeting, Room 104." I turned and made my way through a dimly lit hallway marked by endless doors. Finally, I came to Room 104 at the end and hesitated. I no longer felt optimistic; entering meant that I was giving up everything I had ever held so dear. Running away could feel so, well so thrilling, like every other time in my life. I couldn't live on the edge any longer, though; that was getting me nowhere.

Inside, a handful of men and women of all sizes sat on folding chairs, and a light hum emanated as they chatted and passed tissues. I stood in the far corner and observed. Every so often, one tearful person offered a hug to another. I discreetly took a seat behind the group and forced an awkward smile. I noticed an obese woman across the room, smiling back. I looked harder at everyone. One woman, about sixty, stuck out: she was the size of a pencil.

At seven on the dot, the meeting commenced. Each person explained a little about themselves and their struggles. One woman was a binge eater for nearly all of her life; another, a bulimic for ten years. Hearing their stories didn't ease my nervousness. As my turn inched closer my armpits began to sweat profusely, and my inner thighs became soaked. Finally, everyone turned to stare at me. My voice croaked as I tried to explain *who* I was.

"Hi, my name is Nikki, and I'm a bulimic. I've had . . . an eating problem since I was eight years old. Today is my first time at a meeting."

My body suddenly felt hot, and everyone's face melted into a puddle. What did I just say? *"Hi, my name is Nihkiiianhdimabulhmick."*

"Thank you, Nikki, for sharing! And welcome, we are *glad* to have you."

A peppy lady wearing a shiny, silver jacket from the '80s winked and beamed brightly. Her cheer was infectious; somehow it softened some of the remorse and shed light on the truth. For the first time I was coming to terms with my behaviors; as a result, shame pierced through my mask. She passed a paper asking for contact information and tears rolled down my cheeks. I could finally let go and be myself for the first time in my life. But, *who was I?*

The meeting ended an hour later. I introduced myself to a few people in the group, including the pencil lady. Her name was Lisa. I didn't ask her what her deal was, but we connected right away. I promised to return, walked all the way back to the apartment, and fell on my bed. The question loomed in my mind: should I keep my word and return, or should I not?

The next morning at seven, I returned to the same church, and that night, I met up at the Cup and Saucer with Janet, an older lady who I had met at the first meeting. Janet was a sponsor to a few other people in the group. I enjoyed listening about her life and appreciated her wisdom, but I wasn't ready to spill my guts just yet. If I told Janet or the others about my life, she was going to think that I was crazy, like everyone else. I carried enough personal shit to fill all of Manhattan a thousand times over.

Every day for the next week, I returned to the meetings. I hated them and liked them at the same time. Then on Sunday, a man named Henry turned up to the meeting. At fifty, he had suffered from bulimia for twenty-five years and was in recovery for fifteen. Combined with the fact that he was gay and struggling with an eating disorder, he had had a difficult time recovering until he came out to his family. Something about Henry's story stirred the darkness in my soul and gave me strength. I decided to stand up and share a bit of my past; my body shook, but I did it anyway. As I talked about the abuse from my childhood, and how that had led to my eating disorder, I felt Henry's eyes sinking into me. I also felt something else radiating from him: acceptance. When the meeting ended, he tapped me on the shoulder.

"Hey. I just want to say that your story touched me. I know it hasn't been easy to go through."

"Thanks, thanks, Henry. I appreciate that."

"That's what I'm here for."

He smiled warmly.

How is your program going?"

For some reason, I felt jittery.

"Oh, you mean the twelve-step program. Well, I'm new. I've only been coming to the meetings. I don't have a sponsor or anything."

"I'd like to be your sponsor if you'll let me."

My heart stopped.

"Are you serious? Oh, Henry, I'd be so grateful! I just haven't asked anyone—"

He put his palm up.

"I completely understand. You are me fifteen years ago, honey!"
He scribbled something on a scrap of paper.

"Here's my number, and *that's* my e-mail. When you're ready, just let me know, and we can get started. I'll be happy to help you."

We embraced and he walked out the door. I squeezed my eyes tightly and thanked God for this miracle.

♪♪♪♫

A few weeks in, the sessions with Dr. Kelly seemed to be helping. Twice a week I sat on her velvet couch and poured out my soul. She was more than a therapist; she was a guide. Dr. Kelly was someone who traveled with me into the realms that I usually deemed as too painful to touch. Once there, we worked through layers upon layers of memories of abuse. Most of the time I questioned if Momma and Stephen, and especially Uncle Robbie, had touched and harmed me. If they had, were their offenses valid? Perhaps they had only acted out of their misery, and I had no right to judge them.

Dr. Kelly pointed out that although they were human beings and capable of faults, I was entitled to my basic needs and rights as a child, and never received that. I never lived in a healthy environment and had no chance to give myself what every child deserves: love and security. As a result, I had spent my adolescence and adulthood searching for that love and security in all the wrong places.

She recommended that I visit Dr. James Berry, a psychiatrist with a well-established practice in Gramercy Park. Therapy and the twelve-step program were parts of the solution, and medication could potentially provide another missing piece.

I showed up at Dr. Berry's office on a Monday afternoon at ten past four. I was a little late, but I didn't think that would matter much. Dr. Berry rushed me in and hardly muttered a word. I, on the other hand, filled out a packet of forms and blabbered about my modeling career and infinite history of abuse, eating disorders, addictions, and tendency to harm myself. He blankly stared, and the tears cascaded down my cheeks while I continued. Suddenly, I stopped. I detected a *hint* of annoyance on his face; perhaps I was going over the time limit, and he wanted to leave for lunch. He held up his hand, cleared his throat, and scribbled on a notepad. He gave me a bill that was marked by what appeared to be a three followed by two zeros.

"Here, go fill this."

I tried to read the rest of the scribble.

"What's this?"

"It's called Topiramate. It will suppress your appetite."

He looked me up and down.

"However, I suppose that will only help you in your modeling endeavors."

The slightest smile slithered from the corner of his mouth, like a sheepish snake daring to face the sunlight after a sumptuous spree during the small hours of the night.

I looked around the room.

"Help me? Does he think I need to lose weight?" I thought. This psychiatrist needed a shrink. I paid him, however, and ran straight to the nearest pharmacy to fill the so-called miracle medicine.

Without insurance, three hundred dollars a bottle was going to wipe me off of the financial map. I could work more, call Dad, or one of my former lovers. The last two options made my toes curl into a permanent, crusty ball; I didn't want to depend on someone to pay my way anymore, but I felt helpless. Just a phone call to Dr. Berry was going to set me back three hundred big ones.

Thankfully, the Topiramate worked. I lost my desire to binge almost immediately. I also lost my will to eat entirely, though, and three weeks later, I was twenty pounds lighter. Besides the weight loss, something else started happening, something unexplainable.

It began on Saturday evening, as I flipped through the television and searched for something suitable to watch. I clicked the remote, and stopped; the photo of Granny that sat next to the tv caught my eye. *"Did she just wink at me?"* I thought. I shook it off, clicked through the channels again, and paused. No, I was certain; she *had* winked at me. I stared at her picture for a few seconds. All of a sudden, she winked, not once, but twice. My heart sped up. Shaking, I threw the remote on the floor and shoved Granny's photo under a pile of panties in my drawer.

The next night, the mischief continued. The heavy metal trash-can lid in the kitchen flew off and slid down the stairs several times. Finally, I removed the cover and kept it off, but then the lights in my bedroom started to flicker. I wasn't sure if I was hallucinating, it was a poltergeist, or there was a problem with the electrical wiring. One thing was sure, though: everything started once I began taking those damned pills. I wanted to call Dr. Berry but then thought twice once I remembered that meant paying him with Benjamin Franklins.

Soon, the pills ran low. Instead of calling my lovers for cash, I spent an asinine amount of time picking the scabs on my knuckles and dangling a butcher knife over my arm. Piercing the skin was ir-relevant; fantasy was what I wanted, a distraction from the stress at hand. The reality eventually became louder, though; it ate away at my brain like maggots, millions of slimy, disgusting maggots. *"Three-hundred more fucking dollars! I'm doomed! I'd rather kill myself and just get it over with."*

For a couple of weeks, I hid in my room with a knife and fresh, open sores. Dr. Kelly repeatedly called, until finally, I picked up the phone.

"Nikki, I don't know what is going on inside your head, but I haven't seen you in quite some time, and you've missed far too many appointments—"

I broke down and cried.

"Please help me, Dr. Kelly . . ."

Through waves of tears, I tried to explain what I had been expe-riencing: suicidal thoughts, hallucinations, and the dramatic weight loss. Dr. Kelly instructed me to come into her office immediately.

The following morning, Monday at ten, I hurried in to see her. Just talking made me feel better instantly. She didn't call me "crazy" or laugh, but she gave me a big hug and her eyes teared up a little. When our session ended, she concluded that I needed to eat more because

Topiramate merely created the *sensation* of fullness. I retorted that that meant I was going to have to stand up to my fears. She smiled and firmly pointed out that facing my fears was the point of the treatment, and as long as I continued with therapy and the twelve-step group, I had all the support I needed.

Little by little, I began to eat more and gained a few pounds back. The combined success of therapy and the medication allowed me to focus more of my attention on the twelve-step program. Henry and I dove deeper into the principles, and as we did, I realized that I was missing something profound. There was a massive, gaping hole in my soul that had never stopped bleeding, and the familiar longing for love came rushing back stronger than ever.

❧❧❧

I worked with Dr. Kelly for two more weeks then returned to work at the beginning of March. I gained back all of the weight that I had lost, plus a few extra pounds and felt confident to get back to business. On Tuesday at half past three, Carol called me into her office to take fresh polaroids in a swimsuit. After the first few clicks of the camera, though, it was evident that I had not done well with my time off; the deep lines above her brows told me so.

Every day for a week I went into the agency before and after castings to pick up composite cards or to say hello to the bookers, and every day, I picked up cutting remarks about my appearance; my already thin resiliency was wearing down. Three days later, on a Friday afternoon, Carol pulled me into a corner after we shot a few polaroids for Tommy Bahama.

"I've been looking over these a few times. I don't understand what's going on, but your body has changed *dramatically*. It's not like you've gained weight in one or two places . . . You've gained it all over. What's your diet like?"

I didn't know what to say. Her words brought tears to my eyes. I was never the right size, and I didn't know how to control my body. I went to my apartment, called Dr. Kelly, and she suggested that I make an appointment with a doctor. *Fuck.* I didn't want to go to the doctor. I didn't want any hands coming near my body. I fought with Dr. Kelly for a few days and cried. I locked myself in my room and binged while I thought about all of the horrifying things that could go on in the examination room.

Finally, on Wednesday, I came to my senses and began searching on the Internet. I booked an appointment with Dr. Stark, a highly rated gynecologist on Park Avenue. His website seemed professional enough; perhaps he could help ease my fears and decipher the reason behind the weight gain. I called Dr. Kelly again. She agreed that I had made the right decision and that booking the appointment was a sign of personal growth. She also said that the examination could help me confront any issues about rape and sexual abuse. Shit, when she brought up the word "rape," I cringed.

Two days later, on Friday at eleven in the morning, I didn't feel so sure of myself. I didn't like this "personal growth" shit. I seriously considered fleeing, preferably in the most horrifying fashion. As I sat in the doctor's office, on the stiff red chair, I studied the windows: rows of glass windows beckoned me to jump through them and splatter my fat body onto the busy street. The unsuspecting receptionist with a bubble bun hairstyle steadily tapped her glitter acrylic nails against the desk, smacking her gum and scrolling through her cell phone. I studied those windows again.

"Ms. DuBose, we're ready for you."

I dragged my body off of the chair, down the hallway and into the last room on the left. The whole time, I felt eyes on me. The receptionist passed a gown into my hands and left, hitting her bun on the door on the way out.

I changed into the backless gown and sat on a flimsy, paper-covered chair for twenty, grueling minutes. Suddenly, a short, balding man barged through the door with rows of sparkling, false teeth.

"Well, *hellooo* there! Aren't we pretty today?"

I stared blankly and gave him my best bitch face.

"I'm Dr. Stark, it's nice to meet you, Ms. DuBose!"

He held out his hand to shake mine, and I blinked.

"Never mind! You're in great hands, don't you worry about a thing. I was looking at your chart, and it says here you're a model! Hmm, of course, it's not hard to see *that*! We've had more than a few models in here, by the way."

He laughed.

I shifted in my gown, which caused my naked ass to poke through the back. My cheeks became hot, and I rushed to cover myself.

"Yes, I've been modeling for a while now. I like it. . .I guess."

My gaze drifted from his red, jolly cheeks to glass containers on the counter filled with cotton balls and bright fluids. All of a sudden, another knock came at the door, and a black nurse entered the room.

Within moments Dr. Stark hoisted my feet high in the air like a dead chicken. I was forced to look at the ceiling, my legs, and his happy face. Dr. Stark stared hard then plunged his covered fingers deep into my vagina. I squirmed, closed my eyes, and tried to recall a trip that Pio Catanni and I had taken months ago to Bora Bora. Suddenly, I was basking in the glorious sunshine to the rhythm of Sade, with a tall, chilly Pina Colada by my side. A sturdy woman named Manihi manipulated every inch of my neck and shoulders. The drool began to slide down my chin, and Manihi looked me square in the eyes and smiled. Then she opened her mouth and broke my dreamlike state.

"We're gonna need an ultrasound!"

The beach melted into the bland examination room. Dr. Stark was looking intently into my vagina with a little light, and I tried to raise my head.

"Ultrasound. What's that for?"

He smiled and shook his head.

"Oh, I just want to check everything."

He paused.

"You *may* have some cysts growing."

"*Cysts*? Are you trying to tell me that I have cancer?"

"No, no. Don't worry. We just need to check them out, that's all."

"Don't worry," I thought. *"That's easy for him to say. He's got my vagina in his face."*

My paranoia was interrupted by a hurried knock on the door. The nurse arrived with the ultrasound, and as Dr. Stark ran the wand, his furrowed brow released, and a smile slowly spread across his face.

"Well, it's not cysts."

I closed my eyes and grinned real big.

"Oh, thank God! For a moment there I was afraid I had cancer."

"No, it's nothing like that."

I breathed a sigh of relief.

"But, you're pregnant!"

I laughed then stopped. He was serious.

Every fiber within me wanted to fly back to Bora Bora and stay there until the second coming of Christ. *Pregnant?* My head started spinning as I tried to piece together the events that could have led to this point. Pio and I had had sex in Miami just before I left for New York; our relationship, however, was nothing short of a nuclear explosion.

Dr. Stark lowered my chair, planted his hands on mine and looked into my eyes.

"I know this must be hard."

I detected a hint of sincerity in his voice.

"We deal with this news every day. Fortunately, you know, there *are* options. We're here to help you every step of the way."

I made a face.

"*Help me* with this? What do you mean?"

As if on cue, the nurse walked over and softly placed a stack of brochures next to my chair. I flipped through and instantly felt light-headed. *"They want me to have a fucking abortion!"* I thought. They quickly left the room, and I dressed and paid the receptionist. I ran out of the building and raced through the colorless streets.

A week passed. It wasn't a lot of time to think, but it was enough to weigh my options. Living in Spanish Harlem and raising a newborn on my own wasn't exactly the dream life I had imagined as a kid. One person *could* understand my situation, but I wasn't sure if she would take the news well. I decided to take a chance and called Momma around six in the evening on Friday.

"I can't believe you, Nikki. I don't know what to think about all of this. It's gonna take me some time to process it all. . .I'll speak with you later."

Click.

I threw the phone against the wall and screamed. Fuck, I didn't need that woman; I didn't need her at all. Some days passed, and she called back. I didn't want to answer, but I did.

"I've thought about it, and you *must* keep the child."

"Christ, Mom."

"Think of the consequences if you terminate the pregnancy. I was tossin' and turnin' all week with nightmares. Do the *right* thing! Please!"

"I want to keep it, but I don't know what to do. It has to be Pio's and we stopped seeing each other months ago. God knows he has no intention of raising this baby. How am I going to handle this child on my own? What am I going to do, give it up for adoption? Then it will be in the same—"

"The same what, huh? You scared this child gonna be a lunatic like me? What about you?"

What about me? I was a goddamn, insignificant nothing; a poor excuse for a human being. How the hell could I expect to be a mother? There was a destructive ripple in our family, and this child didn't deserve to be born into it; I couldn't even communicate with Momma. Trying to talk about options seemed to be leading nowhere. She forgot, like most times, that I was her daughter in all this, with genuine feelings.

I needed more time to think. The next day, I headed down to New Directions. I sat in the waiting room with my legs twitching and my arms folded across my growing stomach. I *needed* to confide in someone besides Momma. Hell, this baby was going to come out in a few months—it was now or never.

Claudia, one of Carol's assistant bookers, was finishing an email. Our appointment was in five minutes.

"I'll be over there soon, love."

I stared at the ceiling as packs of wispy, giggling girls strolled by. Five minutes passed, then ten, then thirty. Finally, Claudia walked over. She touched my shoulder and smiled.

"Hey, there. Haven't seen you for a while. You okay?"

I couldn't hold back.

"I—I'm *pregnant*."

"What?"

She stared at me with a pitiful expression.

"Oh, *sweetie*, I'm so, so sorry."

Her voice was soft, like a flower.

"Yeah, I—I had no idea. Shit, Claudia! I feel so stupid."

I sobbed. Claudia wrapped her arms around me for a few minutes and gently cupped my face in her hands.

"Oh, *honey*, I can't imagine what you must be going through right now." Suddenly, her tone deepened and she lowered her head.

"Who's the dad?"

"We don't have a relationship. He's not necessarily the best guy."

She nodded.

"You know, truthfully, this happens *all the time*. We're here to support you every step of the way. In *any* way . . ."

"What does that mean?" I thought.

"What do you . . ."

She stared, and my eyes flickered.

"You mean, other girls have gotten abortions?"

She laughed and flicked her hand.

"Oh girl, yes! You wouldn't be the first one!"

I searched for the words to say, but I couldn't answer. I was lost at sea, drowning again. I couldn't breathe for all of the salty blood that filled my lungs.

꒰꒰꒱꒲

I made the appointment. Thursday morning, at nine, was the next available time, and I took it. It wasn't hard to make the call to the clinic; I was having a damned of a time getting my rain boots on, though. It was pouring already, and I didn't have an umbrella.

I covered my head with my hands and started down the street. The rain drenched my face, anyway, and my boots squeaked against the wet concrete.

Squeak, splash. Squeak, splash.

I sped up, and mascara ran down my cheeks. Through my wet, dirty eyelashes, the pedestrians looked like gray and black squiggles. I hurried down into the subway.

Squeeeaaak, thud. Squeak, splash. thud.

A car opened. I slipped inside and tried to squeeze in-between the mess of people. I grabbed onto the orange strap and took a breath.

Voices; so many voices around me. I covered my stomach with one hand and tightened my grip on the strap with the other. I could feel the people looking at me, but I didn't look at them. Instead, I focused on a spot on the window.

The car stopped. People got off, and more got on. I kept my gaze on the window, though; I couldn't face all of the people. The car stopped, then it started again. My stomach jiggled, and I thought about my baby. *"I'm sorry, I'm sorry for being such a waste of a mother. God, please forgive me."*

The car stopped at Fifty-ninth Street. I squirmed through the crowd and headed up the stairs. The rain came down harder, and I hailed a taxi. Pio had sent me extra, so I could afford it.

The driver stopped at an unmarked brick building. Outside, a stout girl with a wool coat was smoking a cigarette. I paid the driver and stepped out. I walked up to the girl; it was Penny, patiently waiting for me. Penny was an eating disorder survivor from the twelve-step group who had offered to accompany me to the abortion clinic. When I told her about my situation, she listened and never said an unkind word.

We peered up at the somber structure that housed more tales than The Library of Congress, and quietly walked inside. As the elevator climbed, Penny squeezed my hands and held them tightly in hers.

"Are you all right? Do you need anything?"

I started to cry. Fuck, I didn't want to cry in front of Penny.

"Thank you. I'm okay."

We took our seats in the waiting room, and I fumbled through my purse. As I filled out the paperwork, I wondered just how many had sat on my hard plastic chair. The receptionist casually went about her duties. A few more young women trickled in, each pale and stone silent. I tried to keep my eyes away from their stomachs, but I couldn't. My foot began to rattle, and I glanced up at the clock. *Tick . . . tick . . .*

"If I run away, I bet I can find a place where they take care of fucking murderers like me!" I thought.

"Ms. DuBose?"

The receptionist's booming voice threw me into the present; a place otherwise known as Hell. I looked at Penny.

"Here we go."

Penny hugged me and kissed me on the cheek.

"Don't worry. I'll be here."

I forced a smile. The head nurse guided me down a sterile hallway where several other girls sadly sat, clutching their knees under thin gowns. I changed and took my seat next to a girl no older than sixteen. I suppose it didn't matter if she was sixteen and I was twenty-five; either way, we could suffer from the trauma of this at some point in our lives. I closed my eyes and rested my hands on top of my stomach. Perhaps there was still time to escape and save the baby.

"Ms. DuBose? We're ready for you."

It was a good thing that two tall, big-boned nurses came to my side. I wanted to run. But I made the decision to take their hands and walked down the hall. In the operating room, they secured my body on the steel table. That damned hospital-grade paper scratched my back down to my ass crack. The doctor entered the room and waited at my feet. I couldn't see his face behind the mask, but I knew he had no emotions.

The anesthesiologist filled my arm and asked me to count to ten. I inhaled and exhaled.

"One, two, three . . ."

June came. I looked in the mirror and saw a monster of the worst kind: a baby butcher. I wanted to kill it; kill the monster and change myself. If I changed, I could start working again and have the career I always wanted. New York wasn't the place for me anymore. New Directions had made sure of that when they canceled my contract and sent me to their division in Miami.

What a joke to go back to Miami. I scraped by and tried to make a few dollars; a few dollars to binge and purge on. I needed to get out of Miami. It gave me a lot of idle time, and that was the devil for me. In my idle time, I started to look for other things to take the fat off, and I found it in laxatives—that was the real shit.

On the second week of July, the eighth, I got the hell out of Miami and flew to Europe. XXP Models, the esteemed London agency, was my ticket to a *real* modeling career; all the best models went to Europe. As the plane took off and I soaked in the reality of my new life, I felt frightened but excited; the prospect of working and living abroad was daunting. I closed my eyes and tried to relax. *"This is going to be the best thing you've ever done. Living in a new country is going to change your life, and your career,"* I thought. I opened my eyes and sighed; there was no reason to be nervous. London was a chance to start over, and no one would recognize the old Nikki DuBose. *The Monster. The Baby Killer.* I could be anyone I wanted.

The next day, the plane landed, and I settled into my flat near Notting Hill. The sky was somber, but it didn't deter from London's allure. I liked the mysterious and gloomy vibe of the city, and I felt myself falling in love quickly. My attraction couldn't distract from my obsessions, though; I was a fool for thinking so.

I went down to the agency at noon the following day and collected my pocket money. Alice, the head booker, handed me a list of castings, and I began my journey. London was thrilling; I loved the people and the old architecture. But there was one problem: the clients didn't like me.

Two days passed. I woke up at six in the morning on Tuesday and walked to the bus station. The bus was right on time at half past seven. I reached into my purse and fished for some money to purchase an Oyster card, but felt only makeup and candy wrappers. *"Shit, I'm broke again,"* I thought. I checked my purse and found a crumpled receipt from Harrods; apparently, I had spent most of my money on chocolates yesterday afternoon. I felt around and then found another receipt from the pizza place down the street. I forgot that I had bought three large pies last night. *Dammit.* I had no choice but to call Dad again.

Dad wired two hundred dollars right away, but I wasn't interested in saving it. I headed straight to the nearest grocery store and bought bread and candy to binge on. Three days later on the fifteenth, the money was gone, and I still couldn't afford an Oyster card to ride the bus for castings. Hell, I didn't need an Oyster card—it was useless. I didn't need a phone or a map to find my way, either. I had destroyed my cell in the sink during a purge session the other day. None of that mattered.

I left the house at four in the morning on Saturday, the sixteenth, and every morning after that for weeks to get an early start on castings. Walking for ten hours a day was a great way to see London *and* burn the fat off. On some days, I lost my way and didn't show up to castings. On those days, I succumbed to my obsessions; I binged and purged behind trash cans, cleaned myself off and wandered around the city until dark.

When August came, London turned a bit beautiful. It still rained a lot, though, and when the rain came down, it left me hungry for that something that I couldn't satisfy.

Starvation seemed to be the only answer. I wasn't winning in London yet; I wasn't a star. If I pushed myself to the limits and lost a lot of weight, I would feel happy, and my career would blossom. So I pushed, and by the end of August, I was thinner and walking farther. After my walks, I purged in the shower. I could see the sharp edges of my bones, which motivated me to walk longer, purge more, and eat less until the numbers on the scale mirrored my goals.

My plan worked. Alice and the clients adored my appearance. At the start of September, I booked fashion editorials and began to attend posh dinners in the West End. During the shoots, all of the photographers showered me with praise.

"You look lovely, you really do, darling, don't change a thing! Whatever you're doing, it's working!"

"Have you lost weight since these pictures were taken? Can I tell you something, love? You look *much better* now."

"Tonight, there's a dinner at Annabel's, eight sharp. All the girls are coming. Free drinks, food, and of course, lovely company!"

September was proving to be quite the success. Extreme restriction afforded me not only consistent work but companionship for gentleman at high-end restaurants. A whole new world was opening up again; day by day, my transformed body was granting me access to the prestigious high-fashion arena, the so-called crème de la crème of modeling. I felt compelled to please the fashion world, but frankly, I was enjoying the attention.

Mid-September, the designers draped me in Chanel and Valentino as they prepped me for the fashion editorials. The makeup artists painted my face in beautiful colors, but they treated me anything like a work of art. As I twisted my body into bizarre poses and tried to deliver their outlandish requests, I absorbed every ounce of their arrogance and negative energy.

"Fuck, I can't photograph her. I don't like this girl. She's not meant for couture. Period."

"Hold still, *honey*. Don't talk. I'm hired to paint your face, not be friends, got it? Good. We can be friends, then. Just don't open your mouth and speak."

I was angry. Everybody could cut me, and I couldn't fight back. I could drink and have fun, though, I could do that. I headed down to

The Box Friday night on the fifteenth. I needed to shut their fucking voices up and forget about life. I headed to the bar, ordered a vodka, and threw it back. I ordered another one; the warm liquid felt soothing as it rushed down my throat.

After a few more vodkas, I left The Box around one in the morning with a new friend: Harvey, a short guy with a lisp. Harvey was wealthy and well-known around London; he said that everyone referred to him as "The Prince." I went back to Harvey's hotel room, snorted a few lines, and rolled into work the next day. That night, I danced my ass off again with Harvey.

Harvey was attractive. He was sweet and wild, all at the same time. Harvey also had more access to cocaine than all of Colombia; maybe that's what I liked about him.

Every day the following week I went to castings, shot fashion editorials, and walked a few miles back to my flat. At night Harvey picked me up in a Bentley, and we snorted, drank and repeated until the wee hours of the morning. In my heart, I knew sobriety was the only way to achieve sanity, but it felt so fucking good to be high; I felt on top of the world.

September 30. I looked and felt like a raging lunatic. My nose was a crusty, bloody pool and the sores on the corner of my mouth split wide open. My body ached from the late nights and constant photo shoots, not to mention from the nonstop binging and purging. A couple of months ago, I arrived believing my lie, that I could be anyone I wanted, but I was merely a junkie.

October 3. My agency in Miami signed me to a Spanish agency named Soto Management, and now It was time to pack. I snorted the last of coke and swore off the white stuff. *"Focus, Nikki. Just fucking focus, for once in your miserable life,"* I thought. Perhaps Spain could give me the strength I needed to resist drugs and booze.

I said goodbye to Harvey and flew to Barcelona on the sixth. When I stepped off the plane, the warm, Spanish sun melted on my skin; it was comforting, unlike London. *"Maybe London was the problem all along,"* I thought.

At half past eleven, I walked up to Soto's doors. I took a few steps inside, and a lady with a kind face ran over.

"Welcome, you must be Nikki! I'm Amada, your main booker here. It's nice to meet you!"

She wrapped me in a hug, and my body stiffened.

"It's nice to meet you . . .too."

"Why is she so nice to me?" I thought.

She leaned back and smiled. Then she looked down at my legs and frowned.

"You're too thin. I think you should eat more."

I laughed. I couldn't believe what she was saying.

"What? But everyone's always telling me I'm fat."

She shook her head vigorously.

"No, honey. Here, we like curves."

I wanted to kiss Amada on the mouth, but I held back. She led me into a private office and took my polaroids and measurements. The entire time, she didn't utter a negative word. For once I felt free, in a good way. She handed me pocket money, a piece of paper with the address to my apartment written on it, and called someone to pick up my suitcases.

As I walked to the apartment, I stopped a little and observed the beautiful flowers on the ground; the soft lilac and amber petals reminded me of Momma. I walked a bit more and passed by the Mercadona. The smell of bread drifted in the air, and I stopped.

"I can have a little bread. After all, Amada said that I'm too thin. She wants me to gain weight," I thought. I headed inside and began browsing the aisles filled with pastries and exotic chocolates. The sight was thrilling. I could finally eat and not feel guilty about my weight.

Suddenly, my heart rate sped up, and the room felt insanely hot. I stopped and looked around. The insanity was back, and I was no longer in control. I walked swiftly to the front of the store, grabbed a rolling cart, and filled it with every sweet and bread I could find. I paid with my pocket money and walked out with three bags cradled in my arms.

As I pretended to stroll down the street casually, I slipped the food into my mouth. By the time I reached the apartment, half of the food was gone. My bulging stomach pushed my jeans, and the seams stretched. Barely breathing, I started up the stairs and shoved more food into my mouth.

Rrrrrriiiippp!

All of a sudden, I heard a horrible sound and noticed a tiny, shiny object shoot across the stairwell; my button was now an unidentified flying object. I waddled the rest of the way up the stairs and into the apartment. Once inside, I snuck around and searched for an empty bedroom. I placed my groceries on the floor, grabbed a bottle of milk from the bag and tiptoed into the bathroom. As the steam filled the air, I swallowed the milk and stuck my fingers down my throat. The water drenched my face, and I expelled every last chunk into the drain. *"I'm so sorry, God. I'll never do it again. Please forgive me,"* I thought.

I wiped myself off and climbed into bed. The next day I met my roommates: Evelin, an eighteen-year-old model from Estonia, and Vitor, a twenty-year-old male model from Brazil. It was going to be tricky to hide my behaviors from them, but I could do it. I went into my bedroom, shut the door, and devised my plan.

For the next few weeks, I operated smoothly and kept out of their sight. Every day after catalog shoots and castings, I binged and threw up in the shower or in paper bags that I kept in my bedroom. I was the smart one; Evelin and Vitor had no idea, *especially* when I hid the vomit in the paper bags. My knuckles and lips began to bleed and scar again, but I covered them with concealer. Whenever a makeup artist raised an eyebrow at the cuts, I said that I had an autoimmune disease; that always shut them up and even earned me a few sympathy points.

On November 2nd, Harvey sent an email saying that he was in town. Exploring the city with Harvey was tempting; I missed his fun spirit, and work was boring. Jobs were coming easy, but they were not going to turn me into a household name. I accepted his invitation to go to dinner on Saturday night at eight. The reservation was at Gaig, a high-end restaurant on Corcega Street.

I sat down and ordered tapas and some water. Harvey chose a glass of wine, and I decided, *"What the hell, I'll have a sip."* By midnight, I was finishing off the second bottle. Every day after that, we stuck to each other's side and snorted cocaine in his luxury suite. I stopped showing up to castings and on the sixteenth, I told Amada that I was jetting off to Ibiza with Harvey. After all, he was spoiling me, and I didn't have to think about reality anymore.

On the island, Harvey rented a four-thousand-square-foot villa, complete with two guest houses. I sat my things down when we arrived and took a look around. My eyes didn't linger on any of the expensive art or furniture, however, they became locked on the fully stocked refrigerator. I ransacked the food, hid in the guest bathroom and binged for hours.

That remained my strategy for two weeks: ransack and hide, ransack and hide. Then I stopped hiding in the bathroom; I hid in the bedroom, took ecstasy and snorted coke instead. One day, I remembered: work. I stopped snorting coke long enough to email Amada. My nose dripped on the keyboard as I typed.

"Gone for vacation. Not sure when I'll return."

In December, millionaires and dignitaries flew in from all corners of the world, and we spent the month cavorting from one luxurious mansion in Ibiza to the next. For breakfast, I snorted plates of cocaine, and at lunch, I swallowed unmarked blue, yellow, and pink pills. Dinner consisted of dining on the finest seafood and purging it all in the bathroom afterward. Dessert topped everything, though; I made it a point to snort more coke and pop more pills than anyone. The next morning: repeat.

On the outside, I was positive that I was keeping everything under control, but in my mind, I wasn't present with anyone. I was merely existing in an alternate universe where I was either flying full-speed ahead or floating listlessly between walls of nothingness. Life was a nonstop carousel of swirling lights, music, and wild states of consciousness. I was half living the way I had always dreamed, and at a million miles per second.

January came, and I continued my druggy excursion with Harvey. We traveled to Spain, rented a house in St. Tropez, and cut loose in Monaco in a style that rivaled a James Bond film. I kept my nose packed with the white stuff the entire time and sucked on pills. The month came to a close, and we boarded a palatial mega yacht with his friends from London and began the journey around the Amalfi Coast. I tried to maintain first-class behavior, but a few hours into the voyage, I snuck chocolates from the Tiffany bowl in the hallway. An hour later, I ordered a decadent cheese plate and truffle fries from the chef and locked myself in the bedroom. Afterward, I vomited in the bathroom that Harvey and I shared.

Binging evolved into full-blown mania. The next day at seven in the morning, while Harvey ate breakfast with his friends, I called the chef and ordered two plates piled with my favorite foods. In a few hours, I called again and asked for some more. I knew that Harvey wouldn't find out—he was off swimming and tanning. I purged in our bathroom again and forgot to clean it all up.

For the next week, life on board was a dream, and the fantasy was constantly unfolding with surprises. When we pulled into ports during the day, Harvey's celebrity friends gathered in droves to attend the elegant lunches. They danced until the sun came up, and I was beside them, draped in beautiful clothes, swaying to the sweet music. I was one of *them*, one of the privileged and recognized. Who I was, I still didn't know, but it didn't matter because I felt happy.

But even acceptance couldn't save me from slamming back another drink or snorting another line of coke. The more accepted I felt, the more I wanted to destroy myself. From far away, the scenery was breathtaking: the elegant crowd mingled and twirled underneath the stars, and laughed without a care in the world. A closer look, however, revealed a monster lurking in the shadows, binging and purging in a Valentino dress.

The second week in February, on Sunday, the monster came out of hiding. It was the afternoon of the final party of the trip, and as the sun faded behind the Mediterranean, I gazed upon the water and sensed that my mind was leaving me for good. When dinner ended, and the party began, one dancer passed me to the next, and the lights above fluttered like whimsical fairies; I felt like life could always be this perfect. As the evening progressed, I picked up shot after shot of spicy tequila, threw my head back, and laughed without a care in the world.

I awoke, some time later, in a daze. Shadowy faces hovered above me and firmly pressed my body to the ground. I screamed in agony, but that only caused the shadows to push harder.

"Hold her down, she's getting away!"

"She's crazy, I tell you, absolutely mad!"

"I can't stand this bitch. She threw up all over the walls and the toilet. I want her off my ship immediately! What a fucking embarrassment!"

Darkness.

Pale light kissed my swollen cheek. I opened my crusty eyes, and looked to my right. Harvey sat beside me, crying.

"Harvey, what's wrong? Where am I?"

"You don't remember anything?"

"No, I—"

Suddenly, the memories came back.

"There were so many dark faces on top of me . . .people screaming . . ."

"Nikki, you were belligerent last night. You threw up everywhere, all over the walls, the bathroom. You were screaming at me and accusing me of being abusive."

I sat up.

"What? I don't remember that?"

I couldn't believe it. I couldn't believe that I had ruined the premiere celebration of the summer, and now, everyone knew about my secrets. To make matters worse, I couldn't remember a single moment of my insanity. This was my wake-up call. The next day I asked Harvey, the crew, and his friends for forgiveness and opened up about my problems with food. Deep down, I knew that I couldn't touch alcohol or drugs if I wanted to enjoy the moments that life was offering me.

I told Harvey that we couldn't continue our relationship. I couldn't trust myself around all of the temptations that his lifestyle provided. I emailed New Directions Miami from the ship, and they arranged for me to work in Paris. I left two days later, vowing to remain sober, yet knowing that it was going to take one day at a time.

CHAPTER **8**

My Battle with Anorexia
and the Modeling Industry's Love Affair with It

In February, Paris was a city full of glamour and prosperity, ripe and ready for the taking. I instantly forgot all about recovery and focused on work; work was another obsession, another distraction from reality. I assumed that modeling could quench my parched soul, and for a couple of weeks I spent every waking hour in my apartment exercising, trying to prepare my body for victory.

Although the French oozed with a certain *la grâce,* I, did not. One week after another, doors slammed in my face; after a few dozen, I caught on. I was unwanted, with my *American-sized* hips, as they said. My agents offered one suggestion: lose more weight, *comme hier.*

In March, I became desperate. I searched every pharmacy in Les Halles, purchased the highest-grade diet pills available, and restricted my food intake to five hundred calories a day. At first, my plan seemed foolproof, brilliant; the weight melted off, and I felt as high as the summer days in Ibiza. Then, my plan was interrupted when the agency moved me into an apartment on the Champs-Élysées with two other girls from Eastern Europe.

"This should be no problem," I thought. *"I've done this before."* On Friday evening, however, as I unpacked my bags and settled into my room, shame and rage seeped into my blood. The voices talked

down to me until all I wanted to do was hide in the closet and suf-focate. *"You can't let them see you, fat pig. You're a fuck. A filthy, disgusting fuck."*

I didn't get the chance to wrap the pantyhose around my neck, although I had it knotted and ready to go. A few minutes later, *I heard footsteps.* Fucking footsteps and laughter, the kind of loud, untrou-bled laughter that was familiar to the rest of the world; it slit my skin and left me bleeding to death like Momma's butcher knife. I peeked through the crack of the door and caught a glimpse into the other room. The sight caused my heart to shatter into a thousand pieces, and I wanted to plunge the broken shards into my chest.

Behind the thin, ordinary wall was a world that I envied. Two young, willowy models frolicked about their bedroom and discussed the day's adventures. I froze in my spot for hours, while they shared stories of life in Russia and ate muffins topped with hazelnut spread. They practiced pirouettes and stretched their graceful gams as Tchai-kovsky played in the background. At some point, the voices spoke and broke my spell. *"Why can't you be normal like them? Don't let them see you. Go to bed."*

The next day, I mumbled my name to one of the girls as we rushed past each other in the stairwell. Her name was Darya; she didn't know that I existed and shot me a frightened look.

That evening, I introduced myself to the other model, Nonna, but remained in the shadows. As they carried about the apartment day af-ter day and worried about their hectic schedules, I stayed in my room. I absorbed the silence and stared out my dreary bedroom window that faced the side street. I waited *and waited.*

At midnight I couldn't sleep. The shadows woke me up. I turned on my tablet and began scrolling through my Facebook news feed. Suddenly, a notification popped up: a friend request from some guy named Olivier. I accepted, and we started chatting right away. He told me that he lived in Nice, a nearby city, and I joked that if I were ever there, I would come and visit. We talked until the morning, and I signed off and fell asleep with a little smile on my face. Olivier managed to bring happiness into my heart for a moment, but when I woke up, I felt deeply depressed and paranoid. I didn't trust Olivier anymore.

I felt like the fashion industry in Paris had rejected me immediately, and my only chances of connecting with life in the city could happen during my walks to the supermarket. I ventured out a couple of times a day to breathe in the cool air, feel the paper bags crinkle in my arms, and returned to the apartment.

Amidst the paranoia and isolation, though, I secretly longed to connect with someone. Every night I thought about reaching out to Darya and Nonna, but I stayed in my room and binged and purged in the shower while they slept. I scrubbed the walls and floor with bleach, and soon I noticed the chunks in the drain—some of my hair was falling out.

By the end of March, my castings became obsolete, and curiosity got the best of me during my idle time. While my roommates worked in the city, I rummaged through their groceries and binged. After a few splurges, I became sloppy and forgot to replace their food, and on the last Sunday of March, everything went to hell. Darya ran through the bedroom door screaming. Her face red and eyes blazing, she pointed her finger and called me an *American pig*. She was right, though, I was a pig—one glance in the mirror confirmed it. I apologized through tears, but the wall that divided us became thicker. With a heavy heart, I asked New Directions Miami to send me back to Barcelona. Paris was a place not meant for me.

❧❧❧❧

The next day, Monday, I flew to Barcelona, the one city where I knew I had the best potential for success. It was going to be a relief to see Amada, and I couldn't wait to start working again. Life was less complicated in Barcelona, if I steered clear of my demons.

My optimism sank, however, as I entered the front door of Soto Management. I didn't recognize a single person. Spanish pop music blasted overhead, and it felt more like a fiesta than an office. I scanned the room for Amada, but she was nowhere in sight. Everyone seemed to be absorbed in their duties, so I took a seat and waited.

After a few minutes, a young woman named Ana came over and explained that Amada had transferred to another agency after I had hightailed it to Ibiza. Ana introduced me to the other agents, and the hair on my arms stiffened. My senses in Paris had been correct after all—this *was* a time for new beginnings. In the modeling business, hands changed fast and all anyone could do, all they were *allowed* to do, was smile.

Ana wasted no time getting down to business. She sorted through piles of editorials and shoots, took fresh polaroids, and led me into a private room to gather my measurements. As she moved past my chest and down my waist and hips, her lips stiffened like a tightrope.

"Do you think you can . . . lose a *little* bit of weight?"

She squinted and held her fingers a few inches apart. I was trapped; what was I supposed to say? *"No, I'm sorry, Ana. I can't do that. I love to binge on cookies and bread."*

Instead, I smiled.

"Oh, yes . . . I'm fine! Of course, it's no problem. I'll just go to the gym and have it off in no time."

"Perfect."

She handed me a paper with the address to the same apartment as before.

I left the agency and took the long route to the apartment. I also avoided all supermarkets. Four hours later, I arrived; knowing that I had pushed myself to the limits made me feel alive. Once inside, I peeked into the kitchen and noticed some crisp, red apples sitting in a basket on the counter. I snatched one and crawled into bed. My heart raced to pump fresh blood as I realized the magnitude of my feat. If I kept this routine going, in no time my body would exceed Ana's expectations, and I would be nothing but prized bones.

By April, my plan was going better than I had imagined. Ana sent me on one exclusive casting after another, until I wasn't shooting silly catalogs anymore, only editorials with some of the best photographers in Spain. A few weeks passed by, and on the second week of May, my schedule reflected that of a successful model; perhaps it was the twenty pounds I had lost.

As my portfolio expanded and the compliments poured in, though, fear raped every shred of my sanity. Fear fucked my mind and cut me little by little; it told me that if I dared consume anything other than red apples, I would blow up to an unfathomable size and the world would come to a cataclysmal end.

The fear controlled every aspect of my waking reality. I carried bags of red apples to work and turned down all offers to attend dinners with my agents and other models. I was a hermit, but I loved it. I couldn't wait until work ended so that I could take the long route home and relish in the feeling of my bones hitting the pavement. With my daily walks and bags of apples, I was unstoppable, a sheer force of fear-driven nature.

᠈᠈᠈᠈

When September arrived, I no longer recognized myself. I hadn't an ounce of cheer in my veins, and my body was colder than what I knew to be possible. My toes and fingers turned a consistent dark purple, and even wrapped in layers of the finest wool, my bones quivered.

Nevertheless, it was time to bare every inch of my body in front of casting directors and photographers to prepare for swimsuit season. With centimeters of cloth covering my privates and stilettos strapped to my feet, I resembled a stripper. Although I looked like I wanted to tease and tempt the cameras, I felt disconnected from my sexuality. Really, I was losing my mind, and the mere process of putting on a swimsuit launched me into madness.

When I changed in the bathroom before castings, I entered the doorway to the netherworld, I was sure of it. Inside, I met the malevolent forces in the mirror and fell into a trance; the powers taunted and magnified every flaw, ordering me to submit myself to painful routines.

I inspected all of the crevices of my body: twisting, bending, and pinching. My hands assessed the flatness of my stomach, and I inhaled to count the number of bones that poked through my skin. I placed my feet together and compared the distance between my thighs, over and over again.

During the castings, my fear melted into a beautiful facade. If a client approved of my appearance, my ego was overinflated. The deranged girl from the bathroom didn't exist, and I morphed into a self-assured bitch who didn't let anyone stand in her way.

After the castings, the evil forces left the bathroom. I looked, long and hard. Instead, I saw myself for what I was: a skeleton. Bones piled on top of one another, leading up to a gaunt face; the sight was thrilling, erotic. My face was ugly, but at least it was one that others appreciated.

An emaciated appearance was a ticket into the most exclusive fashion gatherings in Barcelona, and Ana invited me to *all* the parties and boutique openings. When I made my entrance, cameras and endless kisses on the cheek bombarded me from all angles. I wasn't lonely anymore; everyone wanted to be by my side. The people bathed me in a warm stream of compliments.

"You've lost *so much* weight, darling! I don't even recognize you!"

"Bonita. You look *muy, muy* bonita. Tu es una princessa de Espana."

"You are the most beautiful woman I have ever seen in my life. I am honored to stand next to you."

They had their model, a living replica of the ideal woman. Their admiration shot doses of pride into my veins, but at other times, it sent me spiraling into depression and suicidal thoughts. Not a single person cared about me or my feelings; they wanted my fading perfection. Their superficial accolades painted over my miserable soul until I could no longer distinguish my true self from the likeness they had created. In the modeling business, only the beautiful image could show.

ↄↄↄ

The dream jobs came fast, and I had to be prepared for them. If my body wasn't in top shape, someone else was always underneath me, climbing my back to snatch everything I had worked so hard for. No matter how special the agents considered me to be, there was a handful of girls available; girls willing to kiss every butt in town and lick the rim, even while I watched. It was simple; as long as you spoke the language of sex, names, and beauty you could get ahead. But my chances were limited. After the rape incident, I knew I could only go so far. Now, I could only rely on my weight to get ahead.

Fortunately, Ana kept me under her wing, and as October gave birth to an array of innovative campaigns and editorials, I was given priority to many of them. My career was shaping up to be more promising by the day; shoots with some of the most sought-after photographers in Spain and glamorous parties filled my calendar. When I thought life couldn't be any more thrilling, Ana sent word of a week-long shoot in Punta Cana in a couple of weeks. The only catch? Before the booking could be confirmed, I had to drop . . . a *few* extra pounds. After all, it was a swimsuit editorial.

Exhausted by the fact that I needed to lose even more weight, I decided to take a break. I had to rest my mind and nourish my spirit, two parts abused for far too long. I went back to the apartment, lounged in bed for days and watched television. Every day, I searched for an inspirational program, but I found only crummy telenovelas and soccer games. All of a sudden, I remembered a name that Henry had brought up one day during a twelve-step meeting: Joel Osteen. I pulled up his videos on my laptop and felt immediate relief come over my body.

He spoke in a calm yet joyful demeanor and talked about the unconditional love of God; I absorbed every word like medicine. I reflected on what *unconditional* meant and had a revelation. Here I was, working in an industry where others based my value on my looks and what I could do *for* them; however, no one in the modeling industry loved or cared for me, so why was I killing myself to make them happy? I was more unbalanced than a seesaw with an elephant sitting on one end.

For once, I looked out the window in my bedroom and noticed the turquoise sky. Despite everything I had managed to screw up, the world still felt beautiful and magical at times. I could sense something good ahead, but I didn't know what it was. One thing was clear: God loved me because I was still alive after all the terrible things that I had been through.

"I am worthy, and I have a purpose. One day this will all be over," I thought. I looked out the window again and observed the gleaming Mediterranean. The sun's rays appeared pure against the window, and the avenues of time seemed distant. Footage from my memory melted, and as the warmth of God channeled into my spirit, I experienced freedom. An inexplicable sense of peace replaced the shell of my lonely, anxious heart. My soul rested with a higher Spirit, and I bathed in the vibrant sweetness.

$$\smile \smile \smile$$

The shrill cry from my cell phone knocked me out of a deep sleep. I fumbled toward the clock and checked the time: half past seven in the morning. I pulled the covers over my head, and without hesitation, the phone rang for the second time. I snatched it from the nightstand.

"Hello?"

"Hey . . . It's your mom. Sorry if I woke you."

"Is everything okay? Why are you calling so early on a Saturday? Do you realize what time it is here?"

"I'm sorry, honey, it's just . . . well, I'm afraid I have some bad news."

Bad news. It was always bad news with her. I rolled my eyes.

"I hate to tell you this, but a few nights ago, Nana had a stroke that damaged one side of her body. She's down in intensive care at Roper . . . blind and deaf. The doctors don't know how long she has to live."

I froze. The phone solidified into a chunk of ice in my hand. Momma continued, emotionless, and the line crackled and fizzled. I tried to grasp—*stroke, blind, deaf*—but I couldn't. Those damned words didn't fit into my world, the one where Nana and I lived together, for all of time.

"M-Mom, I have to go. I'll call you later."

Suddenly, I realized that I never called or wrote Nana. It was too late now—she was dying. Overnight, my precious Nana had transformed into a lifeless mute! *A mute!*

The phone dropped from my hands, and I fell onto the floor. Nana had always treated me like a princess; I, however, had treated her like shit. I was a selfish screw-up! An addict!

"My life is a mess . . .Please forgive me, Nana!"

I whispered the words as I dragged my body across the bedroom floor.

Was this the price of my superficial life? I had made a pact with the devil, and losing Nana was the sacrifice for this artificial wonderland I had created.

۵۵۵۵

The next few days rolled by in a fog as I starved to prepare for my trip to Punta Cana. Every day Momma sent an update on Nana's condition, which wasn't improving. Unable to carry the sadness, depression sank in. I was hungry for love, for the love of Nana.

I contemplated canceling the trip and hopping on another flight to Charleston. How could I possibly work in such a desperate state of mind? On the other hand, if I flew to Punta Cana, what would the family think? *She's a selfish bitch, as always; even on Nana's deathbed, she only thinks about herself.*

On Sunday, I carried on to the airport anyway, dripping with sweat and nausea. As I ventured toward the check-in, I felt a tap on my shoulder. I turned around, startled. A giant, ginger-haired girl with freckles was searching my face.

"Excuse me. Are you Nikki? I'm sorry if I have the wrong person, it's just . . . You look like a model."

I managed half of a smile and a handshake.

"Yes, I'm Nikki. Are you the other model that's coming on the shoot to Punta Cana?"

"Phew, yes! Hi, I'm Cindy. I'm relieved I found you right away! I didn't want to be alone."

Shit. There was no chance in hell I could bail on the trip; my cover was busted. I studied this new specimen before me; grinning from ear to ear, Cindy was sure to stay glued to my side the entire time.

After we checked in and passed through security, two hours remained until departure—two long hours. I jammed headphones into my ears; the last thing I wanted to do was talk. Cindy had other plans. She grabbed my arm and pulled me into a cafe. Ignoring her was useless; she had me cornered without a way to escape. I removed my earphones and looked straight into her eager eyes.

"Yes?"

"Are you hungry? We should eat before we board."

"Here's an idea. Why don't you slice me open and offer my bleeding organs to the monkey gods instead? That would go a whole lot smoother," I thought.

"I ate before . . . before I arrived. But I'll sit with you and have a coffee or something."

She nodded and turned in line to order. I decided to make my move; it was now or never. I slipped Topiramate from my purse and swallowed a couple. Just before I dropped the bottle back inside, Cindy zipped around.

"What's that?"

"What? Oh, you mean my medicine? It's for . . . for migraines. I get them pretty bad when I'm traveling."

A few weeks earlier, I had discovered the Holy Grail of Topiramate. One morning, I dug around and found out that in Barcelona, the pharmacies handed out most medications left and right, no prescription required. That was all I needed to know. On a whim that afternoon, I walked a couple of blocks to the nearest pharmacy, and within five minutes I strutted out, bag in hand, armed with a bottle of my saving grace. However, it was going to take more than Topiramate to save me. On the way back to the apartment I managed to grab a few loaves of bread and milk and purged it all in the toilet, Topiramate included.

Cindy ate a blueberry muffin while I stared out the massive windows that overlooked the runways. A few planes dawdled about, waiting for their turn to fly. I pondered if I could hide in one and plunge to my death as it approached 40,000 feet; dying would be quick and painless, although slow and magical, like a beautiful, somber dream.

"Hey, I hate to be a pain. I know we just met and everything."

Cindy played with the wrapper of her muffin.

"No, it's okay. What's up?"

"Do you think I can have one of those tablets? I also get terrible migraines, at least one a day sometimes. I don't know . . . I think work brings it on."

My plan to be deceitful bit me in the ass. I *had* to lie again.

"Oh . . . I *wish* I could help you, but uh, my doctor only prescribed a certain amount, and I don't have that many left."

She bobbed her head and smiled, but there was something in her eyes that told a different story, and I sensed that she knew my secrets. For the rest of the wait, I flipped through magazines and she picked her nails. As we soared through the skies neither one of us uttered a word.

❧❧❧❧

"God only knows what they think. They'll probably be so disappointed in me that they'll call the agency and send me back to Barcelona. I fucking hate myself," I thought.

As I exited the bathroom and roamed toward the food court, I observed Gracia and Idoya, the photographers, sitting with Cindy. The voices came back. *"Don't go over there. Run away before it's too late!"* All three women stood up and flailed their hands in excitement. I had nowhere to hide.

Madrid was our meeting spot, the final stop before our flight to Punta Cana, and something told me that I was not going to enjoy it.

"Would you like to order some food before we board?"

Idoya reviewed an extensive list of hamburgers and desserts and pushed a menu in my direction. The voices put up a fight. *"This is the first thing she wants to talk about? What's wrong with people?*

Don't touch that shit, fill up on coffee!" I peeked over at Cindy, who was gabbing to Gracia about the variety of milkshake flavors. Fierce rumbles emanated from the pit of my stomach, but I ignored them.

"No, I'm not hungry. I just want a coffee. I'm gonna go grab one, would anyone like something?"

They looked up from their menus and stared. Gracia cocked her head.

"You should eat, Nikki."

"I should eat. What the hell does she know? All she wants is for me to get fat. At least she doesn't have to worry about that. I gotta get out of here," I thought. I smiled, shrugged and walked away until I could no longer see them. I inhaled and exhaled the suffocating air. I needed to go somewhere where I could be myself, where they couldn't find me.

I walked past the food court into the crowds of people and kiosks. Around and around I went, looping between magazine racks and cheap jewelry counters. I noticed a Zara store, entered, and began looking through a rack of jeans. As I checked the labels for the sizes, I suddenly stopped. There was a presence behind me, an evil feeling that I couldn't ignore.

I turned around and saw hundreds of blood-speckled eyes, watching and whispering. *"Help this girl. She's going insane. Help this girl. She's going insane. She's a bitch, you hear, a bitch of the worst kind. I say, she's a whore! A filthy whore. Wash out her vagina, at once!"* The voices sounded loud and soft, all at the same time. I could hear them separately, yet they overlapped. Everyone knew; everyone was watching and judging. I wasn't safe anywhere. I rushed back to the table and noticed that the crew seemed to be engaged in a passionate debate. When I arrived, however, the conversation stopped.

"Are you okay?"

Cindy peered up between bites of her salad.

The voices taunted me. *"Cindy knows. She knows! She thinks you're a freak."*

"Yeah. Yeah, I'm all right."

My heart pounded, and I knew they could hear it. I chewed on the inside of my mouth and sucked on the blood, distracting myself from the incident. Not everyone wanted to forget, however; as we boarded the flight, Gracia reached over and tapped my arm.

"What happened to your coffee?"

﹆﹆﹆

The following evening, I checked into the Hotel de Coralillo and wandered the lush grounds. Cindy and the crew retired to their rooms until the morning. Just before she left, Gracia handed me a wristband that granted free access to food and drinks, including alcohol. Afterward, the voices pulled my attention toward the sparkling bar underneath the palm trees. *"It's so easy to grab a drink or two. After all, it's on the house, dummy."* Without further thought, my feet carried me toward the jolly bartender who appeared antsy to pour a margarita. As my hands touched the bar, however, I froze and remembered Nana.

"No, uh, no thanks. I'm good for tonight."

"Whatever you want honey. I'm not going anywhere."

Nana. I took off across the lawn in a blurred search for my room, dragging my suitcase behind, but every entrance and hallway looked the same; my temperature began to rise, and a razor-sharp pain ripped through my stomach. I stopped and fumbled in my purse for the room keys. Suddenly, I felt an evil presence looming behind me. Shaking, I turned and spotted the blood-speckled eyes that had plagued me in the airport. All of a sudden, the lawn melted into a vision of terror.

I raced and stumbled through the halls, frightened and confused, while the shadows chased me every which way. Finally, I located my room: *323.* I shoved the door open and slammed it shut, then I scanned the spacious suite, making sure the evil spirits had disappeared. I collapsed on the floor in a puddle of sweat and closed my eyes. Out of nowhere, a feeling of serenity came over me. I inhaled deeply and opened my eyes, thankful that the fear had passed. As I took a look around the second time, however, I noticed a large basket with a variety of tropical fruits sitting on the desk, and my heart dropped into my stomach.

I tore into the basket with a blazing passion and devoured the fruit without stopping, choking and wheezing in the brutal process. Then I crawled over to the mini-refrigerator and chugged one bottle of water after another. I slid my aching body over to the toilet, thrust my fingers down my throat and punched my stomach. After several flushes yellow acid swirled in the toilet—nothing else remained. I had to be sure, for Christ's sake, I just had to be sure; I couldn't risk leaving any food in my body. I pushed for the final time, and a strong sour taste circled in my mouth. Relief poured over me; it was over. Shaking and dizzy, I pulled a towel down from the rack and wiped away vomit from the walls, floor, and seat; the filth was everywhere. I crawled back into the bedroom and retrieved my perfume from my suitcase. With the sweet, flowery aroma covering the filth, my secret was safe. I wrapped the dirty towel in-between some other clean towels and bundled them underneath the sink.

As I scrubbed my face spotless in the hot shower, I cried out to God.

"Please, God, take this all away. I'm such a fuckup."

Tears mixed with the water and floated down the drain, right along with the life from my soul. I stepped out into a thick fog and wiped away the film on the mirror; an imposter glared back. Every impulse urged me to crack the glass and sever the face of the fucker. Instead, I closed my eyes, took a deep breath and prayed again, this time for the truth. I slowly opened my eyes and saw myself, soaking wet and hollow. I had to keep *my* face on and hope that the imposter didn't come out to play.

꩜꩜꩜

The next day, Tuesday, whizzed by like a whirlwind, and as usual, I ate only red apples for fear of not fitting into the dresses and swimsuits. The fittings lasted for hours, and to my surprise, almost everything had to be double- and triple-pinned.

"You're smaller than Cindy. We picked you two because we thought you were the same size . . . I guess the agency didn't correctly measure you."

Idoya carefully eyed me as she slipped various outfits over my head.

My mouth was clamped shut. I wanted to say *something*, but inside I was glowing with pride. *"I'm smaller than Cindy,"* I thought. *"Fuck, this is amazing. I don't want to stop. I want to look better and better."*

Evening rolled around, and Gracia and Idoya decided upon a mandatory, sit-down dinner. Cindy suggested an Italian restaurant on the hotel property, the finest for miles. We gathered together at nine, and everyone relaxed as the wine was placed on the table; everyone but me.

"None for me, thanks."

My heart skipped, and my palms began to perspire.

"I love wine!"

Cindy reached for a glass and signaled at the others to drink. All of a sudden, my mind began to drift to a sinister place: images of Nana, ten feet under the ground, gnawed away at my mental meat. My appetite disappeared, along with any reasons for living, but I tried to appear happy and calm. *"Smile, stupid,"* I thought. I curled my lips and engaged in light conversation as if nothing had occurred.

"Madam, are you ready to order?"

I looked up. I had failed to notice the waiter at my side. I stole a peek at the others; they watched me with wide, curious eyes.

"Oh! Um, sorry. I didn't know you were here. Gosh, look at all of these choices, they all look so good! I just need to ask you something, though. You see, my doctor has me on a special diet. Do you have *red apples*? It's all I can have, unfortunately . . ."

I shifted in my seat. The waiter stared at me blankly and paused for a moment, unsure of how to respond. I dared not look at the others again.

"Uh, no madam, this is an *Italian* restaurant. While we do everything we can to accommodate requests, if you want to have something . . . of this nature, you have to dine in your room."

There I was, thrashing about in the midst of the ocean, clamoring for the right words that could rescue me from the sinking ship.

"Okay, thank you. Again, it's the *doctor's* request!"

I lowered my face and locked my eyes with his to enunciate the urgency of the situation. He adjusted his tie and looked around the room.

"I—I'm sorry, madam. There is no way we can grant your wish."

As he walked into the kitchen, I felt the eyes from across the table. It was now or never; I had to flee.

"Well, I . . . I've never *heard* of such a thing! Have you? A restaurant not serving apples? It's just fruit! I have to eat! I can't eat . . . eat *this stuff*. I—I'm sorry. I have to return to my room, if you'll excuse me."

Cindy looked away while Idoya and Gracia sympathetically nodded. They dismissed me all too easily. I knew that they were going to talk about my odd behavior the moment I turned my back. For the rest of the trip, I had an excuse, though; pure solid gold.

I hurried back to my room, ordered a few apples, and picked at one while I watched *I Love Lucy*. As Lucy and Teresa smashed grapes in the vat with their feet, I nodded off.

Somewhere in-between faded dreams of Nana and visions of the future, I awoke suddenly to the blurry alarm clock that read one in the morning. I peeled my sticky body from the sheets and changed into my pajamas. I had to check up on Nana's condition.

I crept outside to the theater area, turned on my tablet, and tried to sit still while the shaky Wi-Fi service loaded. In the distance, a few flickering lamps acknowledged my presence; the stifling air soaked my skin as flies circled my neck and legs. Waiting for the Internet to load was grueling. The knot in my stomach was growing by the second; it was a physical sensation with a mind of its own, able to torture and mock me simultaneously.

Finally, I had service. I frantically logged into my email and combed through miles of unwanted messages. All of a sudden, my eyes rested upon a name that caused me to stop cold: *Christian*. The subject simply read: *"No Subject."* I clicked on it and put my hand over my eyes while the message loaded. Moments later, I peeked between my fingers, and my heart stopped.

Nikki,

Nana's gone. I'm sorry. Please come home. We love you.

Love,
Christian

I dropped the tablet and opened my mouth to scream, but only silence passed through my lips. I clenched my fists and cursed the starry sky. Up above there was no sign of death or anger, sorrow or pain; clear and radiant, the moon shone, and the stars twinkled as brightly as ever.

"God, please take my pathetic, meaningless life! Take it, take it, and just let me be with my nana!" I thought.

Shame shot through my heart like a round of bullets. I couldn't see her anymore; maybe she was looking down, wondering why I didn't say goodbye.

Dizzy, I raced to my room, slammed the door shut, and slid to the floor. I clawed the carpet and tried to produce sound, but nothing. There was only silence, eerie silence. I curled into a ball and stared into space. Suddenly, the tears began to fall, and my voice returned, like a newborn baby crying for its mother.

I cried for hours. I cried until the tears lost their salt; until the breath lost its air. I watched the nothingness, the one thing that brought temporary comfort. The numbness and pain alternated like waves, until I crawled into the shower, begging the hot water to wash it all away. But it couldn't, it didn't; the water couldn't quench my dry, aching soul.

I stepped out of the shower and pulled a shirt over my soaking body, avoiding the mirror. Without the one I loved, who was I? I was dead; my reflection could only reveal a ghost. I fell into bed, weeping with the knowledge that I could never touch Nana again.

After a little while, the rhythms from my sobs lulled me into slumber. I remained content in my dream world until a movement on the left side of the bed stirred me awake. Petrified, I carefully turned to confront the mysterious presence. Crouched beside me was a brown shadow, reaching for my hand. I adjusted my eyes, but it was still there, lingering by my side. I paused. The shadow grabbed my arm and cradled it like a treasure. Something familiar radiated from the creature, an essence that I recognized. Still frightened, I rolled over and shut my eyes tightly, wishing for it to disappear. After a few minutes I looked back, and to my slight relief, it had vanished. Deep down, I felt that I shouldn't have been frightened for it was Nana; she had come to say goodbye for now.

Sunlight broke through the navy blue curtains. I rolled around the sheets for a few blissful, lazy moments, and the harsh memories came flooding back. It was morning in Punta Cana, and Nana was dead. I rolled around some more, and it hit me: it was my day off from shooting.

I skipped breakfast and scoped out an unclaimed beach where the crystal sand stretched for miles. I sat down and gazed onto the turquoise reflections, meditating on Nana and all that we had shared. The warmth from the sun transported my thoughts to a happier place when I was a child in Nana's arms; I had always felt safe there. I allowed the memories to steep in my mind for a while.

My heart became heavy again, and I felt like I needed closure. I wandered over to a path lined with palm trees and broken coconuts and searched for a spot to hold a private funeral. There, beneath some palm leaves, was an untainted patch of sand. I removed the leaves and traced *Nana loves Nikki* in the shape of a giant heart. Here, in this sacred place, our love would stay until the ocean carried it away. I prayed to God and told Nana how much I missed her, then I sang "Amazing Grace" and said my final goodbyes. I knew that she was in heaven, our heaven, down in my heart and soul.

As I walked away, I turned around and observed the makeshift burial ground one last time. I knew that this spot, this moment was our permanent sanctuary.

᠉᠉᠉᠊

Over the next few days, the trip developed exceptionally. I produced some of my best photographs as I hid my darkest pain. Eventually, though, I broke down and told the crew about Nana, and in some way that helped me pull myself together.

In spite of the ironic success that Punta Cana left me with, life was flipped upside down when I returned to Barcelona. Facing the day, for one, became a nightmare because the light inside me had faded. However, I continued to press on. According to Ana, I was on my way to becoming a top model, and I couldn't let that slip through my fingers. The promises of the world rested on my shoulders; I was now an adored member of the egocentric universe, one regarded as the highest echelon of achievement. And yet, the material fantasy droned on like an endless musical loop and blended into the same, dull pitch. My artificial world was spinning faster, and I wasn't slowing down. In November, Ana booked me on more shoots than I could keep up with, but I thrived on the high of it all. I continued to starve and morphed into a creature of the rare, bizarre species; fashion photographers flocked in from every corner, hoping to capture my oddity. Now, I wasn't a *sensual* or *sexy beauty* anymore, but an *interesting-looking* model. In all my life, I had never been interesting, just someone who people wanted to screw, especially as a child.

Wearing the high-end labels was all the motivation I needed to continue starving; one less meal could guarantee another page in a glossy fashion magazine, maybe even more money. If this was anorexia, I adored it.

᠉᠉᠉᠊

In the mornings before work, I stood in the bathroom mirror and dealt with the rituals and hallucinations for hours. The exhausting act began with my bones; running my hands over them one by one gave me a temporary sense of security. I wish I could have stopped there, but that was just the beginning. My flat ass and pencil thighs brought pleasure; however, there was always more to lose. I despised my cheeks, my fatty facial cheeks. The same fantasy always replayed: a butcher knife glistened as I sliced them into a thousand, unrecognizable pieces. Bloody chunks covered the floor, and I stared at them and smiled. *Then*, and only then, was I suitable.

I never uttered a word about my morning customs or horrifying imaginings to a soul. Work was my closest friend. I couldn't confide in anyone real, even if I wanted to.

Besides, every week I found myself in a different place. Ana kept me busy, and there was no time to think about anything other than what city I was headed to. The twentieth of November was no exception. I boarded yet another plane and glanced at my ticket: MARBELLA. It could have read HELL for all I cared, and for all I knew, it did.

But, as the aircraft slipped over the beautiful Mediterranean and landed into the hills surrounded by caramel sands, I temporarily forgot my sadness. It was time to work, and work meant money. A driver quickly whisked me away from the airport and started out to an address that I had scribbled on a scrap of paper.

After a minute of taking in the breathtaking sights, I fell asleep.

"Senora, estamos aqui!"

The driver's firm voice shattered me awake. The car popped and halted in front of a tiny, dilapidated building with the word HOSTEL hanging off of the front. I leaned forward and tapped him on the shoulder.

"Ah, por favor. Esto no esta bien."

He pointed to the address and fluttered his hands in the air.

"No, no senora. Esto es correcto!"

Fuck. The sadness came flooding back.

Realizing that this hostel was, in fact, my arrangement for the next couple of days, I slowly got out and watched as he sped away, murmuring obscenities under his breath. I checked into my room and noticed a handwritten note sitting on the dresser.

Dear Nikki,

Welcome to Marbella!

We are so happy to have you. Sometime this evening Mauricio, the other model, will be joining you in your room.

– S.

I threw the paper in the yellow plastic trashcan.

"Not only do I have to sleep here, I have to share it with a fucking guy."

I showered in the shared, greasy bathroom and settled into bed. Dinner wasn't an appealing option anymore. Suddenly, my heart began to pound, faster and faster, and I could hear its rhythm in my throat. *Lub-dub, lub-dub, lub-dub.* The ceiling squeezed down on my chest, and the room rattled. The walls moved in closer and closer, and just when I thought my lungs might cave in from the pressure, everything released, and the walls returned to normal. A few blissful moments of silence passed, and something floated over my eyes. I looked up; the damned cheap, mint wallpaper had peeled off and was flickering across my face like baked rain. I brushed it off but more fell, and more. I tried to move away, but the ceiling broke. I struggled to breathe for a few moments and finally, I gave up. I let the air go from my body and drifted into the black. All of a sudden, I heard a voice.

"Are you Nikki?"

I snapped back and studied the person that belonged to the voice. At just over six feet, he didn't have an ounce of fat on his muscular body. Curly, brown hair and hazel eyes set off chiseled features comparable to the Greek statues at The Met.

I sat up.

"Y-yes. Mauricio? Shit, you scared me! It's nice to meet you. You must be tired from traveling . . . I know I am!"

"Nah, I'm good. I'll just play some video games on my phone and read the comics."

He jumped on his bed and pulled out a stack of comic books from his suitcase. *"Idiot,"* I thought. I rolled over and closed my eyes.

At five the following morning, the chilly air was bitter and unforgiving. I sluggishly piled into a van with Mauricio and the crew and headed for hair and makeup. Barely a word was muttered as we rode through the mountains and journeyed by the sea. Finally, an hour later, we came to a stop on a remote beach. I got out and surveyed the surroundings: behind thick, prickly bushes on a stretch of fly-infested sand, a makeshift studio had already been constructed for the day.

"Can you change over there, in the bushes, darling?"

Felipe, the stylist, tossed a couture dress in my direction while he puffed away on a cigarette.

I stripped down behind the thorns without a second thought. What difference did it make if anyone saw my boyish body? I had nothing *to* hide. I was a waif, worthless in my own eyes, and expendable to everyone, too.

I put on the dress and checked to make sure that no one was watching. No one was, everyone was busy on their fucking phones. I started my ritual and began tracing over my hipbones with my hands then moved up to my stomach. I felt over my flat ass, rotated my legs multiple times and rubbed my body again. Finally, I twisted from side to side. *"One, two, three, four, five . . ."* In my head, I counted all the way up to thirty and started over again until the voices told me that I could quit. *"Now you may stop. You're safe."* I took a deep breath, composed myself and drifted over to a clump of rocks where Ria, the makeup artist, was eating. She smiled big and offered a bocadilla.

"No, gracias. I ate already."

"How do they expect you to eat bread? You should be drinking coffee!" The voices became louder, and my temperature began to rise. Sweat dripped down my legs; everyone would find out about my secrets now. I peered over at the misty sea. Drowning seemed so natural, so beautiful for such a time as this.

I turned to Ria.

"Por favor, yo quiero una cafe con leche."

She shook her head and motioned for me to sit down on a rock.

"Mira, I don't have any coffee right now. Here, have a seat. I need to get you ready."

I searched for the smoothest rock possible and eased my bony butt down. I closed my eyes, and with every stroke, I could feel my anxiety vanishing. Two hours later, I had a face covered in paint and felt ready to face the day.

I relaxed while Ria patted Mauricio's face with a sponge and smoked a cigarette. Felipe pranced over, opened a bottle of shimmering lotion and rubbed it between his hands. He grabbed my right arm and began applying the lotion to it. Suddenly, he gasped.

"What's wrong?"

He looked at my right arm, then he peered over and looked at my left.

"Your *arms*!"

I looked at my arms, but I didn't see anything.

"What's wrong with my arms?"

"Darling, they're *so* skinny! They're just bones!"

He held my right arm out in the air and examined it, then he looked at me. I forced a laugh.

"It's how my arms have always looked. . .I don't understand."

He stared a bit more, then he shrugged and began rubbing the lotion again.

"Well, you know darling, *all* of the supermodels have super skinny arms. . .It's no big deal!"

Felipe sucked in his cheeks, kissed the air, and began applying lotion to the rest of my body.

The next morning, as I sailed through the clouds to Barcelona, I pondered yet again the price of my success. I was losing my health and for what? I looked out the window and wondered about all of the sufferings in the world. Where was my place in all this madness? Did I even have a place? Perhaps my life had a higher purpose, and being a product in the fashion industry only made me part of the problem.

❧❧❧❧

It was May, and I was tired of getting the damned Skype calls from George about Momma at all hours of the day and night. Over the past six months, I received so many damned Skype calls that I stopped answering them.

On the thirteenth at eight in the morning, my Skype rang. I didn't answer it right away, though; I was distracted by the feeling of my swollen belly and the sight of the toilet in the bathroom. Finally, I answered.

"Hello? George? What . . . what's wrong?"

My heart raced. *"Don't tell me she's dead,"* I thought.

"Hey Nikki, how are you doing?"

George sounded poised in spite of my annoyed state. I closed my eyes and took a deep breath.

"I'm okay, I guess . . . what's going on?"

"I hate playing this cordial game shit. I want to know the truth," I thought. As I paced back and forth in my bedroom, my mind became fixated on the bathroom again. All of a sudden, George unloaded.

"Well, to tell you the truth, I *don't* have good news. Your mom has a serious problem with her drinking."

I rolled my eyes.

"George, you call me almost every day about this!"

"I know, but it's getting worse, Nikki. I took her debit cards away the other day, but she managed to find money somehow."

"Yeah, well, *that's* nothing new."

"That's not all, though . . . she got into a car accident last night."

I froze. *"Not another one of those,"* I thought.

"What?"

"Yeah, Out there on 526. She flipped the truck into a ditch and just left the scene. Nikki . . . we can't find her."

I hung up. My momma: the adult, the child, my everything. I slid to the floor and smacked my head with my fist.

"God, help me!" I thought. I desperately wanted the pain to end, and for our lives to be normal, but life had been chaotic for so long, perhaps this *was* our normal. I crawled into the bathroom and jammed my fingers down my throat. I felt my lips ripping, but I kept pushing; I wanted to see blood flow into the toilet. Time seemed to stop as I purged; the pain was the only thing that existed.

A few flushes, and a couple of sprays; the obsession was easy to hide but nearly impossible to escape. I let the cold water wash over my blistered knuckles and stared into the mirror. The only face I recognized was Momma's; she was all I wanted. Her reflection blended into mine and brought me face-to-face with some disturbing truths. Why was I incapable of taking care of myself? Why couldn't I take care of her? *"God, where are you? Don't you love us?"* I thought.

☽☽☽☾

Two days later, around nine in the evening, George called again with the latest news. He sounded distraught. Momma had returned to the apartment earlier that morning in a laughing, drunken fit. She said that worrying about her was ridiculous and that we had no right to question her whereabouts. She then got into a green van with a strange man and sped off. It was the final straw for George. He decided to go and stay with his mother, who lived an hour away.

"Fuck that woman," I thought. How could Momma laugh about such a serious situation? I hated her for not caring about us, and I hated that I was powerless to do anything about it on the other side of the world. The next day, I called Dad and expressed my frustrations. He suggested that we come together as a family and confront Momma about her problems. A family gathering didn't seem possible, but now we needed it more than ever. If Momma could see how badly her drinking problems had affected our lives, then maybe - just maybe - she would wake up and finally get help, and I could regain some of my sanity.

I booked my ticket to Charleston for the twenty-third. The next day, I went into Soto Management and told Ana that I was going home for a week. She understood, I never went home. However, she was also quick to point out all of the editorials and campaigns on my calendar for the next few weeks. I felt the stress rise in my throat, but not about the work; Momma was the only thing on my mind now.

On the twentieth of May, the camera captured my image in a tawny field somewhere in the Spanish countryside. After eight hours of shooting in furs and silk, I wiped off my makeup, put on my tennis shoes and jeans and embraced the crew. In my spirit, I sensed that I was saying goodbye to a part of my life that I could never recover, and strangely, peace washed over me. There was something brighter on the horizon, but I couldn't see what it was just yet.

"Searching into the light
for the hands that guide me
Wanting your love
completely
Yet I burn naked under the sun
without you
A thousand years pass
still I feel not your
touch
Mother."

—Nikki DuBose

CHAPTER **9**

Saying Goodbye

Three days later, I landed in Charleston. As I exited the plane and descended the stairs, I could feel my throbbing bones knocking against each other. I entered the terminal and struggled to pull my luggage past one loving family after another. After a while, I paused to rest and gazed at my skeletal arms and thighs. I sighed and realized that my bones were my family now, but that was all right; I felt closer to them than with any person in the entire world.

The thought of seeing the family together made my stomach churn and my throat tighten. I rushed into the nearest bathroom, threw my things into a stall and slammed the door. I quietly tried to purge, but nothing came out. I exited the stall and looked in the mirror: a teenage girl, heavy suitcases by her side, was watching me. She had her messy hair combed to the back like she was ashamed of its bulk. I hurried over to the sink and started washing my hands; the soapy water felt soothing on my scarred knuckles. I looked up, and the little girl was still staring at me. I smiled, but she didn't smile back.

I turned around to speak, but she was gone. I whipped my head back, but she wasn't in the mirror, either. An odd feeling came over me. I ran out of the bathroom and headed towards the baggage claim.

Dad was standing by claim number six in his usual, casual way, with a grin that stretched for miles. We sprinted for each other at competing speeds. He won and scooped me up in a bear hug, although he was careful not to squeeze *too hard*.

"I sure have missed ya . . . *man,* how you've shrunk!"

"Thanks, Dad, but I'm modeling, remember? I don't have time for this weight talk nonsense."

I quickly switched subjects.

"Have you heard from Mom?"

Dad's face became as pale as a ghost.

"Why don't we just get goin' now. We got much to do, dontcha think?"

For the next few hours, we talked little and accomplished a lot. Our primary mission was to settle in at the Residence Inn where Momma was hopefully going to stay. As Dad and I checked into the fully equipped suite, I spotted the kitchen and spacious bathroom and suddenly froze. I *needed* to think of something to keep me in that kitchen.

"I can't wait to show ya'll all the Spanish food I've learned to cook! Paella is my favorite."

I happily rubbed my stomach as Dad propped himself up against the kitchen counter.

"Child, if you have half of your momma's cookin' ability, I know it's gonna be *good.* Now whatta ya say about us payin' everybody else a visit? They're all dyin' to see ya."

꒰꒱꒰꒱

We pulled up to Aunt Sarah's house around nine in the evening. The headlights on the car hinted at the crepe myrtle bushes, which sent my nostalgia spinning. *"It feels so good to be back here,"* I thought.

I peered at Dad. He looked at me and smiled big. I sensed he was reading my mind.

"You know, you haven't seen her since you were a little girl if I remember correctly."

My face turned hot.

He parked on the side of the driveway, and I got out. I opened the screen door and squinted. Underneath the porch light, everything was as I remembered: a picture preserved in time, every inch of her wood remained untainted, reflecting the tenacity of the Southern spirit. I knocked on the front door.

"Just a minute!"

I heard some loud shuffling. A few moments later, Aunt Sarah opened: just as the wood that made up her porch, her face had stood the test of time. Beautiful and graceful, every wrinkle was like a river full of stories that I wanted to get lost in. She looked at me with a puzzled expression.

"Well . . . N-Nikki, is that *you?* Well Lord help, come on in. I don't mean to be rude, it's just. . . I didn't even recognize you! Turn around, honey, where's the other half of you?"

"Oh my God, please kill me now," I thought. I laughed, and Aunt Sarah forced a smile.

"Come on in. Wayne, come on in now, everyone's been waiting to see ya'll. Take off your shoes and make yourselves comfortable, this is your home, too."

As Aunt Sarah shuffled me inside, I could almost hear the silent dialogue that was taking place behind my back. *"Why is everyone making a big deal about my looks? For once can't they just be happy that I've finally achieved something great with my life?"* I thought. I looked around and saw Christian and George sitting on Aunt Sarah's velvet green couch; that, too, had remained the same. I embraced them and noticed their eyes asking the same question: *"Who are you?"*

As I eased down next to Christian, I realized that someone was missing.

"Where's Stephen?"

Aunt Sarah howled.

"Honey, I'm not a miracle worker. It took a lot to get all of ya'll here. Besides, do you really want that man in this house?"

I thought about it and sighed.

"I guess not, but at some point, we have to have him."

An hour passed. Everyone stared awkwardly and danced around the elephant in the room. Finally, Dad decided to take the lead and brought up the necessary topic: Momma.

"How are we gonna get Sandy into the hotel?"

I felt my blood pressure rise.

"Dad, I *told you* I could cook. The room has a nice kitchen, and I know Momma will want to eat something if I tell her about the food from Spain and everything."

Aunt Sarah snorted.

"You can cook? Oh, I'd love to see that!"

I put my hand on my hip.

"Of course, I can! I've learned from traveling. Plus, if I invite her over for dinner, she'll just think I've flown here to spend time with her. She won't know the difference."

Aunt Sarah rolled her eyes and shook her head.

"I'm not so sure about that. Your Momma is a wise woman, honey. She's going to know."

"Trust me, it'll work!"

I sat up tall, but inside, my heart was pounding. *"The irony. How am I going to get through this and not blow it? God I need help. I don't know who needs more help, Momma or me,"* I thought. Dad seemed to like the cooking idea, however, and swiftly agreed.

"I don't know Sarah. I think we should give Nikki a chance here. Christian? What do you think?"

Christian folded his arms across his chest.

"I agree with Sarah. It's a great plan, but I'm sure she knows Nikki's here already. She's one smart cookie in spite of her problems."

I dropped my head into my hands.

"God."

Momma *was* smart; so smart, that she terrified me. I raised my head and grabbed Christian by the shoulders. Face-to-face, we were still kids just trying to keep our heads afloat.

"Please just trust me, all right? I won't screw this up."

I looked into his innocent eyes and saw a determined spirit rising.

"I trust you, Nikki, I do. *We* are going to do *whatever* it takes to get her help, okay? I love you, sis."

"I love you, too."

He passed me his phone.

Suddenly, I felt fear in my throat. Christian nudged me.

"Nikki, I'm right here."

I heard him, but I couldn't move. I wondered why Momma never loved herself enough. The woman I admired as a child was now the biggest burden on the family. Christian put his hands on top of mine.

"Nikki, it's okay…"

I took a deep breath and dialed Momma's number. The line rang a few times, and Momma picked up. Her voice sounded heavy and reckless, but lost, like a child. *"Fuck, it's Henrietta,"* I thought.

"Why did you lie to me?"

"I didn't lie to you. . ."

"Why didn't you tell me you were coming home?"

"Mom, I'm so sorry. I *am* here, but I came to surprise you! I've missed you so much that I wanted to do something special for you."

"You're lying, you're lying!"

I closed my eyes and pinched my forehead.

"Mom, *I'm. not. lying.* . .I'm not lying, Mom. I'd *like* to sit down and cook a nice dinner for you."

She paused, and her voice changed back to normal.

"Oh, *no you don't.* Uh-uh. I'm not buying that crock of crap for one minute. You're planning an intervention on me, aren't you . . . *aren't you?"*

I had to think fast.

"Mom, no! Here's the truth, okay? I haven't seen you in forever, and I'm. . .scared. I'm scared, all right? George has been calling me at all hours of the day and night about you, and I haven't been able to do anything about it because I've been on the other side of the world working. Now I'm *here* to see *you* and make sure you're all right!"

She whispered.

"Okay. What's for dinner?"

The next day at five, I drove to Momma's apartment with Christian hiding in the backseat; we couldn't take any chances with her and her strange man. As we passed by her unit, I noted an unusual sight: crooked blinds. I parked the car behind some bushes and dialed her number with Christian's phone.

The call rolled over to voicemail. I dialed again—nothing. Half an hour passed, and we waited in silence by the bushes, looking for any sign of life. All of a sudden, a dark green van jerked into Momma's parking spot and slammed on its brakes. A bony man with a dirty T-shirt emerged, holding a case of beer in one hand and a black bag in the other. He ran up to the front door and slammed it so hard that the neighbor's wreath shook.

I started to cry.

"Shit, what should we do?"

"Nikki, calm down. . ."

"I can't calm down!"

I picked up the phone, and suddenly, it rang. The screen read loud and clear: MOM. I answered.

"Mo—"

"I'm comin', I'm comin'. Just give me . . . a second, will ya?"

She hung up.

She sounded piss drunk, but even in her intoxicated state, I wanted to wrap my arms around her. Christian remained hunched down in the back seat, on high alert like a pit bull.

We sat and waited anxiously for another twenty minutes, but there was no sight of Momma. All of a sudden, Momma's lover came running out of the apartment, looking in every direction. Angry as a bull, he appeared to be on a mission for our heads. Then he stopped, marched back into the apartment and hurled the door shut.

"Shit, Christian, that's *it*, I'm calling the police. Did you *see* the look in his eyes? *I bet you* he has a gun!"

I snatched the phone and dialed 911.

"911. What is your emergency?"

I started to speak but stopped.

"Hello? This is 911. Do you have an emergency to report?"

My mind registered her words, but I couldn't focus for the sight in front of me. A disheveled, severely overweight woman with soiled clothes and bare feet was limping out of Momma's apartment. She began wobbling all over the parking lot. I turned around and looked at Christian with wide, teary eyes.

"What the fuck? That's Mom!"

I hung the phone up, pulled the car beside her and parked. For a moment, our eyes met, and hope rose inside me; Momma *was* in there. I rolled the window down.

"Mom!"

She staggered forward and stared at some unknown place in the sky.

"*Hey*, how's it going?"

All my hope vanished. She hiccuped, stumbled and tried to balance herself on the car. Who *was* this woman and what had she done with my momma? I stepped out, placed my hands on top of the car, and looked her in her glassy eyes.

"Mom, get in the car, please, don't you remember we have. . .a *dinner*?"

She stuttered.

"O-ok-kay, I-let me just go get my sh-shoes on."

Christian chimed in, sounding exasperated.

"Mom, mom no. We don't have *time* for you to go back in there and get your shoes. Please, just get in the car and we'll go buy you some shoes."

She closed her eyes and scratched her head.

"Nah, I'm gonna get my shoes, and I'll be right back, okay?"

She staggered into the apartment and smashed the door shut with a whopping *"smack!"* I felt powerless. Momma was back in dangerous territory, in the arms of a stranger.

"How much longer can this go on?" I thought.

I gazed at the sky. I could see the dark coming in, concealing the last light of the day. Then, a text floated in: *I can't go.*

"No, I'm not giving up on you."

I dialed, and she answered in a pitiful voice, sending me over the edge.

"Mom, if you don't come out of the house *right now,* I'm calling the cops!"

A long pause ensued, followed by some muffled sounds. The line cut, and I looked at Christian.

"Did she just hang up on me or what?"

Christian braced himself, ready to barge into the apartment at any moment. For a few minutes, we waited on pins and needles. Suddenly, the door opened, and Momma exited, purse in hand and ratty tennis shoes on her feet. Barely able to hold herself steady, Christian jumped out, raced over and helped her into the car. As she settled into the backseat, heavy grunts and groans erupted like a harrowing melody. Christian signaled for my attention, and I looked: massive bruises covered her arms like tattoos. *"Why didn't I notice those before?"* I thought. I started the car, jammed the pedal to the floor and didn't look back. The tears ran down my face, but I forced a smile; we were a family again, running away from danger with shreds of love to guide us someplace safe.

♪♪♪♫

A few minutes later, the car rolled over the Arthur Ravenel Bridge. I peered in the rearview mirror at Momma: eyes clamped shut, lips pale as a ghost, body withering in agony. She needed a miracle, something only God could provide. I felt Momma's looming mortality; the alcohol was killing her, and I wanted to kill myself. As the Residence Inn came into view, however, I knew I had to disguise my depression and slip on another happy mask. "All right guys, we're here! Mom, are you excited about our dinner?" I turned and looked at her. She resembled a swollen corpse, but I pretended that I didn't notice. I parked, and we hoisted her unresponsive body out of the car. She wobbled a few feet across the parking lot, and I lost my composure. *"God, what are we going to do?"* I thought. I flopped down on the pavement and buried my head in my arms; my tears flooded the parking lot, and the water began to rise. Suddenly, I felt a delicate touch on my shoulder. I looked up and saw Momma's eyes searching for mine. I looked deeper and smiled; somewhere in those eyes, I saw my mother again. She started to cry softly.

"I carried you in my womb. For nine months I held you inside of me. The breath left me, and I searched for the words to say.

"Mom, I—I know. I love you so much." I reached for her and held her in my arms like a baby; at that moment, she was my little girl. My beautiful mother and child needed love and protection, forgiveness and grace. I had to be strong. I had to love her like never before.

"Let's go in, shall we? You must be starvin'." Momma wiped the tears from both of our eyes. We walked through the hotel and headed for the elevator. As we ascended, Christian suddenly dropped a bomb. "You need to leave that guy. He's no good for you." Momma let out a loud snort and smirked. "He's my buddy. . .This hotel *is* beautiful, honey. You must be doing pretty well over there to afford something like this. God, you know you are *tiny*. I bet I can fit my whole arm in your pants leg."

Christian's face turned a dark red.

"Mom don't change the subje—"

She rolled her eyes and turned to face Christian, her voice firm.

"And what about *you*, mister. What have you been up to? You are *my son*, you know, it'd be good to see you."

Christian leaned in close to her, his bottom lip quivering.

"What have *I* been up to? *I've* been looking out for *you*. Been worried about *you*, you know? *I* spend most of *my time* wondering where *you* are."

Momma threw her hands up in the air and laughed.

"Well, why is everyone so worried about *me*? I'm a grown woman . . . I can take care of myself!"

The elevator stopped on the sixth floor. I stepped in-between them and motioned for us to step off.

"Come on, we have to get off here."

I grabbed Momma's hand and led her down the hallway. With

every step, butterflies tickled my stomach. I realized the potential hell that could unfold inside. I led Momma down to Room 616, slid the key in the door, and faked a smile as I opened it. *"Here we go again, God. Please help us get her to the hospital, so she doesn't die!"* I thought.

I stole a quick peek before Momma could. The view inside was priceless: Stephen, George, and Dad sat in a circle, calm and quiet. *"Jesus, how did they manage that?"* I thought. Momma pushed her way through, and Christian followed closely behind. I braced myself for the worst. She looked at them and opened her mouth to speak, and I caught the overpowering stench of alcohol.

"What are *ya'll* doin' here?"

She frowned at Christian and me.

"I didn't know anyone *else* was goin' to be here."

Dad stood up.

"Well hey, Sandy."

He walked over to Momma and bent over to embrace her, but he couldn't conceal his sadness once he noticed her bruises. I looked at George and Stephen, and they noticed them, too, but I knew that they weren't surprised. *"I wonder what Stephen thinks about those,"* I thought. *"Not that he cares."* Momma pulled back, then suddenly, as if noticing Stephen for the first time, she exploded in a fit of rage and panic.

"Oh, no you don't. Wait *just a minute now*! What is *he* doing here? I want to know why all of ya'll are here. Is this what I think it is?"

The composed Stephen vanished. Mr. Hyde leaped out of the chair toward Momma. Fear opened fire on my mind, commanding me not to interfere; this *was* the man who had hurt me for so long.

"You have a problem, Sandy! Playing the pity party is not going to solve anything."

Momma's face contorted, and she moved in close to him.

"Oh? *I* have a problem? Who's the one who started all of this in the first place? Don't you accuse me, *buddy*. I'll have the police in here so fast—"

Stephen took a step forward and poked her in the chest.

"I'd love to see that! Why don't we tell *everyone* what happened, huh?"

"Oh, are *you* threatening me? You're a real class act, Stephen. It seems that you've forgotten what *you* did! What about all those times downtown? Yeah! The black guys raping me, huh?"

I looked at Christian with big eyes. Momma and Stephen were now nose to nose, screaming at the tops of their lungs. I couldn't take it anymore; I couldn't be the scared child. I jumped up and tried to push them apart. Stephen pulled back and looked at me, stunned.

"Stephen, *stop it*! *Listen to her*. She *needs* someone to *listen* without judgment."

I wondered if inviting Stephen was such a bright idea after all. He continued to stare, and Momma began to sob.

"I *knew* this was an intervention. I knew all of this all along. I'm not stupid, you know."

Dad quietly chimed in.

"Sandy we're not here to hurt you, we're here because we love you, and we want to see you get the help that you need. We've been worried sick about you. You *know* I care about you . . . We all do."

Momma cried harder. I pulled her close to me and ignored Stephen's eyes.

"How do you think I feel Mom, getting these calls that you're missing and could be dead, huh? How do you think I feel, knowing that you've run off with some guy? You don't even know him. He could be a killer for all you know! And all these accidents you've been having, you could die in a second. If I didn't love and care about you, I *wouldn't* be here. I flew here because I love you, and I want *you* to get better. I want to see you become my mom again."

She sniffled and looked at me with weepy eyes.

"I *am* your mom. I've never changed. . .and I'm *sorry* I cost you all of this *money* to come here."

A nasty pain shot through my heart.

"You *haven't cost me* a lot of *money*, okay? I *chose* to come here because *I love you. I love you, Mom*, and I don't like what's happening. Please, promise me you'll get help!"

Exhausted, I broke away and collapsed on the couch. Momma stood, bewildered.

"Get help for *what*?"

I threw my hands up in the air.

"Jesus Christ, Mom. . .*the alcohol*."

She rolled her eyes to the floor and whispered.

"I don't have a problem with alcohol."

A thick blanket of silence covered the room, and Momma looked at all of us, her face growing tense.

"What, *what*? I *don't* have a problem with alcohol! And if ya'll *don't* leave me alone about it, I am *going* to go *home* this *instant*!"

Christian spoke up.

"You have a problem, Mom, and you're not going home. *Period*. Especially not to that jackass."

Momma laughed.

"He has a name, you know. It's Will."

Christian shook his head.

"This is not funny, Mom, and I don't give a shit about. . .Will. . .don't tell me his name, it just pisses me off. Actually, no, I *want* to know his name so that I can bust his ass if he tries to come anywhere near you again. You are *not* going home, end of story. You're staying here for the night, and we are taking you to the hospital to get checked out."

Momma turned serious, and she started towards the door, but Christian beat her to the punch and covered it with his body. Momma began to whine like a kid and tried to break his arms away, but Christian held firm.

"*I wanna go home*, please! *I wanna go home!*"

"MOM, NO!"

"B-but, all of my stuff is there, a-and we made this delicious stew!"

Christian rolled his eyes and kept his chest puffed.

"*We*, who's we? Mom, get some sense in your head. You haven't even seen Nikki in over a year, why would you rather go and be with that dumbass? You're not well."

He took a deep breath and slowed his voice.

"Please, let us take care of you. Whatever you need . . . We'll get it for you."

Momma backed away and looked at all of us.

"Dammit, *fine*. I'll stay here, but I'm *not* going to the doctor, and I'm *not* going to rehab."

George piped up.

"Sandy, I know this must be difficult, but please, think about how worried we are. I love you, and I want you to be healthy and happy again."

Momma's face suddenly morphed into someone that I didn't recognize.

"Oh, yeah? You love *me*? Yeah, that's why you left me, right? Forget it. I'm *fine*! I'm as happy as can be."

Luring Momma into rehab was one ordeal, but steering clear of her love life was another mess of its own. I had to think of something to bring the attention back to the pressing matter at hand.

"We've got to focus on your health right now, Mom. Right now we just want you to be in a place where you are safe."

I smiled and changed the subject.

"Besides, did you forget about the dinner I promised you? It's late now, but if you have an appetite, I have a feeling that my meal might taste better than that crappy soup you've been wanting."

Her face slowly relaxed, and she tried to hide a smile. I walked over, rested her head on my chest and rubbed her thick, messy hair; every strand sparkled like the ocean, and even through the smell of booze, I detected traces of warm vanilla.

"I love you, Mom."

She trembled and cried in my arms, and no one said anything; we couldn't, all we could do was let her be. After a few moments, I kissed her on the forehead and made my way into the kitchen.

All of a sudden, the thought of preparing food sent my heart racing. *"God dammit,"* I thought. *"How am I going to do this? Focus, Nikki, focus. Just make something up."* I took a deep breath and smiled. "Dad, did you go grocery shopping?"

His face lit up.

"I sure did, yes ma'am! Check in the fridge there, darlin'! I bought some steak, shrimp, rice and peppers for that paella you said you like to cook."

I scrunched my nose and smiled until my cheeks hurt.

"Thanks so much!"

I snatched the ingredients from the refrigerator and sat everything down on the counter. *"Shit, this is going to be impossible,"* I thought. Nearby, the family began conversing in a light, happy tone, and I felt anxiety rising. The voices started talking. *"The pressure is on now. You better not screw this one up. They're watching you."*

"Shut up," I thought. *"I can handle this."* I opened the drawer and hunted for a knife to cut the steak. The shiny blade from the big butcher knife caught my eye and beckoned me. I slipped into a sick, but tempting dream world, one where cutting myself felt magical and seductive.

"Nikki, I can't wait to try that paella, pallella? Am I saying it correctly?"

Dad's voice pulled me out of my fantasy. I snapped my head up and faced him.

"Hmm?"

He stared at me eagerly.

"Oh, Dad, it's paella, you've had it right all along."

I forced a laugh and quickly looked at the rest. They seemed to be deep in discussions. My blood boiled; I despised their inability to recognize my growing insanity. *"Fuck you,"* I thought. The anger spread until I couldn't breathe. I looked at the knife again and set it on the counter. My gaze went back and forth between the knife and the food, the food and the knife. Finally, it lingered on the packages of raw steak. I wanted to feel the meat choking me, right then and there, and I wanted it out of my body. My heart pounded, and I struggled to remain calm and in control.

With trembling hands, I tore open a package of raw steak, placed the meat on the chopping block and began slicing. The knife glistened, and I imagined the feeling of the blade cutting my neck. The voices talked to me, though, and kept me in control. *"We don't need a scene, you idiot. Be the good little girl for your daddy."*

I cut the rest of the steak and transferred it to the pan. *"Don't make a sound! Stop it, or else Stephen will get angry."* The voices continued to growl as I turned on the burner. I peered out the corner of my eye to see if Stephen was watching, but he was busy talking to Momma. *"When will you get it through your thick skull? Nobody cares about you."* The voices snickered as I turned back to the pan and watched the meat sizzle for a few minutes. The smell hypnotized me; time and space no longer existed, and I became one with the food.

"Don't let them see you! Eat it, EAT IT!" The voices grew louder until I felt compelled to stick my fingers into the hot pan. My skin blistered from the intense heat, but I scooped out as much meat as I could and filled my throat to the brim, over and over again; the insanity was arousing.

I opened the refrigerator door and wiped my filthy mouth with my arm. A light grin flowed across my face—it was over. I closed the door, excused myself to the bathroom, and turned on the shower. I purged, cleaned up and sprayed my perfume. The smell of vomit faded, but my raging thoughts didn't; they were ever-present, gnawing away on my sanity. My head began to pound, but I forced a phony smile on my face and strolled into the kitchen.

"Supper will be ready in a little while. I've been picking at it, and it's delicious!"

᠉᠉᠉᠊

An hour and a half later, everyone plowed into the paella, and Momma beamed with joy, citing that she could never prepare a meal from Spain, as she was a Southern woman at heart. I watched them eat and chewed on an apple. No one said anything; I told them that I had sampled enough during cooking.

Christian and Stephen cracked jokes about Will for most of the meal, and Momma appeared not to pay any mind. Every so often I looked at Christian, and we seemed to understand that as long as Momma stayed through the night, we could convince her to go to the hospital in the morning. If she left, we knew she would never come back, and really, we were running out of strength to care. After dinner, Dad put on a pot of coffee, and we began a round of Parcheesi. Half-way through, Momma's purse rang. Christian and Momma raced over at the same time, but Momma was faster to reach it. She ran into the corner by the door, pulled her cell phone out, and lowered her voice.

"*Hey.* Yeah . . . I can-I can't talk. Well, I'm here at the Radisson—"

"MOM, NO!"

Christian wrestled with Momma, tore the phone out of her hand and screamed into it.

"LISTEN, ASSHOLE, she is NEVER COMING BACK! Do you understand? GO TO HELL!"

Christian jammed the phone into his pocket. Right in front of my eyes, my baby brother was becoming an adult. He was a stark contrast to Momma, who looked about thirteen years old, twiddling her thumbs and twitching her mouth. Christian pointed his finger at her.

"Mom . . .*Mom.* . .*we, we* are *not* doing this. You're not answering the phone again if that asshole calls. *End of story.*"

An awkward feeling permeated the room. For a few moments, everyone became silent. Then, Momma spoke in a measly voice.

"I'm not a child. I can take care of myself."

Christian's face turned red.

"We know you're not a child. All we want is for you to make the right decisions, and the right decision now is to go to the hospital so that you can get help!"

Momma whined and rubbed her eyes.

"Just *let me call* and explain to him why I can't talk tonight, okay? I at least *owe him that. God,* ya'll just don't *understand*!"

I lost my composure and stood up.

"*Understand*? Understand *what*? That you're living with some abusive guy just so he can give you some wine, huh? You need to go to the hospital to get detoxed, and that's what *you* need to understand. You're still drunk now, Mom! Face it, if you don't do this, *you're going to lose us forever*! You've already lost us. . .in so many ways! Please, for *the love of God*, love yourself and get help. You have *so many people* who love you. *Why can't you see that? God*, Mom! Shit, I just. . .love you so much."

She opened her mouth as if to argue but instead leaned against the wall and stared at the ceiling. Christian walked over to the door and opened it.

"This is bullshit, Mom. I need to get some fresh air."

He shut the door. I looked at the others.

"I. . .I'm done, too. See ya."

I walked past Momma and didn't look at her face. In the hall, Christian was on the floor, frantic.

"What are we going to do?"

I joined him.

"There's nothing we can do, Christian, but pray."

Dad, George, and Stephen came out. Dad put his hand up to his mouth and whispered.

"I think if we just give her a bit of time, she will be all right."

I rolled my eyes.

"Dad, I. . .God, I don't know. I don't know anything right now."

George put his ear up to the door.

"Is she talking to someone?"

Christian jumped up.

"What?"

He burst through the door and screamed.

"GET THE FUCK OFF THE PHONE!"

I hurried inside and saw Momma, nestled on the couch and giggling away on the hotel phone like a child. Christian didn't take it away from her, though; he suddenly stopped and walked away.

"I'm done, Mom. I don't want you if you don't want me."

Momma stopped laughing immediately and hung up.

"Son."

Christian didn't answer.

"Christian, stop! Ya'll want me to get help. . .I'll get help."

She rubbed her face. Christian stopped and turned around.

"No, Mom. We want you to get help because *you* want to get help."

I looked at Momma, and she looked at me. Her eyes quickly faded, and she turned into the little girl again. She drew her hand into her mouth and rocked back and forth. Was it Henrietta or Momma? I went over and sat beside her, pulled her close and caressed her hair. I noticed tiny, purple bruises on her neck. She raised her head, and her eyes morphed back into Momma's.

"I—I want to go, I do. I want to get help. I want to get better."

I managed a smile.

"Okay, Mom. We're so proud of you. Let's get a good sleep tonight and head out to Roper in the morning."

♪♪♪♪

Two days later at nine in the morning, Christian and I drove to Roper Hospital for the fifth time. During Momma's detox, she had almost had a heart attack, and they had transferred her to the intensive care unit. The past forty-eight hours had been a nightmare, full of uncertainty.

As we rode the elevator in silence to the fourth floor, neither one of us said a word; the journey up was draining, and the hospital was beginning to feel like our permanent home. The door jerked and stopped, and we got off. While we slowly made our way down the endless hall, the head nurse came running and collided into Christian's chest.

"*Oh* . . . goodness, I'm sorry, are you all right?"

Christian nodded and laughed a little.

"Yeah, I'm fine, I'm out of it . . . "

"Okay, *good*. Well, ya'll must be on your way to see your mom, it's a great thing I did run into ya."

She giggled awkwardly. I gave her a serious face.

"What's the latest?"

"*Well* . . . she did good last night, but um, we have to discharge her today."

I wasn't sure I heard her correctly.

"Excuse me? *Today?*"

"She doesn't have health insurance, and she's not sick enough to stay on this floor anymore. We don't have any beds on the regular floor to keep her. I'm sorry."

Christian and I glanced at each other, unsure of what to say. I knew that George was covering her expenses, but I didn't know that she didn't have health insurance; we were alike in so many ways.

"We have someone who's going to come in and talk to ya'll. A case worker who handles these things all the time."

I felt my anger rising.

"Yes, but you *do* realize she doesn't have a place to go. If she goes home, she's going to drink again. What are we going to do?"

Her voice turned tight.

"That's what your case worker is for, okay? Talk it over with her, please."

She scurried off toward the nurse's station.

"What in the hell are we supposed to do?"

"Nikki, *I don't know.* Let's just see what this lady has to say."

We hurried into Momma's room: 423. Momma was sitting up, watching tv and beaming. *"Fuck, nothing ever goes right,"* I thought. I smiled and gave her a hug.

"Good morning! How are you feeling?"

"I'm feeling right as the rain. How do I look?"

"You look beautiful, Mom."

"Sandy?"

I whipped around. A tall, black lady waltzed in carrying an official-looking red folder. She stopped at the foot of Momma's bed.

"Hi, I'm Ms. Delford, Ruth Delford, the case worker. It's nice to meet ya'll. Now I've been assigned to you, Sandy, and I need to go over your situation and see if we can figure out something."

I glanced at Momma. Her face turned white.

"Ms. Delford, thank you for comin' but what is this about?"

I cut in.

"Mom, I'll handle this."

"Ms. Delford, our mom needs to stay here for as long as possible. She doesn't have health insurance, and if she goes home, she's just going to drink again. We've been telling the staff this for I don't know how many times, but they haven't done anything to help us—"

Momma started to babble.

"I—I'm in a tricky situation, and I just wanna go home you see . . ."

Christian moved toward Ms. Delford and shook his head.

"No, no, no, Mom! What are you talking about? We had an agreement! Look, I'm going to handle this. Ms. Delford, our mom is an alcoholic, and she's been in the mental hospital twice for trying to kill herself."

I stopped him.

"Sorry, Christian, to interrupt, but I think it's important you know that she has extensive mental health issues, too. Did you see all of that on her paperwork?"

She fiddled through the folder slowly.

"Yes, I did here somewhere . . . "

My throat became hot, and I moved in close to Ms. Delford.

"She needs proper care! Now we have tried to explain time and time again that if she goes home, she's gonna wind right back in the hospital, and it ain't gonna be good."

Ms. Delford held her hands out and took a few steps back. She stuck her finger under her blazer and scratched.

"I understand, believe me, I do. I see this type of situation all the time, unfortunately…"

She pulled out a piece of paper from the folder.

"What I can do is give you a list of halfway houses and centers that are open to taking her, but because she doesn't have insurance, it's going to be tough to *get her in*. The waiting lists are usually very long . . ."

"We'll take it, thank you!"

I snatched the paper out of her hand and sat down carefully in the chair. My back ached from the stress, but something inside told me that this battle was just beginning. Ms. Delford gave us all a thin smile and left. Momma watched on as Christian and I huddled together to plan our next steps.

ﮌﮌﮌﮑ

Two hours later, Christian and I sat in the cafeteria, still considering our limited options. He looked over the list and stared at me intently. "I'm sorry, Nikki. Hey, are you going to eat that yogurt or just play with it?"

I swirled my finger in the cream listlessly. It wasn't an apple, and I didn't want it. I *was* starving, but I couldn't bring myself to eat. I also didn't care if anyone noticed my odd mannerisms, nor did I care if I walked outside and got hit by a truck; discussing Momma's limited treatment options drained my energy. Christian reached over and placed his hand on my shoulder.

"It's all right, Nikki. She's going to be okay."

My little brother, the brave one. He exemplified courage and stability, yet I had the coping skills of a baby. Earlier, when we sat in the waiting room and called every treatment center and halfway house in South Carolina, North Carolina, Georgia and Florida, he kept a steely look on his face and didn't let the constant stream of "NO's" discourage him.

"Maybe you're right it's just . . . I don't know what to do now. Maybe there is nothing more we *can do*."

I rested my head on the table and sighed. Slivers of cold air sent me into a trance. As I drifted away into the nothingness, I heard a gentle yet firm voice. *"There's nothing you can do, huh? Not even pray?"* I sat up and stared at Christian, who was still hovering over the list.

"Did you say something?"

"Hmm? No, I didn't say anything."

I paused.

"I'll be right back. I'm going to use the restroom."

The bathroom: my refuge, my home. I walked in and inhaled the air; it was stale but comforting. Then, I looked in the mirror and stopped in my tracks. My reflection was shifting, and the voices picked up. *"What a disgrace you are!"*

I moved in closer and scrutinized my changing face. Fangs jetted out of a gaping maw, and the eyes . . . the eyes. I looked into one and felt the hope drain out of my soul. The voices taunted me. *"Go on, kill it. Slice it up, you worthless bitch."*

"This is my chance," I thought. I backed up and found myself in an empty stall. I closed the door and reached into my purse. I grabbed a pen, removed the cap, and plunged it into my knee. Suddenly, I felt thick liquid flowing like an unforgiving stream down my leg.

Pain ripped through my body. *"Fuck, what did I do?"* I thought. I looked down: the grisly sight was alluring, but I knew I had to clean it up. I wrapped tissue around my hand, placed pressure on the wound, and cleaned up the blood with water from the toilet. *"Thank God, I have these Band-Aids . . . in case of an accident like this,"* I thought. I pulled a couple of crinkled patches from my bag and peered inside the wound. There was an entire matrix of fibers and tissues deep within. I covered the hole and limped out of the stall.

The voices snickered. *"Keep it together, Nikki. If you don't, you'll end up like that mother of yours. God knows she doesn't stand a prayer."* I leaned over the sink, splashed cold water on my face and looked in the mirror. My reflection wasn't a creature this time, but a skeleton. Bones protruded beneath my dress and my gold belt highlighted my withered waist. I felt the hunger pains more than ever, but I paid no mind. I breathed in and cinched my belt tighter.

I had to walk out the door and pretend that everything was all right. *"Get out there and be the big girl now,"* I thought. The soles of my feet crunched against the floor as I made my way back to the table. My knees ached, and the bones in my butt pulsated like a chainsaw as I sat down. Christian was on the phone; hearing his voice abruptly disconnected me from the torture.

"Oh *really*, you do? Sure, how much is it? Uh-huh. Okay, awesome, thanks so much. Christian. . .Yep. What's your address?"

He scribbled on the paper; there was barely any room left because we had written the information down from all of the other centers.

"Okay—tha-thank you. We'll see you soon."

He hung up.

"Nikki, you *won't* believe this. There's a place right here in Charleston called Ashley Hope that has an opening."

I was shocked.

"What?"

He nodded eagerly.

"Yes! The cost is reasonable, and they said we could bring her in as soon as the hospital discharges her."

I wasn't sure how we had missed it the first time around, but I didn't have the strength to ask too many questions, either. We sunk into each other's arms; hope was within reach again, but it was slippery. We still had another major obstacle: obtaining Momma's permission. I searched Christian's eyes.

"She has to agree. She *promised* she would go! Do you think she would go back on her word?"

"Has she ever?"

I thought about the answer for a moment. Of course, she had, but I didn't want to believe it. More than that, I knew I had to be the bigger person for Christian.

"Okay, I believe with all my heart that Momma's going to go, and everything is going to turn out better than we expect. Honestly, I believe it."

We headed to her room. Momma was watching television again, with the same glistening eyes. She sat up and held her arms open wide.

"Come here and give me a hug. By the way, when am I busting out of here? I want this stupid tube out of my arm."

I stopped by her bed.

"Mom, you know we have to leave tonight, right?"

"Yes, I know."

She gazed out the window and began searching for something outside.

"Mom, I need you to pay attention. We have good news."

Every organ in my body twisted and tightened. *"God, I hope she thinks this is good news,"* I thought.

Her face stiffened, and her eyes darkened.

"What is it?"

"Well, we've found a place for you to stay . . . tonight. It's called Ashley Hope, and it's a beautiful facility. Look, we have some pictures here to show you."

Christian pulled out his phone and started scrolling through the website. He sat beside Momma and showed her photos of a picturesque living room layered with cherry floors and draped in antique furniture. The brick two-story house sat on acres of lush green grass with rose bushes, complete with a wrap-around porch sprinkled with rocking chairs. She slowly went through each picture, and her face softened.

"This is close to where I grew up, you know. Brings back a lot of memories."

Christian winked at me.

"That's great, right? I mean at least you know you'll be in familiar territory."

Her chin quivered, and she threw down the phone. She rubbed her eyes and stretched her face.

"I know I said I would go, but I—I just don't think I can."

The voices laughed. *"Ha! When have you ever been able to trust her? What an idiot you are."* Christian picked up the phone.

"It's okay if you don't want to, but we love you more than you can ever know, and we want you to be safe. Please do this. We're going to support you every step of the way."

Her eyes moved between us like a shy, frightened child, and she squeezed the sheets as if waiting for one of us to reach out and strike her. Then, light broke through her eyes and she smiled.

"All right. I'll go."

"*Thank you, Jesus. Thank you for everything in our lives,*" I prayed.

♪♪♪♫

At eight in the evening, Christian packed Momma's things into a bag, and I emailed Soto Management and requested an extra week off. The idea of returning to Barcelona wasn't appealing anymore; modeling was just a stained photograph in my mind.

Two nurses lifted Momma out of the squeaky wheelchair and settled her into the backseat of the car. The deal seemed uncomplicated enough: Christian and I agreed to split the cost of Ashley Hope down the middle. At only a thousand dollars, it was a steal compared to the regular treatment centers, some of which cost in the range of tens of thousands.

Forty minutes later, the car thumped on a bed of rocks and came to a bumpy halt in front of a wrap-around porch. I squinted and noticed the rocking chairs from the website.

"Looks like we've arrived. How do you feel, Mom?"

She huffed.

"As ready as I'll ever be I reckon. Hurry up and get me out before I change my mind."

We helped her out of the car, collected her things and trudged up the wooden steps. Christian tapped on the front door. I clutched Momma's hand and caressed her tresses. Her face was a shadow beneath the haunting light, and she spoke in a serious tone.

"You look like death, Nikki. You're not taking care of yourself. When was the last time you ate?"

"At the hospital—"

The door swung open, revealing a man about middle age, with messy, red hair. He looked as worn as we felt.

"Hello? Ah yes, you must be Sandy and Christian, and is it . . . Nikki?"

He stuck out his hand, and we took turns shaking it. In his other hand, held close to his chest, was a blue book.

"Yes, that's us. You're Randy, right?"

He smiled, and I noticed a slight gap in-between his two front teeth.

"That would be me."

Christian wiped his head.

"Yeah, we talked on the phone, I believe. Thank you for having us on such short notice."

"We are *more than happy* to help. Come on in and I'll give ya'll a tour."

We entered through an elegant foyer, the kind that is only suited for Southern households. A few seconds later, a man with a kind face and gray hair walked over. His name was Martin, the other founder of the Center. Martin introduced us to a black-and-white collie named Buster, who chose to sit beside Momma for a bit while we chatted.

Randy then led us over to the living room. I immediately noticed the folding chairs and blue books scattered about the antique furniture.

"Please, have a seat. By the way, ya'll must be wondering what these blue books are."

We took seats in a haphazard circle. I wondered if anyone could hear my bones rattling against the metal chair. Randy held the book up in the air.

"This is the *Big Book*, what we use here in our meetings. I don't know what I'd do without mine. Please, Nikki, Christian, take one home."

He put his book down on the seat next to him. I grabbed the *Big Book* and flipped through it. *"Oh, Jesus,"* I thought. Martin began.

"Please don't worry about the mess in here. We just finished our last meeting of the night. You'll have about five a day, Sandy. First one's at eight-thirty, bright and early. Everyone's wandering around the house now, doin' chores or getting ready for bed."

Momma looked around with big eyes.

"I don't know if I can do this. It's all a bit much."

"Hey, I can understand that. I've been there . . .*We all have*, Sandy. By looking at your wrist, I can *guess* that you've just left the hospital."

"Detox . . . "

He scrunched his mouth.

"*Ouch*, that's fresh. *But*, thank God you're done with that!"

He laughed softly.

"You're in a safe place here, and you can leave whenever you want. We won't keep you, but we do ask ninety days as a commitment."

Momma slapped her hands on her knees.

"*Ninety days*? Oh, I can't do this! I've *never* been away from home for that long. What about George?"

I looked at Christian and back at Momma.

"Mom, George will always be there for you, especially now more than ever."

Martin leaned back in his chair and scratched at a patch on his silver head. Randy tilted forward and placed his elbows on his knees. The faint smell of cigar wafted past my nose.

"Now before you write this off, let me tell you my story."

Momma rolled her eyes, and Randy put his hands up.

"Nah, nah now, Sandy just listen, all right. We all have our stories."

He looked around and chuckled.

"Twenty years ago I was working in real estate and living the good life. I was a multimillionaire with a lot of ego to back my success, and my *third wife* was no stranger to the abundance that my lifestyle bought. Shit, I spared no expense to give it to her, I know that."

He laughed.

"Let's just say that I worked hard, and I played hard, but all of my prosperity could not conceal the fact that I had a drinking problem. It took me my entire life to come to terms and realize that I, Randy, was an alcoholic. I didn't *want* to accept it, you see, until the night after I closed the biggest deal of my life in October 1995. I got smashed and unlocked the case to my brand-new semi-automatic pistol."

I glanced at Momma. She appeared curious now.

"I put the gun up to my head, you know, I wanted to blow my brains out. *Boom.* I pulled the trigger, and *nothing happened.* Turns out my wife had discovered the gun earlier and removed the bullets. I cried for hours, alone in the corner of my bedroom, asking God why I was such a miserable nobody, and why I couldn't just die! All of this, when He had just given me another chance."

My heart started to race. I peeked around the circle. Everyone teetered on the edges of their chairs, suspended in utter fascination.

"After that night, everything changed. I got help and got sober. I began to see life through different eyes. I quit real estate, left the thrills behind, and have dedicated my life to helping other people. I can't imagine living any other way. God wanted me to go all the way down so that I could experience His love and grace on the way back up and share that with others. The night of October 22, 1995, was my wake-up call."

Momma shifted in her seat. Like a river in a desert a tiny smile spread, bringing life to her barren face.

"I would never have guessed that you went through all that. During my time at Rayside Heights, I never connected with anyone. I felt like a prisoner."

"This place is different, Sandy. You are among those who have walked where you have. Suicide attempts? Been there, and we will be here to support you as you heal, one day at a time. Now, what do you say? Should we go over the paperwork?"

She nodded cautiously and Randy handed over a folder of documents. For the next half hour, we reviewed everything from itemized costs to the beliefs of the twelve-step program. Momma initialed every paper, but when she turned to the last page, her hand froze and loomed above the final spot marked "X." She threw the pen on the floor and began to sob.

"I can't do it. I don't want to. If I leave my home for ninety days, everyone will abandon me!"

Christian grabbed her hands.

"No one is going to abandon you, Mom! We'll all be here. There is nothing to worry about. *You can trust us.*"

She pulled away and stared off into space. Randy moved closer and attempted another heart-to-heart.

"Sandy, I've been right where you are, and it's hell. I won't bullshit ya. But I'm sitting *here* now because I'm here *for you.* You're not alone. Your family is right here, waiting to help you as much as they can, and we will give you the medication you need. You're making the right decision when you sign that paper, and you will feel so much better tomorrow, and the next day, and the next."

Her brows furrowed and her eyes became as dark and hopeless as the blackened sky. She smacked her palms against her cheeks and bit her lips. Momma was gone; we were now in the presence of Julie.

"No! I can't. I just want . . . *I just want to die!*"

I fell to my knees and pleaded with her.

"How can you say such a thing, to us, your children, after everything we've been through? Look how far you've come, Mom. You have so much to live for. Don't you love yourself enough? We love you, more than you can *ever* understand!"

She folded her arms, shook her head, and the dreaded words squeezed from her tight lips once more.

"I *just . . . want . . . to . . . die.*"

I flew to my feet and towered over her.

"You just want to die, huh? *You just want to die?* If you go, what do you think will happen to Christian and me? Do you know how much we'll miss you? Can you even fathom something like that? When are you going to start loving yourself? Don't you see how much we love you? You're breaking our *hearts. Please, please* sign the paper."

I snatched the pen from the floor and held it in my open palm. With pleading eyes I waited, barely able to breathe for the stickiness in my lungs.

"We just want the best for you, Mom, and you have to try your best. We all believe in you."

Time stretched on like an endless nightmare as I prayed for Momma to break through the delusional clouds. Finally, she seized the pen from my sweaty palm and scribbled her name, sealing her fate for a better life.

❧❧❧❧

May 30, 2012. With only a week remaining in Charleston, my thoughts weighed on two things: the value of my modeling career and Momma's mental state. What importance did the fashion industry hold when Momma was fighting for her life? For the first couple of days, Randy advised us to stay away from Ashley Hope so that she could adjust to her new home. I stayed with Dad and tried to cope with my anxious feelings by purging and starving; purging brought relief from the separation, and starving allowed me to feel nothing.

On June 1, I drove to Ashley Hope and brought along the *Big Book*. Christian promised to visit in the evening, and as I pulled up for the second time around, the Center felt different. The afternoon light created a glow that lifted my spirits, and inside, a handful of people sat in the living room, listening to music and watching movies.

I found Momma on the couch and hugged her tightly.

"Mom! God, it feels so good to see you in here!"

I took a hard look at her: her eyes shined like diamonds, and she had a genuine smile on her face.

"Well thank you, I feel good today."

She laughed, placed her arm around my shoulder and led me upstairs.

"Come on. I want you to meet some of the other girls."

As we rounded the corner and entered her bedroom, I noted the fresh vacuum marks and pulled sheets with rigid creases.

"Can you tell I've cleaned in here? I've needed something to occupy myself besides all these meetings we've been having."

I stopped and hugged her.

"Oh, Mom, you look so happy! I just . . .I'm so proud of you!"

I closed my eyes and smelled her hair; it was like a silky blanket I wanted to unwind in. We pulled away after a few moments, and she reached underneath her bed and retrieved a cardboard box.

"I have your magazines here. George brought them to me yesterday from the house . . . all of them."

She opened the lid, and I froze.

"George snuck by?"

"Yes, yes he did. They let him slip in for a bit to bring me more clothes."

She looked at me.

"I know what you're thinking. Will is gone. I called him and told him to get out of the apartment."

"Mom—"

"He listens to me. Don't worry about it, okay?"

"All right, whatever you say. Just don't talk so much about Will around Christian."

"Your brother will be okay. He'll get over it."

"Mom, let's change the subject, please."

She smiled and passed me a stack of magazines. I looked through the pile: they were all in there, from *Vanity Fair* to *Clara*. I snatched them and flipped through the pages. There I was on full display, smiling and twisting my body into awkward positions to sell clothes and swimsuits. All the makeup and fancy clothes couldn't hide the truth, though: I wasn't happy. The camera may have been blind, but I wasn't anymore.

I've been showin' your pictures to everybody. I don't know, but, I guess it keeps you near."

Her eyes began to water, and I felt a tinge of shame.

"That's so sweet, Momma. You don't have to do that."

"I know I don't, but I want to because I love you and miss you. Now I'm gonna tell you somethin.' You don't have to go starvin' yourself, you understand? You tell those agents they can kiss your butt. What's left of it, at least . . ."

We burst into laughter.

Tap, tap, tap.

"You must be Nikki! Oh, we've seen you in *all* the magazines! You're famous!"

A fair-skinned girl, no older than nineteen and shrouded in blonde curls, hurried into the room. An older woman dressed in a velvet jogging suit followed behind, and I suddenly smelled cigarettes. The young girl started to talk fast.

"I'm Brittany and this is *Sylvia* we're pretty much the mothers of the house what's it like to be a *model* you're so *thin* and beautiful well of course your mom is gorgeous so the looks run in the family but your life must be so exciting!"

I paused. *"If this chic only knew,"* I thought.

"It's hard work. I don't get to eat that much—"

"Whoops! Hate to interrupt looks like we have another meeting now it's half past three will you be joining us?"

I waited for her to say something else. She blinked rapidly, and I started.

"I suppose now is as good of a time as ever!"

I peeked at Momma, who was at the door already, motioning for me to come downstairs.

"Time to use the Big Book," I thought.

$$\text{🌙🌙🌙}$$

". . . And that's when I knew. I knew that I had to take that giant leap of faith and surrender myself to my Higher Power."

Randy stirred in his seat and glanced at the group of twelve, including Buster, the dog, who was sleeping by Momma.

"Thank you, Kieran, for sharing. I'm sure we all have a lot to learn from your story. Would anyone else like to share?"

I peeked at Momma, hoping for her to volunteer, but her body was rigid in her chair. As I scanned the front of the room for a hand, I could feel my temperature rising. The pressure was building; I wanted to say *something*. Suddenly, my right hand awakened as if pulled by an unknown force. Before I could react, Randy called my name, and Momma jabbed her elbow in my side. I tried to swallow the enormous lump that had lodged itself in my throat and began talking, surprised by the words that flowed out.

"Hi. My name is—my name is Nikki. I'm Sandy's daughter."

I couldn't look at Momma.

"I'm sure ya'll have gotten to know her some by now. I'm a recovering drug addict and alcoholic, and I've had an eating disorder since I was eight years old."

Adrenaline coursed through my veins. *"I can't believe I just said that,"* I thought. Heavy noises reverberated throughout the room as rows of bodies rotated in their metal chairs to face me. I had no choice but to continue; I picked up the *Big Book* and gripped it.

"I've been modeling and living this wild lifestyle, and I never thought that I had a problem with alcohol or drugs, although I blacked out every time I drank. I believe that my career has been a safety net for me because it's given me an excuse to continue living in my lifestyle. I went through therapy and a twelve-step group, but then I stopped going."

I took a deep breath.

"I just want to say that I'm grateful for my mom being here, but it's time for me to be honest, too, and get help. I haven't drank or used in quite some time, but I'm out of control with the eating. Thanks."

My face suddenly felt hot, and I wanted to cry, but I couldn't. I looked down at the floor and tried to cover my embarrassment. The voices began to talk all at once. *"They're looking at you, stupid. What did you go and do that for, huh? You sounded like an idiot! Who in here is ever going to look at you and think you have an eating disorder?"*

Randy interrupted.

"Thank you, Nikki, for that enlightening share. We sure are happy to have you, and I know your mom is, too. All right, that wraps up our meeting, for now, folks. Please be sure and come back at eight tonight."

I didn't look at anyone. Instead, I stared at the fissures and grooves in the worn-down wood; they were mesmerizing. *"If I follow them long enough, I bet I can wind up anywhere, perhaps in a secluded land. No one can find me there,"* I thought.

All of a sudden, a woman's voice knocked me out of my imaginings.

"Nikki? Hi, I'm Amy."

I looked and saw a friendly, freckled face peering at me from beneath a baseball cap. I felt paranoid. What did she want from me?

"Oh, hi."

"Sorry, I just wanted to say thank you for sharing your story. I've had issues with eating and hating my body since forever! It meant a lot to hear you say what you did. I admire your courage."

I tried to relax, but the voices whispered. *"She thinks you're stupid. She hates you. She's against you."*

"Thank you, I didn't know what I was saying. I just wanted to help."

Her eyes widened.

"No girl, are you kidding? We always think models are perfect. Guess there's a whole lot more to it than meets the eye."

I chuckled.

"Yeah, it's not all it's cracked up to be. Although my problems started when I was little."

She leaned in.

"Didn't all of ours?"

I snorted. Amy tugged on her cap and sauntered away. I tried to absorb what we had just shared.

꜡꜡꜡

Over the next few days, Christian and I stopped by Ashley Hope at least once a day, and George and Stephen came, too. Although it felt awkward visiting with Stephen again, I put my feelings aside for Momma's sake. Gradually, her spirit seemed to blossom, and her growing positivity made me believe in the power of the *Big Book*. I made a mental note to look at it once I returned to Barcelona, but on the morning of June 6th, I found myself questioning my promise. Time had run out, and I didn't care about anything else but Momma. We stood on the wrap-around porch together; I had my suitcases and a purse stuffed with red apples by my feet. We struggled to keep a light heart about things and eventually, Momma started to cry.

"Oh, I don't want to cry . . ."

"Mom-"

"I hope you know you can give those apples up now. And you better read that book. That long flight is as good a time as ever."

I felt the tears coming.

"I *will*. I promise. I want *you* to promise *me* that you will take care of yourself in here. Now, Mom . . ."

She wiped her eyes.

"Yes?"

I will talk to you *every day*, okay? I love you. I'm so proud of you, Momma."

"I love you, too, sweetie, I love you, too."

She wrapped me in her arms, and we became mother and child again. The tears choked me, but I somehow managed to pull back and mutter that I would return for her ninety-day celebration.

"August is not far away, Mom. I believe in you!"

"I know honey, I know, and thank you. I am sure gonna miss you, though. I'm not good at goodbyes."

"Neither am I."

We stared at each other, and suddenly, her face overflowed with a rainbow of sadness.

"Don't leave me, please! I love you so much!"

My heart couldn't take it; her pain was killing my soul.

"I'm sorry, Mom. I love you, too. We'll see each other again, real soon."

We held each other once more, and I gave my farewells to everyone in the house, including Buster, who followed me all the way outside. I stopped him on the porch and patted his head.

"Not now, buddy, but I wish you could come. Maybe next time."

I blew Momma a kiss and waved as I pulled out of the driveway.

Buster raced behind, desperate to catch up, but soon he was nothing than a silhouette behind the billowing trees.

The next day I arrived in Barcelona. The light Mediterranean breeze felt welcoming, but it couldn't take my mind off of Charleston. I needed to see Momma soon, but I also needed to make some critical decisions first. Something in my gut churned; a sense that if I didn't leave the modeling industry for good, I wouldn't live to see another year. Finally, I composed an email to Ana and reviewed it.

> *Dear Ana,*
>
> *How are you? I had a great time back home, and I'm happy to be back in Barcelona, but the truth is that my mom is not well, and neither am I. I want to stop modeling for good, and I hope you can understand. I'm going to focus on my health.*
>
> *God Bless,*
> *Nikki*

If I sent the email, my career would end, but if I didn't send it, I would die; either way, I had to kill something. *"Fuck this. I want to live,"* I thought. I hit the button. Instantly, a mountain of fear lifted from my shoulders and an enormous smile spread across my face. *"It doesn't matter what anyone thinks!"* I thought. For once, I was doing something healthy for myself.

After I sent the email to Ana, I sent another message to Olivier from Facebook. I wasn't sure how he would respond, but he got in touch quickly and insisted that the invitation to Nice was still open. I decided to take a chance and arranged to meet up with him and his family a couple of days later.

On the evening of the 9th of June, the plane descended upon the heart of Nice, and all I could see for miles was a bevy of shimmering lights blanketing the ground. *"This is the right thing to do…friends and a fresh start…I'll be better in no time,"* I thought. In a few short hours, I was finally going to rest in the countryside, miles away from the distractions of the restless world. I knew my troubles were going to vanish once I had the freedom to focus on myself.

Olivier and his family picked me up from the airport and drove to his grandparent's home in Draguignan, a small town outside of St. Tropez. I was pleasantly surprised; Olivier was even more impressive in person than in his photos. He was strapping, dark and had a way with words. I liked listening to him talk about his passions for art, music, and American culture, just like our conversation over Facebook. I especially enjoyed *watching* him talk because his lips curled and I lost myself in a sinful fantasy for the remainder of the trip. By the time we reached the house, I had developed a fondness for the Frenchman. There wasn't much not to like; his parents and brother, Pierre, and his sisters, Anne-Marie and Anne-Claire, all shared a love for America and the arts, just like Momma. They had what I wanted: love, stability, and a sense of normalcy in a family. I left the van, clinging to them emotionally like a soaked skirt. So what if they didn't know about my secrets; what they didn't know wouldn't hurt them, and I wasn't about to ruin the possibility of a good relationship.

Olivier's dad, Antonio, carried my bags into the house like a gentleman. I met the grandparents, Clairene and Bertrand, and settled into the brown leather couch in the living room. Instantly, my muscles melted like butter. I drifted off into a dream world, and some time later, a tangy aroma flowed from the kitchen and brought me back to reality. The smell was enticing but perplexing. *"I wonder, can I. . . eat? What would that be like?"* I thought. Randy and the *Big Book* came to my mind, but so did my warped perception. I realized that I still felt unworthy, even though there wasn't a camera pointed at my face.

"C'est fait! Are you ready to experience the best French cooking in the world?"

Olivier and his mother, Marido, suddenly burst out of the kitchen. Marido was wearing a frilly red apron and clutching a giant silver bowl. I forced a smile and looked away; I could feel the tension building in my throat. She smiled, shrugged and walked back into the kitchen. Olivier came over and sat on the floor next to me, with his legs spread out.

"Oh, you will *love* it! It's one of her specialties, bouillabaisse. Have you had it before? It's a seafood soup."

I shook my head, panicking.

"Olivier, I can't. I'm not hungry. Do you mind if I just join ya'll in the kitchen and chat?"

He shot me a puzzled look and shrugged his shoulders.

"As you wish. You know, you're really skinny, and I hope you don't mind me saying that, but it's just, your pictures on Facebook, and the modeling ones you posted. . . You don't look like that anymore. Are you all right?"

I rolled my eyes. Inside, my blood boiled, and the voices started. *"He knows! He knows!"*

"Yeah, I—I'm fine. I suppose it's stress from work and my family stuff. "

Dinner was hell. While the family tore through cheese, fresh baguettes, and piping hot soup, I watched. I could almost taste the food; the saliva dripped from my mouth, but I couldn't let them see me eat. The voices sat at the table, controlling every move I made. *"Later when the coast is clear, you can come back. Then you can have it all."* I sipped coffee, and my legs rattled with delirium.

When everyone fell asleep, I snuck into the kitchen. Through the drawers I scoured, consuming food by the handful until nothing remained, not even a crumb. I collapsed on the floor, swollen and disoriented, and thought seriously about murdering my wretched flesh, but the sound of my heart pounding against my delicate skin prevented me. Something caught my eye, and I raised my head and peered over my distended stomach. There, on the side door was a ghastly reflection, a horrifying face! I knew then that it was never going to leave me alone. No matter where I went, The Monster was there, ready to take control of me.

𝄞𝄞𝄞

Summer wrapped Draguignan in a thick mist. For the rest of June, I walked to the town center every morning, purchased apples, and read from the *Big Book*, desperate to soothe my anxious mind. I tried to infuse my spirit with hope and strength, but the walks and reading did little good; the shadows followed close behind and found ways to drag me into their bottomless hole of despondency. At night, the voices came calling, and I found myself face down in the trash, soaked in my vomit.

Olivier and his family failed to discover my secrets, but not my wilting frame. Part of me wanted to confess, but the negative voices told me not to; they commanded me to send him off to the store and purchase binge foods. I used the quiet time to call Momma, and of course, I suspected she knew that I was not taking care of myself, but she never uttered a negative word. Her health seemed to be getting better day by day, but mine wasn't. Our daily talks became the bright spot in my black sky, but they were translucent and frail, a temporary flash of what I truly longed for: divine love.

In my heart, I was searching for eternal love, one without fail or judgment. Desperate in my search to uncover it, I hunted for a Bible one July afternoon. Bertrand just so happened to have both an English and French Bible lodged in the far crevice of the living room bookshelf. I took out the English Bible and retreated back to my room. I scoured through the chapters, hungry to connect with God and receive His love.

As I searched, however, sadness and shame came over me. Maybe I was too much of a mess and didn't deserve God's love. I closed my eyes and took a deep breath; the air stung my raw nose and throat.

All of a sudden, a vision crept over my eyes: it was my life playing like an old film. I saw myself during every phase, and all the choices I had made. I realized that I had spent years bowing down to all the wrong things: drugs, sex, alcohol, fame, the toilet. The knowledge I had acquired from the twelve-step program was gone, washed away by the ruthless tides of my destructive behavior, and it couldn't save me.

Then I saw myself struggling to swim in a crimson sea, persisting against the currents. Each stroke prepared me for a battle that I couldn't see, but actually, a bigger battle was taking place: wrestling between accepting God's grace and succumbing to my destructive will.

The vision vanished, and I opened my eyes. I knew that I had to get honest with Olivier. The next evening, I sat him down on the couch, showed him the *Big Book* and began to share a bit of my story. As I did, tears flowed down my face, and a look of relief came over his.

"You're not the only girl I know who's struggled with this. Many girls in Nice go to the bathroom after they eat and stay in there. When they come out, their eyes are red and blotchy. I suspect what they're doing, but they don't want to admit it."

We talked for hours. As the words poured out, I cried harder and harder. Secretly, I waited for Olivier to tell me to shut up, for him to strike my face or yell, but none of that happened. He wasn't Stephen, and I didn't know how to react, so I just cried.

By the time we finished talking, it was the morning, and I came to the realization that I was in love. In this tiny French village, I had discovered my best friend. I felt like God had sent someone to love me back to wholeness.

As the days passed, however, and Olivier and I grew to know each other more, I couldn't separate myself from my demons; they clung to my back and tried to stop me from getting too close to him or his family. The voices continued to tell me to manipulate them into buying binge foods, and they demanded that I only allow Olivier into my room at certain hours of the day. When we spent time together, he told me that I was beautiful, but I saw only that horrid freak that deserved to die. He tried to hold my hand and kiss me, but I always pulled away; pleasure felt like an alien force, and it sent me running. The voices screamed over every sweet word that came out of his mouth, and they said that I deserved nothing—especially love.

Now it seemed that love was not the ultimate healer, that the Bible and the *Big Book* were wrong. I tried to combat the negative voices and continued to pray in my bedroom alone, hoping for an answer.

Marido and Clairene were concerned about the amount of time I spent alone in my room, but I assured them that I enjoyed the serenity. Clairene thought otherwise and spread the word *anorexia* around the house. I told Olivier that her gossip was ludicrous, and how on Earth could she believe that I had anorexia? To prove her wrong, I locked myself in the bathroom one night and studied my body. In the mirror, I saw fat hanging off of a large frame, so I grabbed a bottle of diet pills and swallowed a handful, then purged in the shower and noticed that blood was flowing into the drain.

The next morning, I could barely speak, but I got down on my knees next to my bedroom window, and through whispers, asked God for forgiveness and healing. Afterward, I sat for a bit and stared at the olive trees in the yard. I noticed a tiny yellow bird with black markings hovering among the trees, and in my spirit, I heard a gentle voice. *"Write. Write your story for everyone to read."* The yellow bird fluttered in the branches for a few moments, then it stopped and stood motionless, with a single eye locked on mine. I felt powerless, unable to move, and sensed a strange presence drifting over me. The bird flew away, and strength suddenly flooded my soul. I knew what I had to do.

I snatched my laptop from the closet, headed straight for the office, and started a blog on my modeling website. I filled it with a dozen pages, each one detailing some of the darkest periods of my life. I felt in a trance; I couldn't hear, move, or feel anything around me. The next morning around nine, I finally turned the laptop off and rubbed my eyes, exhausted but thrilled that my diary was online for the world to see.

Writing turned into a drug. The more I wrote, the more I needed to write to feel okay. However, every time I sat down to write about my personal struggles, the maniacal voices told me otherwise. *"Wait till everyone gets a hold of this. You're a joke! You'll never, ever have a chance to model again. What in the hell were you thinking, bitch?"* I tried to ignore the voices and forced myself to read the stories over and over; when I did, the desire to harm myself went away. I realized that I had another ally, a comfort in the darkest of times. Writing empowered me, which was something that modeling never did; it only demoralized me.

⌁⌁⌁

When July came, the benefits of writing started to wane, and I struggled to communicate with Momma and Olivier. I spent the majority of my days in my bedroom, yanking my hair and pulling at my skin to try and quiet the voices, but they didn't go away; they left me in a nightmarish world. As always, I eventually came out of them, and when I did, I hungered for God's love.

One Tuesday evening, after the second round of delusions and obsessions subsided, I hurried into the office and turned on my laptop, frantic to find relief. I searched on the Internet for an Overeaters Anonymous group, unsure of what I would find. Within a few moments, however, I found a long list of possible solutions. One group, in particular, caught my eye.

"Binge eaters, anorexia . . . Wait a minute, what's this? A *Christian-based* twelve-step group?"

I clicked on a link, and it led me to a purple page with a cartoon angel at the top. It seemed innocent enough, but I had doubts. *"I don't have time for religious hypocrisy. I need the real deal,"* I thought. All of a sudden, the gentle voice came to me again. *"Trust me."*

I sat quietly for a moment and contemplated the voice. *"What the hell,"* I thought. *"Guess that's my sign."* I clicked on the link to join, entered in all of my information, and hit the "send" button. Afterward, I let out an enormous sigh.

2

The next morning, I awoke before the sun and tiptoed down the hall to check my email. I was surprised to see a reply already from the Christian recovery group in my inbox. I clicked on it.

Dear Nikki,

Welcome to our group. We are happy to have you! I hope that you will find nothing but love and support here. Please feel free to scroll through our database of members and email anyone you feel led to. We believe that God restores all, and we stand in faith knowing that He can heal whatever is happening in your life, including compulsive overeating, anorexia, and bulimia.

There are many mentors available to help walk you through the twelve steps, and I am accepting new sponsees! If you are searching for a sponsor, please ask.

You are in my prayers, and remember, I am proud of you for taking this monumental step!

God Bless and Keep you,
Monica

Tears rolled down my cheeks and an unexplainable feeling of love melted over my body. I didn't know Monica, but I instantly felt connected to her. I sat for a few minutes, unsure of how to respond. Finally, I gathered the courage and replied. I explained my current situation; I felt safe enough to expose my fears and struggles without worry of judgment.

Our relationship grew online in a short amount of time. Within a week, Monica agreed to act as my sponsor and sent me a heap of spiritually-centered recovery material every day. I found solace in our exchanges; in many ways, her sweet spirit reminded me of Nana. She also challenged me and brought to light the inner work I needed to do. Before long, I craved abstinence more than anything.

Soon, I wanted to know more about Monica. Who was this woman helping me heal across a computer screen? I messaged her one evening and asked if she would share. She emailed back right away with a bit of her story.

Twenty years ago, Monica was filled with a lust for life. She loved singing and was relentless in her journey for pursuing it as a full-time career. Eventually, Monica became famous, and with that fame came a huge sacrifice—her health. She developed anorexia and lost her dream, along with her angelic voice and sanity. For years she underwent inpatient therapy, during which time she gained an excessive amount of weight. Her current situation made it impossible for her to leave her house, and she had to breathe with an oxygen tank strapped to her body.

My soul rippled with waves of compassion. I thought that my life was bad, but here Monica was, in the midst of her suffering, helping me through my pain. She understood my dreams and agony *and* offered me endless hope, advice, support, and love. Monica saw me for who I was on the inside, and I couldn't see that myself.

♪♪♪♪

I broke the good news about Monica to Momma while trying to eat a few lousy chocolate-chip cookies. The crumbs caused my sticky fingers to tense up, and my throat tightened, but I persisted. I was determined to win the battle and consume them without purging. Momma's voice sounded light and vibrant, and that eased my tension a little.

"Well, I'm proud of you for doing that. I hope it works out with Monica."

I chewed the cookies slowly.

"Thanks, Mom."

"We've been talking again, you know."

I stopped chewing and wiped my hands on my leg. The crumbs spilled all over my thighs and onto the chair, causing my blood pressure to escalate dramatically.

"Mwa Mwam?"

"Me and your dad . . . We're good friends, can you believe it? After all these years. Guess the sky *is* blue sometimes."

I swallowed. The cookies went down slowly, in a heavy bulk and caused me to gag. *"Fucking disgusting,"* I thought. I shivered.

"Mom, what do you mean, *good* friends?"

She continued in a happy voice.

"Well, sobriety is hard nowadays, but it's given me clear thoughts on the good ones. Your dad and I have bonded. That hasn't happened since—"

"Since I was a baby?"

"Pretty much. He's sweet, your dad."

"I know, Mom. He loves you. His love has never died."

I picked up a handful of cookies, shoved them into my mouth and rolled my eyes.

"You think your old mom is crazy with all these men, but I'm tryin' to do the best I can."

She laughed and my heart began to race. The cookies in my mouth couldn't go down fast enough. I stared at the ceiling and tried to meditate on Monica's advice. *"Stop, breathe, and pray when you feel like you want to give into any harmful behaviors."* After a few moments, I swallowed and took a deep breath.

"Mom, I love you, I—I have to go. I'll call you tomorrow. Love you."

"Okay. Talk to you soon. Love you, too."

I ended the Skype call. All of a sudden, I felt a rattling sensation in my body, which upset my nerves further. The colors in the computer room started to bake under the intense heat, and I knew it was only a matter of time before I snuck into the kitchen and ravaged every shelf in the refrigerator. *"I have to beat this. God help me!"* I thought. Sweat poured down my legs as I prayed, and suddenly, I broke away and bolted into my bedroom.

I slammed the door, locked it and grabbed the Bible, desperate to squash the claws that were now tearing apart my stomach. I fell to my knees and prayed again, but the harder I prayed, the more I longed to escape to the kitchen and binge. Visions of knives cutting my body danced across my mind; I wanted to tear off my limbs and chop them into a thousand pieces. The voices provoked me. *"That's it, kill yourself, bitch! Cut it, cut it up!"*

The call triggered an ongoing desire to dismantle myself. For days, I kept my distance from Olivier and his family, but by this point, they considered my strange behavior as normal. I lied to Monica as well, and told her that my recovery was going smoothly, but really, I walked to the pharmacy most mornings and purchased diet pills. Later, I purged them in the shower, afraid my body would swell.

At night, I binged for hours, until the veins in my stomach poked through the skin. During the day, I went on starving strikes, and that triggered the twisted desire to stab myself. The longer I went without food, the more detached I became. I needed to feel stimulation, albeit pain.

After a while, I came to myself and called Momma again. Our calls were the only thing that kept me going, and Momma was the happy one. But on the third week of July, that changed. It was a Wednesday evening, and Momma's voice sounded distant. Her head was miles away, and she mumbled on about her fears of abandonment. She said that she was afraid that her relationship with George would end again. I told her that this was all anxiety and figments of her imagination, and urged her to push all negative thoughts aside.

After an hour, we hung up. Momma's state of mind put me in a bad place again. I wanted to talk to Olivier, but he was away on a trip to Paris. Eventually, I binged and purged to release the stress.

The next day, I decided that a good cleaning could get my mind off of Momma, so I started washing my clothes and scrubbing the floors with a fiery will. The sheer movements drained my energy, but it also alleviated my jitters. A few hours later, I finished, and the bottom floor looked spotless. The voices told me to clean upstairs, too, but I ignored them. I gathered the clothes from the dryer, put them into the laundry basket, and headed toward the bedroom. The door felt heavy against my shoulder as I propped the basket on my knee and jiggled the brass handle. Suddenly, it released. I turned around, and the basket tumbled to the floor.

I couldn't believe what I saw; I couldn't believe it one bit. I blinked a few times, but it was there in plain sight. Floating above my bed was a faceless phantom, wearing a hooded robe and carrying a scythe. It turned its head and stared, and all I could do was gaze into its dark, bottomless hole. I mustered a few words to Jesus and suddenly broke out of the trance. I covered my face with my hands, felt for the door, and darted out of the room.

I ran into the office and switched on the laptop. There was only one thought on my mind. *"Pray for Momma. She's going to die!"* I pulled up a picture of Momma on Facebook, placed my hand on her head, and began to pray for protection. The computer screen felt warmer than usual, and I studied her face: an eerie glow surrounded her.

I continued to pray, then I turned off the laptop and edged back into the bedroom to check for the entity. I opened the door carefully and peeked inside, but it was gone. I sighed and opened the door further. Golden light reflected off of the walls, producing a comforting glow. I looked down and saw the clean clothes scattered all over the floor.

I turned on the all the lights in the hall and settled into bed. *"When will all this ghost crap stop?"* I thought. I stared at the ceiling and rubbed my eyes, pulled the covers over my face and tried to fall asleep. *"Oh well, it doesn't matter . . .I should try to sleep . . .I'm sure Momma will be fine."*

For hours I tossed and turned and wrestled with the nagging feeling in my gut. Around four in the morning, I rolled out of the sheets, wandered into the office, and turned on the laptop. A notification popped up immediately on Skype: a new voicemail from George.

I dialed his number, and he picked up on the second ring. The anxious knots in my stomach felt like they were bleeding.

"Hello, George. Is everything all right?"

He cleared his throat.

"I don't know the best way to say this, but your mom walked out of Ashley Hope this morning and took Buster with her. We can't find her. . .No one can. I can't reach her on her phone because it's turned off . . ."

I fell to the floor in a dizzying heap and crawled over to the couch to push myself up. Shaking and in tears, I tried to understand what George had just said.

"What do you mean, *she left?*"

"Nikki. She's gone."

❧❧❧❧

A few days passed, and Olivier returned. I replayed the details of Momma's escape and hoped by some miracle that she would call, but with every passing of the sun, my hope sank deeper into the ground; there was no word from Momma. On the first of August, I forced myself out of the fog and called Christian. A few minutes into the conversation, we decided that it was time for tough love. We had to look forward and cut Momma out of our lives, even if she came back and ripped the skin off of our backs begging for help.

The next morning, I felt happy and lighter in my spirit. With Christian by my side, I had more support. As the day progressed, though, I sensed that I needed to let go of something in prayer, but I didn't know exactly how to say it. I got down on my knees by my bed and waited until the words came out.

"God, I've never been the child. Will you give those years back to me? I want to be a child now."

Afterward, I felt a release down deep in my soul, but also an intense amount of pain in my throat. The following day, I knew that I couldn't isolate in my room any longer, especially if I wanted God to give me the life I never had. Summer was coming to an end soon, and I needed to make a critical decision: was I going to stay in France and develop my relationship with Olivier and his family or return to Charleston? Without Momma on my mind, I could focus on the things that I wanted.

I decided to stay with Olivier and give myself a chance to experience love. Day by day, we spent a lot of time together and talked about life, our wishes and goals. On the inside, I felt like I didn't even know myself, but spending time with him gave me a spark of hope to continue dreaming. Little by little, I let Olivier into my heart, but something was bothering me. I couldn't shake off the warped perception of myself. I still saw a frightening beast and couldn't understand why Olivier wanted to love me. Sex was out of the question; the more weight I lost, the more I felt confused about my sexuality. Why would Olivier love a freak like me?

As I struggled with trying to show my true self to Olivier, Momma resurfaced and left drunken voicemails over Skype. I replayed them and could hear Will in the background, smashed to smithereens, but neither one of them left any clues as to their whereabouts. Olivier reminded me of the pact Christian and I had made. I didn't return her calls, and in my soul, I felt at peace.

A couple of weeks went by, and I started to doubt my decision to cut Momma out of my life. Perhaps Momma needed me to lean on for strength and support, and I was only adding to her problems. Olivier could sense my growing depression, and on the morning of the twenty-fifth, he suggested that we have some fun and visit Marineland, the nearby theme park in Antibes. The thought of going outside and interacting with animals and humans was terrifying but exciting at the same time. It reminded me of my Disney World days, and could be what my heart needed.

We took his grandparent's vintage car and arrived at ten, just in time for the killer whale performance. We watched in amazement as they soared through their bottomless tanks like giant birds in the sapphire sky. Afterward, we stopped to take a picture with one of the killer whales. I stood in front of the tank and smiled big; Momma was front and center in my mind. We purchased the photograph, but when I opened it, I froze. The killer whale was floating upside down, on its back. All of a sudden, I felt a stabbing pain in my stomach; sadness sunk in, and childhood memories flooded my vision.

"*I have to get out of here,*" I thought. Shaking, I gripped Olivier's arm, pressed through the crowds towards the gate, and bumped smack into a giant dolphin statue. Suddenly, I remembered the Native American sculpture Momma had kissed at Disney World and felt an intense desire to imitate her pose. As Olivier took my picture, I tried to keep a positive spirit. "*We will look back on these photos some day and laugh,*" I thought.

We headed to the car and made our way back to Draguignan. Soon, the sky started to drizzle, and then it began to pour. Olivier leaned forward far in the seat and wiped the windshield. By the time we reached the house, we could barely see a foot in front of us. For the first time, I saw fear on his face.

"It never rains, not like this. Go into the house and I'll park."

I bolted inside. It was dark, and I called out, but no one answered. I went through every room and turned on the lights. The wind suddenly blew the wooden windows open in the kitchen and ripped through the hall.

I hurried into the kitchen and tried to close the windows, but the wind was too powerful, and the panels tore from my fingers with a vengeful fury. I moved over to the table and rocked back and forth on a chair. The windows continued to slam open and shut, open and shut, and soon, the lights began to flicker. In the midst of the fury, I became a child; afraid to leave the kitchen and terrified to stay.

The raging storm persisted through the night, and at some point, it stopped. I tiptoed into the bedroom and opened the door; Olivier was fast asleep in my bed. I crept over to the other side, crawled under the sheets, and realized that I hadn't eaten the entire day. "*Tomorrow, tomorrow I'll eat,*" I thought.

The next morning, I sat up before my eyes had a chance to adjust to the naked light. Strangely, energy flowed through me, and I felt eager to start the day. Olivier was still sleeping, and I glanced at the clock. "*Six-fifteen. Hmmm. It is early, though. Maybe I should try and sleep,*" I thought. I tossed and turned for a while, but I couldn't bring my body to rest.

Glimmering shadows guided me toward the kitchen. I rubbed my face; there was no sign of turmoil from the night before, and everything looked to be in place. My eyes scanned the room and rested on the refrigerator. I didn't feel hungry, but I reached inside, pulled out a container of yogurt and grabbed an apple from the fruit basket.

"This looks . . . disgusting."

I walked into the office and turned on the laptop. I opened the yogurt, peered at it, and threw it into the trash. *"Shit, I'm so screwed up,"* I thought. *"I need to go back and look at my stuff from Monica again."* I sat down and began scrolling through my email for recovery material.

Ping!

A notification on Skype suddenly popped up. I squinted. It was from Dad.

"Hey Nikki, I need to talk to you."

"Why is he messaging me? Doesn't he know what time it is here?" I thought.

I ignored it and continued reading through emails.

Ping! Another message.

"Nikki, how are you?"

"God! What does he want? It's too early to Skype . . ."

I started typing.

"I'm all right, Dad! I just woke up. How are you?"

Immediately, he wrote back.

"I'm okay. Listen, I need to talk to you."

I scratched my face and rubbed my nose.

"Can we do this later? I'm in the middle of my recovery time."

"Nikki, I'm afraid it can't. This is important."

I wiggled in my seat.

"But I always save things until after my recovery time."

"Nikki, no. . ."

I rolled my eyes.

"Can you call me later?"

"Nikki, your mom died in a car accident last night."

❧❧❧❧

Once upon a time, there lived a little girl in Charleston with a big heart and a great lust for life. Although she held a fascination for the world, she was helpless to explore it. Braces covered her legs, and whenever she walked, she took stiff steps. Her adopted mother and father prayed every day for her limbs to move with grace, but the doctors gave no hope. They learned to accept the fate of their precious child, and they did their best to make her life comfortable.

When the rain came down, she listened in bed and delighted in the sounds. Shadows from the drizzling water reflected off her bedroom walls, causing her to drift into a fantasy universe. It was an enchanted place, filled with underwater fairies that guided her to faraway lands. In these lands, she was free to run through lush fields full of magical flowers.

She went to her special world as often as she could, and with every trip, she felt the strength returning to her body. Soon, she believed that she was invincible, just like every other girl and boy. But the strength lasted only in this place, and not in her waking life.

One day, as she relaxed in the grass and peered up at the powder blue sky, she noticed a dove as white as snow, soaring in-between the clouds. She watched in amazement as it glided through the atmosphere like an angel before descending and landing on her shoulder. Suddenly, she felt an overwhelming sense of joy and peace; this presence was familiar, and she recognized it as the spirit of Jesus. Her body softened, and she was infused with a new strength: a healing power full of grace and love.

Light shone into her eyes, and she inhaled and drifted into consciousness. The little girl returned to her waking life, but she did not feel Jesus leave her. She yawned and sat up on the bed, and as she turned her body, she noticed a peculiar sensation in her legs. Her eyes widened, and she threw off the covers and gazed down. She slid forward; one of her feet touched the cold wooden floor then the other. She allowed herself to continue rising while holding onto the bed and released to find herself standing without braces. She took a step, and another, and for the first time in her life, she walked by herself.

This little girl was my momma, Sandy.

A week later, I landed in Charleston again. As I stepped off the plane I breathed in the sticky air and tried to hold onto the recent memories, but it was no use; without Momma, Charleston would never smell the same. Some part of me believed that if I could have gone back in time, I could have saved her. But time was nobody's fool; the bitter reality of her death crushed me with unrelenting weight.

Olivier and I headed toward the baggage claim and saw Dad immediately, dressed in his normal way. One thing was missing, though: his trademark smile. Even his eyes had lost their sparkle. I collapsed into his arms, and our shirts became soaked with grief.

We rode in the car for thirty minutes in awful silence. Then we entered an unfamiliar neighborhood and rounded a few streets, and Dad quietly announced that we had arrived at our destination. I smashed my nose against the glass to have a peek; the tires groaned as they pulled into the driveway of a sleepy, yellow house with dark green shutters. It started to rain, and Dad turned off the engine.

"Where are we? I thought we were going to stay at your house?"

"No, no. This is *Mary's* house. She used to live next door to your momma a few years back, remember? Honey, I told you, but I guess you forgot. It's all right, sweetheart."

Dad glanced at Olivier and winked. *"I don't remember him telling me that,"* I thought. I got out of the car while Dad gathered my luggage. The front door was slightly open, and I took a few steps inside and inhaled. A presence like the breath of God filled my lungs. Mary came running from the hall and hugged my neck. She looked better than I remembered. Her hair was copper, and wild curls dropped down her shoulders.

"Gosh Mary, you look great! Thank you for inviting us into your home. I don't know what to say."

"Not a word! I won't hear a thing."

She lowered her voice.

"*Nikki*, I am sorry to hear about Sandy. I should be the one telling you that I don't know what to say. Except, I'm here for you, and I love you."

"Thanks."

Her voice became lighter.

"So, how are *you* doing, I mean. . .You've lost weight!"

Dad coughed. I spun around and shot him an annoyed look. He smiled, but I didn't smile back.

"*What*? I have a bit of a cold, is all . . ."

I glanced at Mary and clenched my teeth.

"I'm *fine*. Modeling had me on a strict diet, but I quit now. I'm tired, can I *sit down. . .please*?"

"Yes, but. . .can you please introduce me to this handsome man first!"

I suddenly remembered Olivier and my body became hot. How could I have forgotten about him? I whipped around and checked on the porch. There he was, trapped in the nasty weather and waiting to come inside.

"I'm sorry! Olivier, please come in. Dad, why didn't you say anything? God, Olivier, I seem to have no sense or manners!"

For the next hour, we sat and shared a pot of coffee, and I nibbled on an apple. Mary was intrigued that Olivier was from France and could play the guitar. As they talked, I stared into my coffee cup. The black liquid was hypnotic, depressing and soothing. I wanted to interrupt and talk about Momma, but I couldn't open my mouth; an invisible force held my tongue. After a while, Mary went into the kitchen and retrieved a silver tray piled with sugar cookies. They ate and chatted, and I picked at a scab on my finger. I peeled off the scab, and it became a string of skin. I pulled and pulled, and soon, I had removed miles of bloody skin, down to my stomach. I kept pulling until Mary called my name.

"Nikki! Earth to Nikki? Yoo-hoo!"

"Hmm?"

"Are you okay? You look like you're off in your own little world. Would you like some cookies?"

The voices started. *"Don't eat the fucking cookies! Don't you dare."*

"No."

Mary grabbed a package of dented Kools and pounded them against her palm. Her brown eyes narrowed.

"First, I'm gonna smoke one of these, and then we're gonna cook supper. How does that sound?"

I looked at everyone and sighed.

"Sure. Whatever you want."

She stood up and smiled.

"It'll be my pleasure, honey."

The rain was pouring harder now. Dad joined Mary outside as she puffed away underneath the awning. Olivier took the chance to hold my hands and plant a kiss on my lips, but it didn't do anything for me. I pulled my hands away, closed my eyes, and inhaled deeply. As I blew out the air, the front door sprung open. I opened my eyes and heard the voice that sent life racing through my blood.

"Where's my sister?"

"Christian!"

I pushed a stunned Olivier out of the way and climbed over the living room furniture to get to Christian. I could barely see his face for the tears. We hugged each other and didn't let go.

"I've missed you, Christian. I'm sorry."

He was strong and didn't cry one bit.

"No, Nikki, I love you. I love you."

Olivier carried his bags into the spare guest room, and Christian sank onto the bed. I sat down and pulled my knees into my chest.

"I want to know the details. Tell me. Tell me what happened."

Christian stared.

"Nikki I don't know if you're well enough."

I rubbed my eyes and slapped the floor. For Christ's sake, I *had* to know.

"*Stop it. I'm fine.* I deserve to know the truth, don't I?"

He cracked his neck and sighed.

"You *deserve* to know, but I'm not sure if you *want* to know."

My eyes widened.

"I want to. . ."

"Really, we don't know how she died. It was all weird. . .the circumstances. That guy could have killed her in an attack, or it could have been because of drunk driving."

My heart stopped.

"Go on."

"I was at my dad's having dinner. Well, first of all, you know Mom and I hadn't talked in a while."

"Yeah, I know."

I peered at Olivier. He was calm and quiet. *"How can he be so peaceful right now?"* I thought.

I looked at Christian, and he continued.

"All of a sudden, I noticed some blue lights flashin' by the living room window. I got up to check, but then I heard someone knock at the front door. I opened it, and a couple of police officers were standing there with these. . .*looks* on their faces, and I knew someone had died.

"One took off his hat and said, 'Are you Christian, son of Sandra Pierce?' I said, 'Yes, what's wrong?' He looked down and said, 'I'm sorry to have to tell you this, son, but your mom just passed away at the Medical University.' How do you respond to news like that?

"Dad was hysterical. The officers tried to calm him down and explain what had happened."

I cried again, harder.

"Wh-what?"

Mom was in Myrtle Beach that morning, visiting Amy. Remember her? They went to Ashley Hope together."

I wiped my eyes.

"Yeah. . .I remember."

Christian sat up.

"Nikki, I don't want to tell you anything that's too hard."

I sniffled.

"No, no. I have to know. . .I do."

He leaned forward and started.

"She was at Amy's house, drinking, and guess who else she was with? That asshole."

I suddenly felt powerless and full of rage at the same time.

"Mom got so drunk that she peed her pants. Amy tried to convince her to stay, but Will pushed her to go back to Charleston. The interesting thing is that later the police found your dad's number in one of her jean pockets, and Amy had heard them arguing about Mom wanting to call your dad. Now I don't know what possessed her to get in that truck with Will and drive, but she did. She decided to come back to Charleston, and at some point, she lost control.

"Witnesses say that they saw the car flip several times. It hit some trees and landed in a ditch. . .Will died on the spot."

Olivier came over and put his arms around me.

"Mom flew through the windshield and landed fifty feet from where the accident had occurred. She was airlifted to MUSC and the doctors tried their best to save her, but. . ."

I stopped him.

"But, they couldn't."

His face fell.

"They couldn't, Nikki. She died alone in the hospital from blunt force trauma to the chest. The officers brought us one of her tennis shoes and her purse."

Every breath suddenly felt painful. I fell into Olivier. Christian hurried over and rubbed my hair.

"I wanted to believe that it was a nightmare. I can't believe she's gone, Nikki. I miss her so much. . ."

All of a sudden, the rage overpowered everything. *"Fuck you, Mom. How could you leave us?"* I thought. Momma had always wanted to die, and she finally got her wish. Now, she could never come back. The more I thought about Momma, the angrier I felt until finally, I exploded from the pressure and screamed.

"WHAT DID YOU EXPECT? We NEVER had a MOTHER. The person we knew, wasn't her. I don't know who that was."

I ran into the other bedroom and slammed the door. If I stayed in bed long enough, maybe I could die, too.

🎝 🎝 🎝

Two days later, on Tuesday morning at eight, Mary rolled my body out of bed and prepared me for Momma's private viewing. She brushed my thin hair, pulled a black dress over my head, and looped a gold belt around my waist. The belt went around several times, and she let out a gasp. I avoided her eyes, though, and stared off into space.

At ten, we all piled into Dad's car and headed to the funeral home. As we pulled up to the address, I frowned; the parlor was merely a small brick building in a deserted parking lot next to a Taco Bell. *"Mom deserves better than this,"* I thought.

Dad parked underneath the only tree, a paltry weeping willow. I stepped out of the car and let the sun sit on my skin for a few seconds, but it did nothing to warm my bones, and I shivered fiercely. Christian put his arm around my shoulders and led me inside.

Immediately, something took over my mind. I floated along the floor, in a dream-like state. The receptionist spoke to me, but I couldn't reply. Dad and Olivier nudged me toward a pair of chestnut doors, and I stopped cold. Dad tapped me.

"Nikki, are you okay? You look like you've seen a ghost."

I stared ahead while they each grabbed my arms and guided me inside. I took one step, two steps, three steps, four. The room was foggy until the brown color came into view. I suddenly slipped back to reality, and in that wooden box, I saw my dead mother.

I drifted over to the casket. Momma was wearing a man's suit, and a rubber mask covered her face. That *thing* was a cruel illusion of what Momma was, what she had always been to me. I peered closer and noticed some dark purple spots by the hairline. I stared at the hair, and then realized, it *was* Momma's hair. I knew her hair anywhere. Her glorious hair, even in death, managed to shine like the ebony sea, and I longed to caress it.

I bent over and kissed her cheek. The room disappeared, and Momma and I floated in darkness. For an endless amount of time, we sank farther and farther into the black and smiled without saying a word. Suddenly, she opened her mouth as if to speak. I reached for her hand, but she pulled away, and I fell back to Earth. Then, someone grabbed my arm.

"Nikki, are you all right?"

I turned, stunned. It was Christian.

"You know Mom loves you, don't you?"

"Of course, Nikki. You know I love you, right?"

"Yes, yes I do."

We cried, and I wondered if our tears would flow down and reach her heart. Secretly, I believed that we had magical tears, ones that could bring her back to life. I cried and cried, but Momma didn't move. After a while, they came and took us away. As the door closed behind, I looked back one final time. I knew that part of my soul was in the casket with her.

The next afternoon, the final viewing began. As the extended family trickled in, I rushed into a corner next to Momma. I curled up in a chair, hid my face and tried to drown out the useless chatter. After a while, something sharp poked my arm. I removed my hand and saw Nana's sister, Aunt Cecilia, dressed in a velvet blazer and long, ruffled skirt. Her face was more hollow than I remembered from childhood. She coiled her lips like a snake and narrowed her eyes. I leaned on the arms of the chair and pushed myself up.

"Hello, Aunt Cecilia, thank you for coming."

She tried to force emotion.

"I *love* your momma. I don't know what to say, Nikki. I'm sorry."

I sighed.

"Thanks. Momma loved you, too."

She moved in closer until her giant glasses nearly touched my nose. Then, she hissed.

"There's something else I need to tell you."

I held my breath.

"No one in here is *brave enough* to say it, but *you need to gain weight.*"

I exhaled and breathed in fresh, bloody anger. It took all of my strength to keep from strangling her crinkled neck. Aunt Cecilia turned around and walked back into the swarm of family. The voices started to laugh. *"She's just like all the rest."*

My head began to spin. I frantically scanned the crowd for Christian, and spotted him with Aunt Sarah on the opposite end, next to a table with a stack of Bibles. Our eyes met, and Aunt Sarah bent over and whispered. Amidst the noise, however, her voice reverberated across the room.

"What's *happened* to Nikki? She used to look normal."

My heart picked up the pace, and all eyes turned toward me. *"I can't escape them!"* I thought. Momma wasn't the focus anymore, I was. I took a few steps toward the exit and tried to catch my breath, but it was no use; a thousand different voices started talking. *"They're monsters! Get away! Get out of here!"* I turned to run but I couldn't. I stood frozen, waiting for them to tear off their masks and devour my flesh.

☽☽☽☾

At noon the following day, the old pipe organ blasted "How Great Thou Art" as relatives, friends and strangers poured in through the church aisles and offered their hugs and sympathy. Dad, Christian, George, and Olivier sat to my left, and Stephen mingled about for a while, laughing in his usual way. Just as the song came to an end, I noticed one of Momma's old lovers, a woman named Melinda, slip in through the back entrance and take a seat at the last pew.

Stephen came over and sat next to me. *"Oh, God,"* I thought. He winked and gave me that slick smile. I turned my gaze back toward the front and tried to meditate on Monica's words. *"Forgiveness is for you, not the other person."* I sighed and shifted uncomfortably. *"Jesus, how can I forgive this man?"* I thought.

The preacher, Pastor Mitchell, marched up to the pulpit and opened his worn Bible. He raised his big hands, and the room became eerily quiet. He opened his mouth, and nearly shook the church with his booming voice.

"As we gather here today to honor the life of Sandra T. Pierce, we reflect on her past, but look forward to the future, trusting that *God* is working *all* things together for good. Jeremiah 29:11 states that God has a future *for all of us*, one filled with hope, and though this is a time for mourning, it *will not last.* For Sandra's children and family, I leave you with the knowledge that when you place your trust and faith in Him, He will never leave you nor forsake you. Look to Him for your comfort and strength."

Pastor Mitchell continued, and I reflected on his words about hope. Hope of any kind seemed bleak; I wanted to believe him, but I couldn't see anything past my grief and anger.

Thirty minutes later, the service drew to a close, and we gave our final goodbyes to Momma. For the second time, I noticed that my tears trickled onto the casket. They left stains on the satin, and I closed my eyes and prayed. *"God, please give these to Momma and tell her that I love her so much."*

I felt someone squeezing my shoulders, and I opened my eyes and looked. It was Stephen, and I froze. He kissed the top of my head. I heard the gentle voice in my spirit. *"Let it go. There's no use in holding on to that anger. He has his faults, so did your Momma. Don't you?"*

An electric shock ran through my body, a moment of realization. *"I'm not perfect. I have to forgive him,"* I thought. I turned and gave him a genuine hug for the first time in my life.

◗◗◗◖

On the afternoon of the ninth, we headed to Mount Pleasant Memorial Park. Momma had clear wishes: she wanted to be cremated and spread over the Cooper River. In spite of our sadness, it was a beautiful day; the sunlight reflected off of the water and stroked the azure sky. We gathered on the dock and took turns talking about Momma, in the ways that we wanted to remember her. Christian smiled as he spoke about all the times they used to scour through the neighborhoods, hunting for buried treasure. Dad mentioned her absurd sense of humor, and George reminisced about their first date on the Isle of Palms. I gazed at the water and muttered about the teacup ride at Disney World. For a little while, we stopped and stood in silence, then Stephen piped up. He laughed and looked at me.

"Sandy was the *best* wife and mother in the *entire world*. I'll miss everything about her, I'll tell you. I know you will, won't you, Nikki?"

He winked at me, and I clenched my jaw. Suddenly, the gentle voice came back, as soft as the breeze that blew over the top of the river. *"Remember forgiveness, Nikki. This is the perfect time to practice."* I didn't want to forgive him a second time, but I did, right then and there. I smiled and nodded.

"Yes, I will. I'll miss Mom until I see her again."

Christian and I headed over to the side of the dock, and we opened the urn that contained her ashes. We took turns pulling out her remains by the handful and watched as they slipped between our fingers. The wind lifted them high into the air and down into the water like endless songs—Momma's songs.

The ceremony was a quick breath of air, a moment in time, and in an instant, it was over. Afterward, only traces of her remained in the quiet waters below. The gentle lapping of the waves created a calming melody for our aching hearts. She was gone, but we could never forget her.

As I looked out, the familiar rage started to rise again in my belly. I hated mental illness with a burning passion; it had taken Momma away from us and stolen her away from her own self.

In the end, Momma's demons destroyed nearly every aspect of her life and many facets of our relationship. Sometimes I caught glimpses of what I *thought* was the real Momma, but I never knew what to believe. For a while, I wrestled with the anger and pondered Monica's words about forgiveness and love. Finally, I settled with the knowledge that it wasn't my job to understand Momma, only love her, and I let it all go.

As we packed up and headed toward the car, I made a critical decision in my heart: to honor Momma and live my life as a light for others. I couldn't do it on my own, and I knew it would take supernatural strength, but with God's help, I could defeat my inner demons and spread hope.

Scattering Momma's ashes at Mount Pleasant Memorial Park.

CHAPTER 10

Weathering the Storm of Recovery

The *thought* of victory filled me with a fiery determination, but I faced tremendous obstacles: where was I going to live, how was I going to survive financially, and *how* was I going to recover? That night, I wrote to Monica, and she encouraged me. She said that pushing through the tough times developed my spiritual muscles. I didn't have any muscles and figured that spiritual muscles were better than none.

Going back to Europe and living in Charleston were both out of the question; I needed to heal first. Despite our issues, Olivier insisted on loving me, and I knew that I had to allow love into my heart. We decided to live together and settled on New York City. We packed, said goodbye to the family and headed off.

On the fifteenth of September, we settled into a small, makeshift apartment in Jersey City. It was only a thirty-minute trek to Manhattan, but after my first attempt at walking, my legs shut down. Olivier became my nurse and ordered me to stay in bed.

As the month went by, I rested more and more, but I didn't get any better, I only became worse. I felt depressed, my gums bled, and my hair fell out. Parts of my digestive system stopped functioning, and my toes and fingers turned purple again. The bones in my body ached like salt rubbed into giant, open sores.

I was fighting a vicious battle between starving, binging, and purging. On some days, my mind told me that I couldn't eat, so I starved.

On other days, the voices commanded me to binge and purge. It was a moment-by-moment struggle to survive, but I kept swimming.

When October came, I wrote to Monica, got honest again, and told her that we needed to start over. Tears, blood, and bits of vomit dripped onto the keyboard as I discussed the state of my health, my true feelings toward the family, and how I hated myself. In less than a day she responded and included her phone number.

A call seemed simple, but hours dragged by as I rubbed my sweaty fingers over Olivier's cell phone and tapped it against my teeth. Why was it difficult to talk to someone who cared for me? As I sat in bed, contemplating the question, I suddenly heard the sweet voice emerge from the ceiling. *"Let the light in. It won't come unless you allow it."*

I then had another profound realization: for most of my life, I ran from love and *abused myself*. Even after the abusive people left, I continued to control and mistreat my mind, emotions, and spirit. I picked up the phone and called Monica, desperate to hear her voice.

As we talked, an intense love filled my heart, and I sobbed. I promised to talk to her on a regular basis and re-committed to recovery. Over the following week, I woke up early and called her. We talked for hours, and she taught me many valuable lessons.

The most profound lesson I learned was that as a child of God, I had unique gifts to spread to the world. This shocked me because I was clueless as to my worth, and didn't see myself as God's child. Although therapy and writing helped me to explore the past abuse, I was holding onto a lot of pain and had not been able to heal in part because I had continued to put myself in situations where other people could control or exploit me in some way. Monica said that I was not my face or my body, but my heart and soul and God loved and accepted me completely.

In mid-October, I purchased *The Life Recovery Bible* and workbook, two Bible-based recovery books centered on the twelve steps. The deeper I dove into the material, the more I began to understand just how much of an addict I was—to everything. I meditated on passages from the Bible and answered questions that pertained to my character. Each response required sheer honesty; the more sincere I was, the more I stood to learn and grow.

Monica said that part of recovering meant loving my true self, which hid behind multiple masks. I identified some of those masks as work, the need to please others, fame, food, and substances. What was more important: the disguises or the real me? I told Monica that I was afraid to see my natural self behind the masks, but she didn't judge me, she only poured on more love.

She taught me another valuable lesson. What was my motivation? I needed to *want* to do the right thing when there seemed to be no reward involved. My sole incentive had to be love, for God and myself. Therein was another issue: I knew God, but I didn't *know* Him. A grimy residue remained from my childhood. I equated God with religion and religion with perfectionism and abuse.

The wealth of knowledge was overwhelming, and as the days passed, I meditated on it all and prayed when I felt tempted. I ate a little more, but continued to purge. At the same time, Olivier got a job working at a real estate firm in New York City, and I felt disappointed that I couldn't contribute. I knew that I shouldn't feel guilty, but the voices worked overtime to distract me.

Blogging about my recovery was healing, but I yearned for more. One evening, as I struggled with what to do, the still, small voice nudged me. *"You can get a job as a writer."* I knew that the voice was coming from the Holy Spirit, but I rejected it. *"Why would anyone hire me as a writer? Who is going to see any value in me?"* I thought.

The voice wouldn't leave me alone, though. *"Just try. I'll be with you."* I mustered up the courage and searched for jobs online. Olivier helped me construct a polished resume; when I saw my work history in print, the negative voices began their torments. *"Who's going to hire a washed-up, addicted model? You can't even make it through college!"* I ignored them and chose to trust God.

On the twentieth of October, I received an answer to my prayers. Olivier's former boss offered me a position as an editor and writer for a luxury website. With this job, I could work in the field of my dreams and write from bed.

Immediately, my confidence grew. I discovered a few talents and thus, new pieces of my identity. Every day as I worked, I gazed out the window at a tiny piece of the sky and reflected on two years prior when New York City represented the pinnacle of good looks, fortune, and fame. The idea of modeling still tempted me, but deep down I knew that a magazine cover couldn't validate who I was on the inside; beauty wasn't bad, but it wasn't everything.

One night I had a dream, and in this dream, I stood frozen in the middle of a room full of shattered mirrors. I looked distorted, but I sensed that my real identity was coming together and that something within me was shifting. Suddenly, I broke free, and I reached down and picked up a shard. I caught a glimpse of my face and knew that the transformation I sought wasn't going to be without pain because the madness in my subconscious fought to destroy me completely.

Then the room became dark, and a flickering light appeared in the distance, revealing the evil voices that had haunted me for most of my life. Their inhuman shapes and images became visible, taking on shades of hatred, guilt, shame, and sadness. Within the voices were the familiar voices of others; those who had hurt me in the past were continuing to live through my malicious words and thoughts.

As the light came towards me and illuminated my features, I saw myself in the fragmented glass as perfect and complete. The forces warred against me, however, causing a split down the middle of my face: on one side was The Truth, on the other, The Beast. I awoke, covered in a pool of sweat. I knew that I was locked in a spiritual battle, and it was going to take a divine miracle to heal me.

❧❧❧❧

In art, miracles can be depicted with light and beautiful colors or with scenes of tragedy, smudged by oil and darkness. As October came to a close, Jersey City was in a state of panic. Hurricane Sandy was fast approaching, and the city resembled a ghost town. Olivier and I chose to stay and ride out the storm, though. I stopped working and sat trapped inside the apartment, without access to binge food, Olivier made sure of that. Now I had to face my greatest fear for an unknown amount of time: myself. The thought made my emotions run rampant.

Something else brought my nerves to the edge, an odd feeling that I couldn't shake: the name, *Sandy*. A little more than a month since her funeral, Momma's presence was stampeding up the East Coast. A hurricane in the Northeast was rare; her wild spirit reflected in the weather, erratic and untamable. Was it crazy to believe that her soul had been the force behind the bizarre storm the night she died? This time, I was sure that the storm was a sign from God; the supernatural rains could bring a blessing or a curse.

The afternoon of the 26th, I watched the *News 12* weatherman predict Sandy's path of destruction and silently prayed for protection. Two days later, Olivier pulled a chair next to the window and observed the air transform into an unearthly pink. In the evening, the trees began to scrape and bang against the windows. I stared at the branches; they resembled long, stringy hands. Fear whispered that it was only a matter of time before they lifted me out and carried me straight into the blinding darkness, but I didn't listen.

The next day, gusts of wind raced sideways, and cracks of thunder split the heavens. I refused to flinch, though. To me, Sandy *was* Momma, and the hurricane was becoming a comforting presence.

At night, while the rain and lightning continued, Olivier warmed up some soup with a few crackers. I hesitated, but finally I put the spoon to my lips and swallowed. I sat and waited for the insanity to take over, but nothing happened. I took another sip, and after a while, another. The soup ran down my swollen throat, and I heard the waves crashing against the apartment.

As time continued, the winds eventually died, and the water level dropped. In the morning, we tiptoed outside and surveyed the mess. The cars looked like sailboats; they glided for miles through the garbage and tree infested waterways. I took a closer look and noticed the damaged homes all around us. Walls and roofs had been gashed or removed, leaving behind fragile shells where stable structures once stood. We inspected our apartment, but there wasn't a scratch. Stunned, I looked out at the damaged homes once more, and tried to grasp how we had managed to escape the devastating effects of Sandy's brute strength. Olivier tapped my shoulder, and I followed his gaze toward the sky. There was a double rainbow; it was then that I realized God's grace had been upon us the entire time.

❧❧❧

Whenever I look at my reflection today, I just see me. Sure it changes, but that's because I'm changing and I'm okay with that. There's no monster, and if one does appear, I fight back with positive, loving thoughts and words. Monsters don't like it when you fight back because then they don't have the power anymore.

Something else happens when I think and say good things about myself: my reflection becomes bright, as glorious and radiant as the light that pours from Heaven. In the light, I feel free, free to be myself, and to embrace every flaw and fear. I have the freedom to accept my mistakes and the mistakes of others. In the light, I understand that what's important is not that I'm rich, thin or beautiful. I have something that neither money or fame can buy: I am loved, a child of the King. He gives me real peace, of mind and spirit. I know that I'm God's child, and for me, that will always be enough.

Grateful to be me. Los Angeles, 2016.

Epilogue

The real storm happened *after* Hurricane Sandy. Yes, I've written a book detailing some of the darkest moments of my life. Yes, I've been sober from drugs and alcohol for five years and freed from my eating disorder for three and a half years. My entire life changed when Momma passed away; I saw my life reflected in her darkness. Sometimes our darkest hour turns out to be our brightest if we choose to learn our lessons.

The decision to love myself has impacted my life in ways that I never imagined. Besides becoming healthier, I am a full-time writer, give talks regularly on my recovery, and am an advocate for child sexual abuse survivors and those suffering from eating disorders. I also serve on the executive boards of Peaceful Hearts Foundation and Project Heal SoCal Chapter. Working with Matt Sandusky to help fellow survivors and change laws is a surreal experience.

School worked out in the end. I'm studying psychology at California Southern University and averaging a 4.0. Not bad for a girl who failed out of college twice, although the goal is to try my best, and take things one day at a time.

Recovery has not been easy, though. Getting to this point been challenging; a path filled with violent whirlwinds that have tested my strength. A part of me thought that recovery was going to be a walk on easy street, but it's been the opposite. I've had to fight like hell, every moment, for my life.

I wanted to eat and resist the temptations, but my mind was screwed up. I had no idea how to eat because my disordered behaviors started when I was eight, during the critical stages of my development. At twenty-seven, I had to approach food and life like a child in an adult's body and did so at home with the part-time guidance of a team of professionals. That team included a sponsor, a mentor, a psychiatrist, and a therapist.

Along with medication, I went into therapy, and I went until I found the right therapist. A combination of cognitive behavioral therapy, art therapy, and other experiential therapies came together to help me confront the underlying issues such as the childhood sexual, physical, and emotional abuse. From there I was able to tackle the other coping mechanisms such as the eating disorders, substance abuse, and sexual and work addictions.

The monster that I saw in the mirror was a result of body dysmorphic disorder or BDD. I continue to see my psychiatrist; he is understanding, and we have honest discussions concerning my body image and negative thoughts. In 2015, he diagnosed me with clinical depression, as well as having a set of symptoms known as psychosis, which helped me to understand many of the hallucinations and delusions I have experienced for most of my life. I still hear voices and sometimes see and smell things, but the medication I take combined with working on my spiritual, mental, and emotional health has significantly improved my life. Now I talk back to the negative voices, replace them with positive thoughts and go about my day. Even when I have a bad day, I have learned that that's okay too, because that's life and the most important thing is to reach out to my therapist or someone stable and share my feelings. There is always someone out there willing to listen, and I gain nothing by isolating.

For me, recovery is a life commitment, and I have to practice my unique set of healing tools every day to ensure that I stay on track. I am a firm believer in the twelve-step program. Throughout this book, I refer to the *Big Book*, which is the main text used by the Alcoholics Anonymous program, and the *Life Recovery Bible* and its accompanying workbook. The truth is that neither the books nor the program saved my life. It's the inner work that I did, and the moment-by-moment choices I made to submit to my Higher Power and apply the information. For a long time, I went through cycles where I read the information, and it didn't do anything for me; the recovery comes when I read it and *apply it.* Going through the steps and staying away from triggering people, places, and things are just as critical for me, so it's a combination, it's a lifestyle—a life commitment as I previously stated. And that's why leaving the modeling industry was so important for me to do.

Gaining a spiritual identity was paramount to the initial part of my recovery process and is an ongoing component to my self-care. I am not religious although I am respectful of other's religious beliefs and spiritual practices. Through the miracles that happened in my life and recovery, I know that there is no way I would be alive if it weren't for the healing power of God. In the world today, people want to have reasons and scientific explanations for everything, and I am one of those people! But let me tell you that when you have a messed-up life like I had, and you surrender your life to God, there is a supernatural healing that takes place, and it transforms your world forever.

I want to share some steps and key concepts that have helped me along my healing journey. Recovery looks different for everybody, but if my experiences can be of some benefit, then this book serves its purpose.

Critical Steps

1. I went for many years without realizing how the abuse from my childhood was affecting my life. Once I became aware, however, it put many things into perspective. Forgiveness is not for others; it's for us. If we are holding onto anger because of something that someone has done to us, it can manifest into all sorts of illnesses.

I sat down one day and wrote letters to all of the people who had

WASHED AWAY: FROM DARKNESS TO LIGHT

hurt me from my childhood, including the individuals who had sexually abused me. In them, I expressed my sadness and rage, and how I felt that the abuse had taken away so much of my life. I sent out one letter to one of my abusers, and never heard back, but I made peace with the situation because the point was to forgive and let go.

2. As an addict, I was unaware of how my life was affecting others. Working through the steps with my mentor helped me to see how my pain had become its own entity. Before I could grow, I had to humble myself. I wrote separate letters to the same people as before, and I told them that I was sorry because I had lived my life in a way that had hurt them and countless others. It was a constant process, and still is a continuous process of asking for forgiveness, receiving the forgiveness, and letting go.

3. Coming to terms with my mom's death has been extremely tough, but the more I confront my issues and educate myself about mental health, the more I can cope with her passing in healthy ways. My mom had severe mental health conditions, and they weren't her fault. Dissociative identity disorder results from trauma, and bipolar disorder is believed to be a product of a chemical imbalance in the brain. My mom was also adopted, a victim of domestic violence, and an alcoholic. There is a saying that, "hurting people hurt people," and I think my mom was acting out of her pain.

4. I wrote a letter to my rapist and then I threw it away. Honestly, I felt so confused and numb when I wrote that letter because I struggled with those memories for a long time. Through the grace of God, though, I was able to forgive him. I still question myself, and I know that that is common for many rape victims.

5. Many people will not agree with me when it comes to abortion. Why did I write about my experience with abortion? It's not because I want to state if I am for or against it, so please, spare me the messages about how I'm going to Hell. I believe that God forgives, and he remembers our sins no more. I'm also looking forward to seeing my child in Heaven one day. I shared that experience because one of my main missions with this book is to *reduce the shame* around marginalized issues.

How did I start the process of healing over the loss of my unborn child, when I knew that I had made the decision to end the child's life? I asked for forgiveness, wrote out my feelings in a letter, and Monica and I prayed and talked about what it was like to feel that grief. Her support was the beginning, and therapy was the next step. Today, I still struggle with some sexual issues and grieve over the loss of my child, but I am getting better, one day at a time.

Key Concepts

1. Having the right attitude has been just as important as practicing forgiveness. When I made the decision to leave the modeling industry, I was forced to confront all of my destructive behaviors and truths head on. Life was not fun anymore; it was painful because I had to face my *real self*. On top of it all, I had to recover, and there were many times where my family and I thought that I was going to die; living became a moment-by-moment process, not day-by-day.

But pushing through, and working with my mentor helped me to understand that having the right attitude was essential to my recovery because *life is life* and it is not going to change according to my feelings. If it did, then I'd float around on a pink, fluffy cloud all day and avoid pain and growth! That's not realistic, though; to rise higher, we have to feel pain. Keeping the right attitude makes the growth process tolerable, and it helps to develop our character, which is necessary for every stage of life.

2. Having the right attitude came in handy because recovery was not a quick process, and **I had to learn how to persevere.** During year one, I sat in my house and learned how to eat for the first time since childhood. I started with juices and soups and still remember how it felt when I drank them and kept them down. I hid in the bathroom from Olivier and cried because I thought that the world was going to end. But guess what happened? Nothing bad! The world didn't end. Instead, I started to eat, little by little, and over time, I got better because I faced my fears head on.

Since then, I have fallen many times and have been sick more than I can count, but what do you know? *I'm still here!* I've perse-vered, and I want you to, too. Recovery is possible. *Never give up.*

3. Transforming my image, and the way I see myself has been one of the hardest parts of recovery. I am everywhere I go, and so I have to constantly remember to think loving thoughts to myself, and speak kind words. There are still days when I really do not like the way I look, and when that happens, I try to stop and make time to do something nice for myself. This isn't always practical, but it's impor-tant because I am.

Knowing that I am a beautiful and confident woman sounds em-powering - and it is - but it comes with a lot of pain and inner work. I used to see all kinds of things when I looked in the mirror, and I couldn't tell if what I was seeing was the result of hallucinations, body dysmorphic disorder, or just my general low self-esteem. As I studied from *The Life Recovery Bible* and my intimate relationship with God grew, however, I learned that my worth was not rooted in anything superficial. Nothing that society tells me I am, I am. So over time, the hurting, little girl from Charleston was set free, and I gained a new image: *God's child.*

4. One of the main themes of this book is identity, which coin-cides with image. **What is your identity rooted in?** When I left the modeling industry, I was *terrified* because my identity was grounded in what other people thought about me, and that made me a people-pleaser, instead of a God-pleaser. When I stopped working and started recovering, I had limited contact with many people, including those in the modeling business, and guess what? None of those people that I tried so hard to please all those years stayed at home with me and helped me recover.

Because my identity was wrapped around so many different ad-dictions and superficial achievements, when all of that was taken away, my faith was tested. It became critical that I grounded myself in the Word and learned who I was as *His Child.*

Galatians 3:26 states, "For ye are all the children of God by faith in Christ Jesus." Revelations 1:6 (KJV) declares, "And hath made us kings and priests unto God and His Father . . ." When I learned that I was a part of the Heavenly Royal Family, it changed the way that I looked at myself. I began to walk taller, I held my shoulders back, and I spoke words of love to my reflection. Now, I know that I'm a queen and that I deserve the best. My recovery starts with a heavy dose of self-love in the morning and meditating on goodness throughout the day.

5. I had to get rid of the victim mentality to move forward in my healing journey. I couldn't become a victor until I stopped believing that I was a victim. Victim and victor sound similar, but the only thing that separates them are the last two letters; a small difference, with an enormous impact. Sometimes in life two letters is all it takes - or that extra dedication to recovery - to make a substantial change.

Victims blame their problems on others, whereas victors step up and create their successes in spite of their problems. Victims choose to see the negative in every situation; victors, the positive. I had a victim mentality for many years, and as a result, I lived in negative circumstances. Although mental health issues are not the sufferer's fault, at some point the individual needs to take personal responsibility for his or her recovery. I blamed everyone around me and didn't take the necessary steps to seek help for my problems. Recovery has given me such a tremendous gift; it has helped me to see that although many terrible things have happened to me, I have a choice to continue changing for the better. I believe the same will happen for you if you make some small adjustments in your thinking.

6. Finally, but most importantly, I want you to know that **God is a God of hearts.** I was looking for love and acceptance for most of my life, and that led to a plethora of destructive behaviors and heartbreaks. By the time I surrendered myself and sought recovery, I was a broken, messed up person, and I didn't think that anyone could love me. But, God knew who I was on the inside, and He loved me. *He adored my heart.* And whoever you are, wherever you're at, God loves you. He has a purpose for your life that is so great, it will *blow your mind.*

CPSIA information can be obtained
at www.ICGtesting.com
Printed in the USA
LVOW11s0117310317
529137LV00001B/82/P